FROM THE BRINK OF DIVORCE

Books by Anne Kristin Carroll

FROM THE BRINK OF DIVORCE

WE BECAME WIVES OF HAPPY HUSBANDS (*with Darien B. Cooper*)

FROM THE BRINK OF DIVORCE

An Evangelical Marriage Counselor's Advice on How to Save Your Marriage

ANNE KRISTIN CARROLL

A DOUBLEDAY-GALILEE ORIGINAL
GARDEN CITY, NEW YORK, 1978

The stories in this book are true, and the people are real. However, to protect their privacy, names, physical descriptions, places, dates, and other identifying details have been changed.

Quotations from the following versions of the Bible are used throughout this book: Amplified (AMP) (The Amplified New Testament, © The Lockman Foundation 1954, 1958, and are used by permission. From The Amplified Bible, Old Testament, Copyright © 1962, 1964 by Zondervan Publishing House. Used by permission.); Living Bible (LVB); King James (KJV); The Modern Language Bible by Berkley (Berkley); American Standard Version (ASV); Ryrie Study Edition (Ryrie); New American Standard Version (NASV); The New English Bible (NEB); Phillips Translation of the New Testament (Phillips); Beck New Testament (Beck); Williams New Testament (Williams); and New International Version New Testament (NIV).

Permission to quote material from the following sources is gratefully acknowledged:

Christian Living in the Home by Dr. Jay E. Adams, Grand Rapids, Mich.: Baker Book House, 1972. Used by permission. *Love Poems for the Very Married* by Lois Wyse, 1972, Thomas Y. Crowell Co., Inc. Copyright © 1972 by Lois Wyse. By permission of the publisher.

ISBN: 0-385-13131-3
Library of Congress Catalog Card Number 77-12843

Printed in the United States of America
First Edition

Library of Congress Cataloging in Publication Data

Carroll, Anne Kristin.
From the brink of divorce.

"A Doubleday/Galilee original."
Bibliography.
1. Marriage. 2. Divorce. 3. Family—Religious life.
I. Title.
HQ734.C323 301.42

This book is especially dedicated to my mother, Reba B. Jones, with my devout love and affection.

It is jointly inscribed to those women whose love, prayers, care, friendship, and counsel have exerted a sustaining and dramatic influence in my life: Ruth M. Denis, Freda Brooks, Merle Foster, Darien B. Cooper, Mrs. Price (Willis) Horton, Xara Ward, June Webb, Beth Dial, Constance Wilson, Anne Allday, Sydna Franklin, Sada Wheeler, Dot Decker, Glenda Grimsley, Camilla Cruikshank, and Barbara Wyche.

FOREWORD

Before I got any further than the introduction I found myself profoundly involved with the emotional depth of what one on the "brink of divorce" must experience. Although I cannot empathize with anyone in the book because, praise God, I've never been there, I can look objectively at the content, sympathize, and see the fantastic impact such a book will have on its readers.

Anne's approach in communicating symptoms, personal real life stories, solutions and constructive assignments, cover every aspect a reader needs to keep him or her thoroughly engrossed. One cannot possibly feel that they are left hanging. Her thoroughness seems to cover every problem with a workable solution and should provide hope beyond measure . . . hope in the midst of unbelievable odds.

I found myself taking notes on areas of my own marriage where I felt I was falling short. Though I credit God for blessing us with a fantastic marriage, I realize that no marriage "has arrived." There is always room for improvement. This book speaks not only to those whose marriage is on the brink of divorce, but to those whose marriage seems solid. Keys to growth are expressed and outlined so vividly that anyone can benefit by applying the concepts communicated. To those who find themselves in a fairly stable marriage these concepts can be like spiritual vitamins. When applied and absorbed into the bloodstream of the marital relationship a healthier marriage results . . . one that has an added resistance to the ailments and contaminating influences of the world. For the marriage that is ailing and perhaps on its last leg, the application of these concepts can be like a healing ointment that not only cures but even removes scars!

While I was reading this book and preparing to write this foreword, my husband came in the door after playing golf and wanted to talk about his game (and you know how golfers are—every shot, every hole). I hated to put the book down because I was so engrossed. The temptation to go on reading was so strong, but I had just read the chapter on "The Communication Blackout" and I was convicted to follow the concepts I had just read and agreed with so strongly. It is strange how we can fall so short when it comes to the *application* of the very truths we believe in ourselves and teach to others. I've loved Anne as a dear friend for years and I find I love her even more for teaching me so much through this book.

The powerful thread that I find woven between these pages is the thread of God's personal love for each individual who reads this book. This thread entwined with the threads of hope are so well communicated that I find them irresistible. These threads multiplied can make a rope. Hang on! This rope can save your marriage!

In God's love

June Webb

PREFACE

You are about to read a miracle book. Why? Because of its unique conception and birth. As we are open and available, walking, moment by moment, in His Steps, it is amazing the wonderful opportunities the Lord brings into our life. Over vast distances He brings people, ideas, and dreams together at one precise instant to further permeate His glorious message. Truly His timing is a wonder to behold.

Briefly, this is the unusual account of how He brought this book into existence. For years many of us who are active in the field of counseling, writing or speaking on marital problems, dreamed that one day God's pure concepts could be shared with the secular world. A number of Christian authors, including myself, have written on this subject in one form or another, but in general only the Christian publishers were interested in such works.

In August 1976, while lying in a hospital bed recovering from a double cervical disc fusion, I received a letter. The note was from a longtime personal friend, Dr. Charlie Shedd. He said that a religious editor at Doubleday was searching for a Christian writer to develop a manuscript which would clearly share how couples on the brink of divorce could save, salvage, and bring their broken marriages to an exciting new fullness, happiness, and solidarity.

I thought, "Dear God, You can't mean me." As if God didn't recall, I said, "Lord, I just co-authored a similar type book, and Lord, I'm already working on a new book on Your principles for child-rearing. It is half finished. Shouldn't I complete it first?" Continuing with my excuses, I said, "Anyway, Lord, I can hardly sit up. Physically I won't be able to begin writing again for months. Father, I appreciate the honor, I realize it is the answer to years of prayer, but don't You have the wrong person?"

I continued to pray, shared the opportunity with Christian friends and we prayed. The answer kept coming back, "God gave you an assignment, Anne!" One day, in a combined state of joy and confusion, I asked Hermine Black. "Hermine," I said, "you know some days I feel so inadequate for this job. Why me?" In her beautiful and simple way she said, "Because you are God's child." Hermine spoke the words, but it was God's message to my heart.

I call this a miracle book because God implanted and nurtured a dream in the heart of Richard May, a religious editor at Doubleday. Richard described his vision to Dr. Charlie Shedd, who was then residing in Hawaii. Dr. Shedd related this exciting project to a woman named Anne Carroll in Atlanta, Georgia. Isn't it fantastic how God used three people, thousands of miles apart, two of whom had never met, to accomplish His plan!

At 2:30 on a Saturday morning I awakened from a dream that was so real, the pain so fearful, that it took a while for me to realize it had only been a dream. I went back to sleep and the dream returned. The dream in essence was a partial replay of the worst part of Jim's and my life together. He was leaving me for someone else. There is no point in describing the dream, except that upon awakening the second time I was filled with every pain, fear, despair, every emotion that many of *you* are feeling right now. The almost blind devastation of trying to hold on to someone you love, almost more than life, and having to watch as they calmly, callously, or unfeelingly slip out of your love, your life.

When I finally realized that again I'd been dreaming, I just turned over, put my arms around Jim and cried. Then I thanked God that He'd let me remember all the pain, intensely recall the feeling of a marriage on the brink. I appreciated remembering how many of you are feeling, and I prayed that the Lord would *continually* bring to mind the depth and seriousness of each thought I shared, each word I wrote. I asked that He constantly remind me of my responsibility to you and to Him in every single word I share, James 3:1.

I was glad to feel each biting, tearing ache because it again reminded me of how dear my love for Jim is and how often I take it for granted.

To the critic who felt my interviews and stories were and are too graphic, too dramatic, I can only presume she never faced losing her mate, never confronted divorce's horrid face. To those of you who are, I pray with all my heart that from the gut level honesty that the couples in this book have shared, you will see, even through your despair, a ray of hope, a true lifeline to a new relationship, a miracle within your reach!

I *know* there is no pain like that which you may be experiencing now. If I could talk to you face to face, I'd humbly beg you to give God's concepts a chance. This book shares His concepts and how they were applied to transform lives just like yours into beautiful, loving relationships. Some may be graphic—I'll admit to sharing the agony with you—but if you're at the point of divorce you want *truth.* You need to know how deeply others have felt, how far they fell, and how they rose from the very pit of marital hell. It would be nice to write of sunshine and flowers, but at the moment I don't think you can relate to them. But I pray that you will and that in a short time the darkness you're experiencing will be only a bad dream, a forgotten memory, just as Jim and mine is.

It is Jim and my combined prayer, in conjunction with many other Christians, that the Lord will use each word, each page, each concept to bring your marriage from the brink of divorce to the enrapturing satisfaction which God planned and intended.

I would like to express my humble appreciation to everyone involved in the preparation of this book. A special thanks to the couples and individuals who shared their personal stories. For some, reliving the pain and heartbreak of past mistakes was indeed traumatic. The subjects' direct, frank confessions are in no way meant to be viewed as an exposé. In love these precious people were willing to allow me to delve and dissect their deepest personal thoughts, actions and reactions, in the hope that through their experiences a life-giving seed of hope will take root in *your* heart. It is their prayer that the realization of divorce doesn't have to be your finalé. Each felt that if only one marriage was saved from the brink of divorce, to happiness and true marital fulfillment, then their revelations will have been worth the pain.

Because of the personal nature of this book, many names and/or locales, for obvious reasons, have been changed, but *all* of the situations, pain, heartbreak, lives and ultimate joy and happiness are true.

I'd like to express my personal appreciation for the hours of final typing by Cheryl Glaser, and months of editing by Dot Baker.

I was privileged and honored to have had the assistance of Rev. Howard Dial, who has taught the original languages of the Bible (Greek and Hebrew) on a college level, and whose knowledge and instruction were invaluable.

My personal gratitude to Dr. Charlie Shedd for his confidence in originally recommending me to Doubleday.

I am deeply indebted to Richard May of Doubleday, who was a constant source of inspiration and the epitome of Christian advice and encouragement.

For their hours of guidance, wisdom, knowledge, suggestions and faithful insights, Darien Cooper, Mrs. Price (Willis) Horton, Harriett Crane, and June Webb deserve my eternal thanks.

A very personal and special tribute to Dr. Loui Bayne, Dr. Donald Grady, and Donna Dorsch, without whose care the writing of this book would have been totally impossible.

My deepest love and appreciation to my three guys—my husband, Jim, and our sons Michael and Ronald—for their constant love, support, patience and help during the writing of this book.

"Thank you, Lord, for the privilege of sharing Your all-encompassing love and Your transforming Word."

In Him, because of His Grace
Anne Kristin Carroll
1977

CONTENTS

FROM THE BRINK OF DIVORCE

CHAPTER 1

THE BITTERSWEET YEARS: AN AUTOBIOGRAPHY

How to save a marriage wavering on the brink of divorce . . . a subject often talked about, yet seldom accomplished. The divorce statistics in the United States show us that more and more couples are failing in what should be the most fulfilling, rewarding relationship of their lives.

Perhaps you picked up this book in a last faint attempt, almost afraid to hope that you might discover the elusive answers to your crumbling marriage. If divorce is the only solution you or your mate can see for your marriage, most likely you have already tried every idea, scheme, tips from well-meaning friends, and you don't expect any more from this book than you have uncovered elsewhere. "I've tried everything, I've done my best, what else can I do?" you ask.

Before you toss in the towel, before you sell all the hopes, plans, and dreams you had the day you said, "I do," let me tell you that there is hope, whatever problem is ripping and tearing at the very foundation of your relationship! I don't mean temporary patches which sooner or later fail and leave you floundering in pain, but real answers which will change your marriage from heartbreak to happiness.

As you read you will learn about *real* couples who learned and applied the concepts shared within; you will find that you are not alone in your pain, your disappointment, that many others have gone through a like crisis in their marriage and escaped divorce to find a more fulfilling marriage than they ever expected. Certainly, if this book were based on my ideas, my views, or even on my experience, or that of any other human being, I couldn't be so positive of the answers it holds, but it isn't; these are God's answers and *they work.*

Before we proceed, my husband, Jim, and I would like to share with you a bit about our lives, and how, at the most hopeless point of any couple's relationship—after we had been divorced well over a year—these concepts first came into our lives.

THE FINAL DECREE

In a few minutes it would all be over. Soaked with fear, pain, disappointment and rejection, I shivered as I stood in the judge's chambers. My eyes wandered over the walls covered with books, the cold leather chairs, past the secretary busily taking notes, and back to the judge's face. He was speaking, but his words were like the monotonous grinding of a motor, and my mind simply couldn't register them clearly.

Is this what divorce is—one man rhythmically reading legal terms, with obviously no awareness or feeling for the cutting finality of his words?

I wondered if they even realized I was real, a person. How frigid the words were. Running from the horrid reality around me, I began to recall all the dreams, the plans for the boys, the schools they hoped to attend, the fine young men they were becoming, and our expectations for a fulfilling future. I had to swallow the urge to scream: "What happened? I don't understand. When did it start to fail? What did I do wrong? How could this be happening to us? Dear God, this isn't the way it was supposed to be."

I watched as the final papers were prepared. What a small piece of white paper, what power it had, how deadly it was. It said that in the eyes of the world Jim and I were no more! All the love, memories, hopes and dreams of a lifetime were dissolved. On a flight from the solidarity of the moment, my mind whirled back to the beginning.

THE YESTERDAY OF OUR LOVE

Only a few days after my divorce from my childhood sweetheart, as the mother of a young son, I found myself sitting in a smoke-filled bar. My date had suggested we come here, but as the evening wore on, I became more and more uncomfortable. I sat on the edge of my chair, doing my best to look "hip," but I had only been in a bar once before and I was sure everyone was aware of how insecure I felt.

Bored, scared, but trying to "fit in," I wandered from my table into an adjoining room. A very attractive young man walked up to me and said, "Hi, Anne." My mind spun, wondering how he knew my name. Noticing my confusion, he said, "I'm Jim. We met last week. Don't you remember?"

"Oh, yes," I said, trying to recall who he was and who had introduced us. Before I could visualize the previous weekend, he said, "How about going to a party?"

"Well, I really would like to," I replied, "but I have a date in the other room who probably wouldn't like the idea."

"Doesn't matter," he said. "My date's in there too. Let's just sneak out the back door and they'll never know what happened."

The idea did appeal to me. Grant, the guy I was with, had a severe case of octopus hands and I wasn't in the mood to spend the evening trying to outmaneuver him. Jim had a happy, warm smile, sort of reminded me of a big puppy. His all-American-boy looks, broad shoulders and wavy brown hair, I felt, would be a vast improvement over Grant.

I mustered my courage and said, "Love to. Where's the party?"

"Sin Alley," he answered, as he opened the door and led me to his car.

"Sin Alley! Oh, holy cow," I thought. I had heard about the area, when friends joked about it. In the early sixties it was a mass of adjoining single complexes in the southwest area of Houston, Texas.

When we arrived at the party, Jim was a bit surprised when he discovered I neither danced, smoked, nor drank! I still think that that was his main fascination with me for a long time. He had never met a twenty-one-year-old, especially a divorcee, who acted like an escapee from the Victorian Era.

That evening, he did his best to teach me the current rage in dancing, the Twist. He'd explain and I'd attempt. Someone should have had a camera, because I am sure it was a very funny scene. Finally, in *total* desperation, he went to the bathroom, got a towel, and returned saying, "It is sort of like drying off after a shower." I started to tell him I didn't take showers, but I knew I had given him enough shocks for one evening, so I picked up the dumb towel and tried, and tried, and tried. But all the patience in the world wouldn't co-ordinate my feet, my bottom, or any of the rest of me.

After that evening, Jim and I became inseparable. I was working for Mitsubishi International, and modeling for a large fashion house. I think Jim enjoyed sharing my limelight; I know I enjoyed having him there.

But I was running from the failure of my first marriage, and sick with the knowledge that my father, with whom I was extremely close, was dying of cancer. My whole being cried for love, security, and I had a desperate desire to belong to someone again.

Six weeks after Jim and I met, we were wed in a simple ceremony at the county courthouse! Certainly, neither of us was ready for marriage: I was running scared and Jim was just playing a fascinating new game. Obviously, the depth of the commitment he had made had not registered, because the next day, while swimming, he introduced me as "one of his friends"! If I'd been smart, I might have guessed right there we were headed for trouble.

When the marriage game became boring, Jim desperately tried to regain his status with the swingles. He was more captivated with pads, partying, and playing than he was with the permanent live-in he'd acquired.

I'll admit, when he did come home he was met with a dramatic display of tears, insinuations, and accusations. There wasn't a peace-filled moment for either of us during that time. Even with the birth of our precious son Michael, I was still doing my best to win the "martyr of the year" award.

My daddy died two weeks before Michael was born. In my agonizing search for *real* answers to my tormented existence, and with passionate hope of reaching my father in the life beyond, I became deeply involved with the dark world of the occult. Particularly in the readings of Edgar Cayce, I felt I'd found the answers to my intellectual Christianity. Of course, like anything the Devil plagiarizes, there were no lasting solutions here, but I continued to mix my intellectual Christianity with my occult beliefs for a long time. Unfortunately, the few real Christians I knew never suggested that I consult the Scriptures to see what they had to say about horoscopes, mediums, etc. The experience would have been a rude awakening for me. You see, before my marriage to Jim, I had already attended one college and studied theology, and you would have thought I'd have known better, but at this point I was too desperate. I would have reached out to anything. All along I wanted to know God, I wanted to follow God's will for my life. I just didn't understand how.

The next few years were filled with a few ups, but many, many downs. Then Jim's employer transferred us to Atlanta, Georgia. After our move, we were happy for a short time, but having had a live-in maid all my mothering days, I had never had to be responsible for the children. Responsibility is a hard lesson to begin learning at twenty-three. Jim wasn't much help; he was as immature as I.

If Women's Lib had existed in the early sixties, I would have been a choice candidate. I hated housework, but more than that, I "felt" that I was wasting my time and talent being a wife and mother. I wanted a maid, a job, freedom, and money of my own. As my aspirations and interests turned from home, so Jim's also began to change. During this time I felt I had desires that Jim just couldn't fill. In fact, looking back, I can see we had almost switched places. Anyway, as I relied on him less, he began to search for someone who did need him.

Soon the problem of "other women" had to be faced. Audaciously, I felt the solution to this new problem was relatively simple; all I had to be was smarter, prettier, or sexier than my assumed competition. I say "assumed," since I blatantly accused Jim of more entanglements than the six-million-dollar man running in high gear could have managed. Proverbs 14:1 (AMP): "Every wise woman builds her house, but the foolish one tears it down with her own hands." That was me.

As my solutions failed to produce the expected results, I became more desperate. I imagine many who are reading this book have tried similar tactics. Mata Hari couldn't have been more proficient than I. I became a master at checking for lipstick stains on Jim's shirts, inspecting his car for hairpins of the wrong color, or a carelessly dropped earring. Of course, I kept a perpetual surveillance on the address book, watching for the entry of any unfamiliar female names.

Occasionally, while trying to track him down, I would call the old bar where we had met, ask for Jim, only to hear him yell from the background and hear the bartender say, "Anne, he says he ain't here!"

Naturally, when I found concrete evidence, heartbroken and crying, I would flaunt it in his face. Needless to say, all these antics produced was unnecessary pain for me, guilt for Jim, and with each confrontation our relationship was further damaged, and the gap between us became wider.

The next solution to my growing marital problems was a new nose! Bet some of you haven't thought of that one yet. In my race to conquer my competition in the beauty contest, I took stock of myself in the mirror. I couldn't find anything I could dramatically change, with the exception of my patrician nose. I made arrangements with a plastic surgeon to take the patrician out of my nose. I was working so hard on that outer beauty that I never even considered my inner ugliness!

A cute nose didn't do it. A new hairstyle didn't work, and neither did all the new fashions. Many nights I lay in bed listening until the wee hours of the morning for his car. I couldn't sleep; I was consumed with thinking about who he was with, where they were, and what they were doing. Night after night, I lay there with the same old thoughts running through my tormented brain, crying, dying as each hour slipped by. I was forever wondering where I had failed, why I'd failed, what he wanted, what would it take to make him happy.

A cold chill would run through me when I heard the car pull into the drive. I'd lay there torn as if two women possessed my body. One of them wanted to reach out, touch, forgive. She was filled with happiness because he was home, her whole being wanted to run and enfold him in the arms of love. The other woman was filled with bitterness, hostility, despair, and she felt cold and icy inside and could only turn away, wanting only to hurt him as she had been hurt.

As the heartbreak continued, I happened to drop in to see my neighborhood physician. As I shared with him some of the upsets in my life, he said, "What you need, Anne, is a pill."

"Well, I sure need something, and anything that will stop this torment and anguish would be a blessed relief," I responded.

I was a prime candidate for the pill habit. Problems that I couldn't solve, questions with no apparent answers, and a desire to escape the pain of the whole thing. That afternoon's visit to the doctor began a habit which would last for almost four years.

It didn't take long for me to like the escape the pills provided. In a short time, I took anything that I could *legally* get my hands on—Benzedrine, Dexedrine, Librium, Valium, Elavil, etc. Uppers to wake up, barbiturates to relax or sleep, anti-depressants to keep from facing my ever-mounting problems, and a lovely variety of tranquilizers thrown in for good measure. I lived from one pill daze to the next. It finally reached the point that even if there were no pressing problems in our lives, I still took my precious pills just in case one came up! It never dawned on me to get to the source of my upset, nervousness, etc. If I *felt* nervous, if I *felt* insecure, if I *felt* afraid, I just took the appropriate pill, and the feeling was gone. Of course, the source of the problems still existed. I was totally intent on treating the feelings instead of the cause. Perhaps some of you are doing the same thing right now. In true southern, Scarlett O'Hara fashion, as far as problem-solving was concerned, there was always tomorrow!

After four years, an article in a local newspaper caught my attention. I realized, as I read, that I was taking twice the dosage used to treat persons who are institutionalized. Right then and there, I decided that I should either be off the pills or in an institution. You can't play detective in a hospital, so I chose to kick the pills and, miracle of miracles, I did.

Of course, there was the issue of what would happen when I was confronted with another crisis. Without my pills, with no hope, having searched the world for answers, suicide seemed beautifully tempting.

I didn't want to do something dramatic, or to cause my children more pain and embarrassment than need be, so I quietly sat down one evening to make suicide plans. That must have been the longest, loneliest night of my life.

When morning came, I had almost finalized my plans when the phone interrupted me. The call was from Xara Ward, a woman I hardly knew. During the course of the conversation, she asked me to attend a ladies' Bible class with her.

It was certainly good she couldn't see my face. I, who had studied theology in two schools of higher learning, had searched Christianity for answers, and she wanted me to go to hear some housewife teach the Bible! I almost laughed, but since I hated to hurt her feelings, I agreed to go.

When we arrived, there was a young woman teaching in the basement of a neighbor's home. Her name was Darien Cooper, and I had never heard *anyone* speak with such knowledge and authority about the Scriptures. When she spoke of Jesus, she just radiated, you *knew* immediately that she was talking about her best friend.

Taken as I was with Darien, I wasn't at all sold on the merchandise she was pushing. That " 'Christ is the answer' stuff is all right," I thought, "if your biggest problem is getting your husband to take the garbage out, or persuading your children to hang up their clothes, but if she had problems like mine it wouldn't work."

The Lord is so gracious, He held me together for another week so I could get another dose of truth. This time everything was different. It was as if Darien had prepared her message especially for ME!

She said that God had a plan for *my* life. She explained how much God loved *me personally*. I understood for the first time why I had never experienced the abundant life Christ promised. I learned that *I* was sinful, and that sin separated me from God. But God in His merciful love sent His Son, Jesus Christ, to span the chasm between a perfect God and sinful Anne. All these years I had been trying to be good enough for God. At that moment, I realized that I could never be good enough to fellowship with a Holy God, but that through my acceptance of Christ's payment on the cross for *my* sin, I could then have a personal relationship with Jesus. I, Anne, could have a living, moment-to-moment relationship with the Son of God!

Of course, the answer had been there all along. I just had never clearly understood before. I knew at that moment that this was the answer for which I had been searching all my life.

I ran home, glowing with my new-found friend, Jesus, but

laden with my total ignorance of His Word, and of His concepts for man, woman, and marriage. Naturally, that didn't stop me; I politely began to stuff Jesus Christ down Jim's throat.

After nine months of living with a female Billy Graham, Jim had had it, and he demanded a divorce! I thought I had all the answers and I couldn't believe what I was hearing.

"Mrs. Carroll, Mrs. Carroll," the judge called. "You didn't answer my question."

"I'm sorry, Your Honor, I was thinking of something else." Here I was again. It wasn't a nightmare from which I would awake; Jim had actually asked for a divorce, and in a few minutes it would all be over.

My mind frantically wondered, How could this be happening? When I became a Christian I thought that all my problems were solved. Those I couldn't manage to patch up myself, I *presumed* God would fix. But that wasn't, and isn't, how it works.

IT'S A MIRACLE

Perhaps some of you are like me: once I get a taste of a new idea, I take it and run, never bothering to read the directions which are enclosed. Christ had something to teach me, but He patiently waited. Feeling I had made a royal mess of my past life, hurrying to establish a new one, I revisited the singles circuit. Of course, the more I pursued happiness, the more I searched for fulfillment, the more elusive they became. Then the party lights began to look grimy in the sunlight, and I realized I was seeing the same lonely faces at every gathering, every party, every "political" meeting. When I'd tried everything, when all my bright ideas had burned out and my brilliant schemes had failed, then I discovered I was almost back where I had begun.

I fell on my knees and prayed to my Father in Heaven: "Dear God, I have tried everything. I did everything I thought was right. I did my best. Why didn't it work? Lord, I'm so tired of trying. I appreciate Your help and friendship in the past, but from now on, You can just count me out. I quit." You know, this is what He had been waiting for. I could almost hear Him say: "Great! Now, Anne, I can begin My work."

A year and a half after our divorce, after seeking help through friends or counseling and finding only discouragement, frustration and a million unanswered questions, the Lord led me to a dedicated Christian counselor, Mrs. Price Horton. This wise woman of God showed me Anne as she truly was! She took me directly to the Scriptures to explain the problems Jim and I had faced and failed. After an insight into the problems, from the Word of God, she shared *the answers*. That's what I had been looking for all along. Answers! What an experience.

As I became teachable, God began to show me that He had created man and woman, that He had performed the first marriage ceremony and had foreseen all the problems with which I would ever be faced. I realized that in His Word could be found *all* the concepts which related to my life as a wife, a mother, and a woman, and to marriage as He had planned it for each of us. Then I got serious about learning each and every concept and, as important, how and when to apply them. I must admit Mrs. Horton had some unique ideas in the area of application. Almost like a child I began, one concept at a time, learning, understanding, then applying when the opportunity arose.

But now, before I go any further with my story, I'd like you to read Jim's impressions of our life together.

MAN ON THE RUN

I remember the first time I saw Anne. "What a doll," I thought, taking in her blond hair, huge blue eyes, and the soft angora sweater she was wearing. Naturally, she was with a date.

But Anne was a girl that was hard to forget. And the next week, when she walked into the club, I went up and reintroduced myself. I had no intention of letting her slip by me a second time!

I had never met anyone twenty-one who was so wide-eyed and innocent. Why, there was a whole world I could show this gal. I found her lack of worldly sophistication fascinating. (When one of my buddies tried to date her, she got quite hostile.) I found her high-school-type loyalty embarrassing. But there were so many things special about her that in a few weeks I asked Anne to marry me.

It wasn't your usual wedding ceremony. But I wasn't taking

the whole thing very seriously anyway. We dropped down to the courthouse one afternoon and were married. I even forgot that I had an Army Reserve meeting that night. Later, on our wedding night, I went off to the meeting and sent Anne out with some of our friends to celebrate without me!

The following weekend we went apartment hunting. We found the apartment we wanted. There was only one problem—we couldn't move in until the first of the month.

The solution seemed simple enough to me. I'd just shove my roommates into another bedroom and move Anne in with us! Anne was none too thrilled about the idea, but she didn't make too much fuss. However, our first small argument occurred when I found out that she was going over to her momma's every day—to take a bath!

"You have got to be kidding," was my reaction.

"No I'm not," she said. "There's no privacy here. And until we get our own place, I'm going to continue to go home."

We did get that new place and for a short time playing house was fun. But now there was always Anne home waiting for me, always Anne to account to for my time, for my actions, and in due time the fun wore thin.

I missed the free life of a single man. I felt no lasting commitment to Anne, so I returned to my former friends. Making the rounds with the guys, partying and playing were more exciting than the same person and the same routine every night.

Anyway, by now Anne was pregnant, and she was moody and cranky much of the time.

If I did happen to get home before she went to bed, it was always the same scene:

"Jim, is that you?"

"Yeah, Anne."

"Where did you go after work?"

"Nowhere."

"Nowhere! I guess you were nowhere for the last four hours . . . Are you listening to me? I asked you where you've been. Don't you realize that I'd like to get out of this place sometimes? Good grief, you never think of anyone but yourself."

About this time, she'd start crying. I'd feel like a dirty heel for upsetting her. But, of course, I easily forgot that feeling when the next afternoon arrived and I had the choice of going home or dropping by the club or a friend's apartment.

Our lives pretty much followed that pattern until I was promoted and given a large territory in the Southeast. For a short time after we moved to Atlanta, things changed between us. I had made a commitment to myself that if I took Anne to Atlanta, I was going to make some dramatic changes in my behavior.

Atlanta seemed to have the magic touch for a time. Anne seemed happy, and I was perfectly satisfied learning to be a good husband and father.

Slowly things began to change again. Anne was an only child, protected, and a bit spoiled. She had had the services of a maid while the children were young, and after the initial fun of playing mother wore off, she became frustrated, confused, and unsatisfied. In time, she arranged for another live-in, then secured a job!

Anne had never been away from home, nor beyond the reach of parental control before, so she was experiencing her first taste of independence. She became more and more involved in her work, and spent less and less time with the children and me.

If that is what being good gets you, I decided, I'd just find someone who wanted to be with me, someone who needed me. Obviously, Anne didn't.

In a short time, our lives had revolved back to the nightly scenes. By this time, Anne realized that she wasn't as interested in work and a career as she had thought. In time, she became aware that she wasn't the only female on my mind—and boy, that did it.

No Nazi general could have held better interrogation sessions than Anne. I must admit that she had developed into quite a detective. Everywhere I went, I expected to turn around and find Anne standing there with that accusing look. Finally, I decided if I was going to be accused of everything in the book, I might as well try to live up to the reputation.

What the heck did she want? When I tried to be a good husband, she ignored me. When I reverted, she harassed me. Women! The only thing I really knew and believed about Anne was that, in her own way, she sincerely and deeply loved me, but she sure had funny ways of showing it.

I thought, after almost eight years of marriage, that I knew Anne pretty well. But one day, right out of the blue, she came home, grinning from ear to ear and sounding like a tent preacher on a Saturday night. I certainly wasn't prepared for this.

Night and day, day and night, she told me about how she had searched for answers all her life, and finally she truly understood.

"Jim," she'd say, "you have got to listen. I just know that Jesus Christ is the answer to all the problems we have had for years."

She'd almost force me to sit down while she read to me how to become a Christian from a little booklet she always carried around. I couldn't understand it. I had been raised in such a formal religious atmosphere, and all this "saved and new birth" business sounded foreign to me. Anyway, I went to church a couple of times a year, and I didn't see any real effect that had on my life. I couldn't imagine why she thought some miracle could be wrought with this "Christianity" she'd found.

She told everybody. If she wasn't talking religion, she was sending out tracts. Then her new-found friends, Xara and Darien, showed her how to write a testimony, whatever that was. Lo and behold, the next thing I knew, she began to speak publicly! That did it. I couldn't stand it any more. The way she was going, I wouldn't have been surprised if she had ascended Mount Sinai and tried to receive a second set of commandments. That's when I let her know I had had it.

Surprise covered her face. She had actually believed that all this Jesus stuff would miraculously solve all the problems in our relationship.

I don't recall too much about the actual day our divorce was final. I just didn't care any longer. I wanted to escape the pressure, responsibility, condemnation and pain.

During the next year or so, things didn't dramatically change between us. I still took her to all the big business functions. She had become so close to many of my important customers that to show up with anyone else would have been the kiss of death. The closeness of our immediate group, plus the excellent job Anne always had done in entertaining my clients, kept the pressure on me to stay on a civil basis with her.

About a year and a half after our divorce, I began to notice a change in Anne. I couldn't believe it. When we were together, there were no more sermons, no more questions, just a smiling face. When I'd leave, I'd sense that Anne really liked me just the way I was!

Of course, I'd seen Anne go through some pretty tricky forms of manipulation before, so I just backed off and waited for this new spell to run its cycle. Occasionally, I'd push her just a bit to see how far she was willing to carry this new approach of hers. But as time passed, and I tested and tested, she remained consistent. It wasn't a game. She was really different.

Things between us got better and better. It was pleasant to be with her. She seemed calm, happy with herself, and undemanding of me. The inner beauty which radiated from her became a magnet.

Finally, I realized what a jerk I was. I wasn't the only man in the world who could see what a striking, intelligent, caring woman she was. If I didn't start playing my cards right, I might end up losing her.

Two and a half years after our divorce, I asked Anne to marry me again. This time there was no quick civil ceremony . . . and I didn't run off to an Army Reserve meeting that night.

In the company of a couple very close to us, we were married in a quiet ceremony by Dr. Charles Stanley. Anne wrote the ceremony that reunited us. Later, some of our friends gave us a wedding reception—something we'd missed the first time around.

After our remarriage, things were different. Home was a fantastic place to return to, and I found that more and more I wanted to be there with my family.

Anne was so different. She made me feel so important, so needed. I encouraged Anne to begin speaking to women's groups. This time Anne had something to say. She'd discovered God's concepts for herself and for a happy marriage, and she was busy sharing them with anyone who would listen. Darien Cooper and Anne have probably helped save hundreds of marriages as they shared God's concepts through talks, tapes and seminars. Recently, with Darien, Anne co-authored her first book: *We Became Wives of Happy Husbands.*

Anne talks away from home, but at home she seldom says anything. I haven't seen that little tract she used to preach to me from in a number of years. Anne learned the truth of I Peter 3:1. The less she said, the more I saw the truth through the life she was leading.

It is clear, though, that the truths Anne found in the Scriptures have totally remolded our existence. I am firmly convinced that I would never have reached a point of understanding Christ, His death and His plan for man, any other way.

POINT OF RECONCILIATION

When Jim asked me to become his wife, two and a half years after our divorce, it was only because I had learned to apply new concepts to my life. Jesus wonderfully ignited the fire of emotion and devotion between us. He taught me to respond to Jim in a different way.

All of life's problems were not solved at that moment in our lives. It has and will always be a process of working in and through God's concepts for Anne as a wife, a mother, and a woman; and for Jim as a husband, a father, and a man.

Daily I claim the promise in Psalms which says: "Delight yourself also in the Lord, and He will give you the desires and secret petitions of your heart. Commit your way unto the Lord—roll and repose (each care of) your load on Him; trust . . . also in Him, and He will bring it to pass." (Ps. 37:4–5 AMP)

I don't question Jim's comings or goings any longer. When he gets home I just let him know how glad I am to have him here with me. The Inquisition is out and love is in. Now I sometimes wonder what to do when, instead of being out late, he is home early and in town as much as possible. I told him the other day I thought I would write a book someday on how to adjust to a transformed husband!

As I continued to learn, Jim began to become the man God has created him to be. In time, he began to graciously assume a husband's normal responsibilities. Jim's maturing has ultimately lessened my load, emotionally and physically. Now I can relax and enjoy his love, protection and emotional support. Praise the Lord, NOW I can enjoy being a woman!

Certainly, Jim and I aren't without problems, but Christ never promised that; He only promised to be sufficient for each day. I can say that we have a deeper, sweeter relationship now than we ever had before. Often I recall these words in Song of Solomon: "Many waters cannot quench love, neither can floods drown it." First Corinthians 13:8 also speaks about the everlasting qualities which God intended for marital love.

Jim has grown before my very eyes. He has become everything I ever wanted in a man, not by my forcing him to change, but by my allowing Christ to change ME!

I hope no one reading this feels that Jim and I are special, isolated cases. Believe me, it wasn't miracles or luck that reunited us, but the application of God's laws. Through them we learned to love again, trust again, share and communicate.

We are still growing in our relationship; I hope that we always will be. I know that many of you feel that you can't stand the mess you are in one more day; you are frantically searching for a pill, a quick cure. But believe me, there are no pills to take, no instant cures for an ailing marriage. Whatever state of decay your marriage is in, it didn't happen overnight; and, depending on the number and severity of your problems, it usually can't be turned around in a day, either. Oh, there are those rare exceptions. I have counseled with some who were so intent, so ready, that they saw changes occurring almost every day. But that is not the norm. Usually a marriage on the brink of divorce needs a firm dose of God's eternal concepts, applied with patience, work, and firmly grounded in a personal trust in God, a day at a time.

What an opportunity, possibly the *greatest* you will ever have—the opportunity to save your marriage, to save your relationship, to save your family! How could you possibly excuse yourself if you closed this book and never tried?

Just think what wonderful things, what marvelous new experiences, may be waiting for you. The decision is up to you. *You* can accept failure without trying, or *you* can reach out, trusting, and put into practice God's eternal concepts and promises.

There was a song which was often played when Jim and I were divorced. It used to tear my heart apart. It was called, "We Almost Made It This Time." Even now when I hear its sad refrain, there is a silent tug, a reminder to hold close the love we almost lost. Those have to be the saddest words in the world: "We Almost Made It This Time." Don't make them yours.

There is no reason why your problems can't be solved. God's word has provided us with *all* the answers to life's dilemmas. His solutions are clear and direct, and you should *expect* changes as you earnestly apply them to your relationship. There is no reason to discuss and debate your torn relationship for days, weeks or months. *Today* is the time to act. As you learn the concepts, you'll find changes happening in varying degrees every day. The more you learn, the more you trust and apply, the quicker the situation will be reconciled.

I'm sure you will be encouraged by this precious promise: "Now glory be to God who by His mighty power at work within us is able to do far more than we would ever dare to ask or even dream of—infinitely beyond our highest prayers, desires, thoughts or hopes." (Eph. 3:20 LVB)

CHAPTER 2

CHANGE CAN START WITH YOU

In your unceasing search for answers, you may have begun to feel isolated and frustrated. You've probably rummaged through bookstores and libraries searching for books written for couples with crumbling relationships, only to find that many of the suggested solutions take two consenting partners to put into operation. You have discovered books which deal with suggestions on how to encourage your husband to remember your birthday, how to induce your wife to run a more efficient home, or how to make your marriage more stimulating, when yours needs a complete overhaul, not a battery recharge. Perhaps in seeking counseling you experienced the same old problem: most of the qualified counselors would only see you if your mate also consented to counseling. I don't condemn the counselors who use this approach; unfortunately, most of us who have reached the brink of divorce are fighting a lonely battle to save our marriages. Now you feel like screaming: "I'm alone, nobody cares whether this marriage lasts but me. Can't anybody hear me, won't anybody help?"

You've been told so many times that it takes two, that you are about to succumb to the pressure of well-meaning friends who say: "You can't change things alone; just let it go." You have been running, searching, sustained only by blind faith, but now that too is failing, and you are beginning to reason that if there were any solutions for you, certainly someone would have written about them, someone would have shared them with you. You have just about had it, and you are ready to quit. Well, don't!

It would be wonderful if all troubled marriages were made up of two people who were willing to try and work things out, willing to seek help, willing to try again. This idealistic situation seldom exists. If yours is one of these rare marriages, you are blessed and should find the bridge back to a rewarding relationship much easier.

Usually, there is only one mate willing to seek answers. Possibly your mate is convinced that there are no solutions. Sadly, often by the time you've become serious about finding help, your mate has already found other things, other people to fill the void your relationship didn't provide, and isn't interested in trying to salvage your marriage.

If you think there's no hope because you are the only one in your relationship who wants or cares enough to try to save your marriage, you are wrong! In my experience, most torn marriages are brought to new life, new vitality, by the interest, basically, of only *one* party. Some of the people discussed in this book were once in exactly the same situation you are in now.

One woman shared the following story of how one person, applying God's concepts, can make a dramatic change in a bad situation.

She said: "After fifteen years, our marriage had deteriorated until there was little left. I tried talking, nagging, manipulation, everything I could find in books, but to no avail. I tried new hairstyles, lost weight, bought sexy nightgowns, everything I could think of. While I was trying the world's solutions to our crumbling situation, Eldon was becoming more and more involved with a woman in his office. Then one weekend, without my knowledge, he left the country to secure a "quickie divorce"! As soon as he returned, he married the "other woman"! He returned to St. Louis, dropped by the house, picked up his clothes, told me what he had done, and left.

Needless to say, I was devastated. I didn't know what to do, who to turn to. I was a Christian, but I had been running my life my way, not God's, for a very long time. Like many others, when a tragedy befalls us, I fell to my knees and beseeched the Lord to do something to save our relationship. He beautifully supplied me with two answers.

First, I had the opportunity to learn God's concepts of marriage, as Anne shares them in this book. Secondly, I called our family lawyer, and he told me that the divorce my husband had obtained was not valid in the States, and his new marriage was therefore illegal.

Of course, Eldon wasn't too pleased about the failure of his "quickie divorce," but he went forward with plans for a conventional one. As he proceeded, I studied God's Word, and began to apply His concepts to our relationship. Eldon noticed the change in me, the peace he found when he visited the children, but still he proceeded. Finally, our day in court came. As we sat outside the courtroom waiting for the court to convene, we talked. I shared with him some of what I had learned. I told him I had learned that I had often been the cause of our unhappiness, and no matter what happened in the future, I wanted him to forgive me. He sat quietly for a time, no response came from his lips, but silent tears began to stream down his face.

As the bailiff announced the start of court, Eldon turned to me and said: "Melinda, I don't understand all that has happened to you, but I have seen actions which speak louder than the words you say. If you are willing to try and forgive me, I would like to walk out of this building and come home. I'm not sure we can make it, but there is a quality about you which seems to be giving me the strength to believe it is worth another try."

We walked quietly out of the courthouse and returned home. Starting over certainly wasn't easy, but as I daily studied God's Word (Col. 2:27), moment by moment applied His answers to our problems, our lives took a miraculous change. God's answers, His concepts, weren't temporary patches. I know from experience, because it was eight years ago that God moved in and divorce moved out. From the bottom of my heart, I can testify to the fact that "With God anything is possible, and nothing is impossible." (Luke 18:27)

BUT MY SITUATION IS DIFFERENT!

In the midst of emotional turmoil and pain, you feel completely isolated. The further the problem has progressed, the more frantic and fearful you have become. Some of you have shared the overt details of your pain and rejection with everyone who would listen. Others have been faking a happy marriage so long that now you can't bring yourself to admit to anyone that it is about to collapse. In each case, you have failed to find the proper answers.

Many people I've talked to have expressed a common thought. They've said: "Anne, I'll understand if you can't help me. You see, our situation is quite different." In our loneliness and fear, most of us feel that way. I certainly did. In fact, I would risk saying that the statement "Our situation is different" is the most used introduction that a counselor hears. I wish you could read the hundreds of evaluation sheets handed in after seminars. You'd soon discover that the same basic problems are shared time after time. Certainly, the circumstances change, but the basic corroding forces rear their destructive heads every time. The Scriptures speak to this point in I Corinthians 10:13 (AMP): ". . . no trial . . . has overtaken you and laid hold on you that is not common to man . . . belonging to human experience . . ." As human beings, we all want to be a little special, a bit unique, and God created each of us with unique talents and abilities, but when it comes to our basic desires, basic problems, we find there are many passengers in our boat.

As part of the human race, we have like qualities. We breathe, get hungry, require sleep, love, sex; and just as we have basic needs and desires, we have basic problems for which there are basic answers. What this really means is that you aren't alone, someone somewhere feels just like you do, has experienced the same pain, the same disappointments and failures. What does make a difference is not the problems, but your willingness to become a survivor and solve them.

HOW CAN I MAKE A DIFFERENCE?

"Well, it is nice to know that I'm not alone in my problems, that others have faced like circumstances," you say, "but that still doesn't tell me how I, alone, can make any permanent changes." To share with you how the changes you alone make can affect your entire marital relationship, let's first look at the following situation.

Virginia was married to a confirmed alcoholic. For years, Ben had come home drunk. Virginia had cried, screamed, hollered, and clearly let Ben know what a worthless, rotten person she thought he was. When Virginia learned what was precipitating Ben's drinking, she realized that she would have to make some severe alterations in her own behavior. Basically, she wasn't the problem, but she was actually feeding the problem. You see, like most alcoholics, Ben knew he was hurting her. He knew he wasn't the kind of man he should be. He didn't need Virginia to tell him. What he did need were excuses for his behavior, and unknowingly Virginia had been providing many of them. Her constant nagging about his drinking only gave him the excuse to drown her voice in liquor. Her criticism only gave him the excuse to justify his indulgence by thinking, "Any man who had to live with a wife like her would drink too."

When Virginia realized she was contributing to his indulgence, she began to change her responses. The next time Ben came home roaring drunk, Virginia greeted him with a smile, offered to make him dinner, or run him a warm bath. The initial shock almost sobered him up. At first Ben responded to Virginia with more hostility than before. He resented her not fulfilling her old role. He fought hard trying to get her to fight, to help him justify his actions. But Virginia continued to respond to him in love. By changing her behavior, a vacuum was created, and Ben couldn't respond in his normal way, because the circumstances were different. Of course, none of us likes our status quo changed; Ben didn't either. But in time, with love and patience, he began to see himself for what he really was. He began to clearly understand his real problems instead of the rationalizations he'd contrived over the years. Ben was then ready for help and change.

Certainly this is a drastic illustration, and I don't propose that every alcoholic wife or husband is transformed overnight by simply changing your reaction to him or her. There are many other basic factors involved, which we will discuss later. What I hope you will see in Ben and Virginia's story is that action creates reaction. When you change the action, or the reaction, you require your mate to make changes also.

As Ben initially revolted against Virginia's change because it placed him in a different position, so your mate may also. The shift in a relationship is often resented because it is either not believed, or because it demands that we re-evaluate our position and make changes which are not natural, or may be uncomfortable, or new to us. Often a mate will test to see if the change is real. Perhaps, like me, you have tried so many personality changes or forms of manipulating before, that they feel you are just on a new kick, and it probably won't last long. Remember, an act is just that, an act, and sooner or later, if there is no truth in it, your mate will see through the façade.

A clear-cut shift in your reaction and relationship to your mate may initially be disturbing and confusing to him. It is rather like learning a new set of action and reaction patterns. Sometimes unlearning old ones and learning new ones can be a slow, painful process, particularly if your mate hasn't voluntarily chosen to do so. In time, the mere circumstances will demand change. Your wife can't scream about never having money of her own if you sit down, make a budget together, and allot her a certain amount a month, plus extra for her. If your husband has refused to talk to you because he says you don't have anything in common, learn about his interests, learn about his work, learn to be a good listener. His reasoning and excuses are destroyed and a warm, new situation is created.

Some of the above suggestions only represent superficial changes in a relationship, and do not deal with the root problems, but they are examples of how change occurs. The whole basis of relationships is founded on action and reaction. When changes are made, right or wrong, they, by their very existence, demand other changes. Voids create vacuums which have to be filled. It only takes one person to change an action or a reaction; therefore, it only takes one person to make changes that will ultimately change a whole relationship.

BUT I CAN'T CHANGE

You say you have tried to change your actions and reactions in the past and failed. The idea of forcing yourself into a different life pattern, constantly thinking positive, pumping yourself up as you face the next crisis, only to find you don't have the inner strength, doesn't excite you. Well, I don't blame you. If in the past you tried gritting your teeth and smiling when you felt like screaming, if you acted gracious and loving when you were actually boiling over inside with bitterness, jealousy or disgust, then you didn't really change, you were only playing a game. I know that when I did this and pressure was put on my act, the curtain came down quickly, and I threw in the towel and reverted to my nasty old self.

When I said you can make dramatic and lasting changes in your marriage alone, I meant without human support and help. The only way to make true, honest transformations, ones that don't crumble with the first assault, can only be found when you are plugged into the ultimate power source. Human effort alone will result in failure. You may present a great first night, but the show will never have a long engagement. Only with the power that is available through a personal relationship with Jesus Christ can this miracle be accomplished.

Some of you are saying, "But I prayed, I went to church."

That isn't what I'm talking about. I am speaking of a personal, daily, moment-by-moment dependency on Jesus Christ to make changes in and through you. As a Christian, you can't say "can't," because, as you recall, in I Corinthians 10:13, God says you can!

This whole concept will be explained in Chapter 3. For now, remember Philippians 4:13 (AMP): "I have strength for all things in Christ Who empowers me—I am ready for anything and equal to anything through Him Who infuses inner strength into me, that is, I am self-sufficient in Christ's sufficiency." And you will be!

A PROBLEM OR A THREAT

Too many people live in a state of fear and insecurity because they view every problem that arises in their marital relationship as a threat to its very foundation. Many of us become very unrealistic when we think of our own marriages. If we were at work and the typewriter ceased to function, we forgot to mail out the monthly statements, and the boss screamed at us for forgetting that important client's call, we would realize it had just been a bad day. On the other hand, if the oven overheats, dinner is ruined, we forget to pick up that favorite suit from the cleaner's and our husband rants, raves and says he wishes he had married someone else, we panic. The situations are the same; only our reasoning has changed. Less pressure is put on our marriages when we learn to recognize problems for exactly what they are and nothing more. Utopia doesn't exist, and every relationship has disturbances. Whether or not these disturbances become blown out of all proportion is our problem. Sadly, we usually get caught up worrying about them, talking about them, rather than solving them.

Problems are just that and nothing more, unless we make them so. For instance, a bad cold can be very unpleasant, uncomfortable, temporarily debilitating, but you wouldn't assume for one minute that it was a terminal disease. Certainly, you wouldn't call all your friends, relate every symptom, then say your eternal goodbyes. We do that in marriage. A problem arises, we panic, certain that divorce is right around the corner. Most of us share, with anybody who will listen, all the pain and heartbreak we are experiencing, and then relate how hopeless our situation is. Beyond making molehills into mountains, we often plant a corrupting seed in our mate's mind. Did you ever realize that what you see as a threat may be viewed differently by your mate? Maybe he or she didn't see the issue as important at all, but when you made so much of it, when you mentioned that it could lead to divorce, you actually set the thought in motion!

Since divorce has become so prevalent, more and more acceptable even among Christians, we are all too willing to see everything as a threat to our marriage, to see divorce as the cure-all to all marital differences. When you are standing in the forest of marital problems, the tree of divorce may seem to bear sweet fruit. But those of us who have actually tasted it will tell you that the fruit is quite deceptive; it looks tasty, but it is bred in bitterness, resentment, pain, heartbreak, discouragement, despair, and failure. It certainly wasn't the taste we expected; it left us hungry and wanting.

You can't proceed with any real effectiveness in problem-solving until you stop using divorce as a scapegoat for failing to assume your responsibilities. I know that it is a hard statement to swallow, but you can't progress if you continually think, "Well, if this doesn't work, we can still get a divorce." The word itself should be stricken from your vocabulary.

Perhaps you view divorce as "the way out." The word itself suggests freedom, elimination of pressure and pain. You are convinced that next time it will be different. If you want out to marry that "right person," divorce appears to be a sweet release.

Unfortunately, in our desire to find the ideal situation, we carry with us the unresolved conflicts of the last marriage. We therefore face not only the unsolved conflicts of the first marriage, but the new problems which will ultimately arise. For example, the problem in your first marriage may have been a critical spirit. Mate number one stunk up the house with his smoking, he drank too much, he was undependable. You complained, nagged, but to no avail. The more you criticized, the worse the problem became. Now mate number two doesn't have the social graces to which you are accustomed, and try as you might, you can't change him. Certainly, the situation is different, but the critical spirit which wasn't resolved in marriage one is now affecting marriage two. Or in the first marriage your mate often flirted, commented on the attractiveness of members of the opposite sex, and in general kept you in a constant state of jealousy. Of course, partner number two never flirts, and never starts drooling when an attractive girl comes on the TV, but the other day you met him for lunch, and were surprised at the beautiful blonde he'd just hired. Jealousy began to swell in your soul, and you became suspicious and miserable. Here again the circumstances are changed, but the basic unresolved conflict still exists.

I knew a lovely young woman a few years ago. In sharing some of her marital strains with me, she said that communication was their main problem. Their intimate discussions had digressed to note writing. A few months later, Ginny was killed in a terrible car accident. In time her husband remarried. The second marriage seemed to have been made in heaven. Susan was a more competent housekeeper, the home was run more efficiently, and she and Greg had a wonderful relationship. But as time passed, Susan and Greg began to have serious problems talking. Greg finally told Susan that he and Ginny had had the same problem. The situation had changed, the person was different, but Greg took in to this new relationship all the unsolved problems of the first.

Unfortunately, divorce is usually not the cure, since sooner or later the problems still have to be faced in one form or another. Don't delude yourself into thinking that divorce is the panacea for a sick marriage. Isolate your problems *right now*, face and solve them; then you can experience true happiness and fulfillment right where you are planted!

If you know your mate is involved with someone else, you are hurting terribly. I know sometimes the pain gets so great that it actually becomes physical. I know—I have gone through exactly the same kind of hurt time and again. Only then I didn't realize how much my words and actions were the root cause of it. If you are hurting now, no matter what the cause, and you feel that running to a lawyer and getting a piece of paper will cure the pain, believe me you can't imagine what "finalized" pain can be like.

WHAT ABOUT HIS HELP?

I'm not telling you that if you truly want to save your marriage, if you sincerely trust and rely on Christ and apply the concepts for a happy marriage, that you will be too busy to hurt. That would be a lie. I can't tell you that there won't be setbacks: there probably will be. But remember, your marriage didn't get where it now is overnight; it didn't get there all by itself, and the return process is like growing—sometimes it's slow, sometimes it hurts, but the end results are worth so much. If you take the correcting of your problems one day at a time, remember that you are not alone in your desire to save your marriage. The help of an Almighty God is available to you. Psalms 34:17–18a (AMP): "When the righteous cry for help, the Lord hears, and delivers them out of all their distress and troubles. The Lord is close to those who are of a broken heart . . ." Isn't that fantastic! God loves you more than you love yourself, and He even loves your mate more than you do. Since He established the institution of marriage (Gen. 2:18), He wants more than anything in the world to have your relationship reconciled. You can relax, knowing He promised (1) Hebrews 13:5 (AMP): ". . . He (God) Himself has said, I will not in any way fail you nor give you up nor leave you without support. I will not in any degree leave you helpless, nor forsake, nor let you down. Assuredly not!" (2) I Corinthians 10:13 (AMP): "For no temptation—no trial . . . had overtaken you and laid hold on you that is not common to man . . . But God is faithful and He can be trusted not to let you be tempted and tried and assayed beyond your ability and strength of resistance and power to endure, but with the temptation He will always also provide the way out—the means of escape to a landing place—that you may be capable and strong and powerful patiently to bear up under it." (3) He promises us that He will be sufficient to see us through anything. (II Cor. 12:9) (4) In II Corinthians 9:8 He promises that He will support us, bless us, so we may be strong enough for whatever problems we face.

Perhaps as you read the next few chapters you may feel that these concepts won't work. You may think that God's directives are totally opposite to all human feelings and ideas. God clearly speaks to this feeling in Isaiah 55:8–9 (AMP): "For My thoughts are not your thoughts, neither are your ways My ways, says the Lord. For as the heavens are higher than the earth, so are My ways higher than your ways, and My thoughts than your thoughts." You might think of the concepts this way: If you are familiar with skiing, you know when you began to ski, your first instinct was to lean back into the slope. It was natural, it seemed right. But what happened? You fell flat. When you were willing to do the opposite, to defy human logic, to risk and lean away from the hill, then your skis became firmly implanted and you were off on a lovely adventure. The same is true in life. God's concepts are often totally contrary to our nature. Remember Proverbs 14:12 (AMP): "There is a way which seems right to a man and appears straight before him, but at the end of it are the ways of death." When we are willing to lean away from the hill, to depend on Him to know what is best for us, to depend on the Master Designer to show us what will work best in our lives and marriages, only then do our lives and marriages become the wonderful adventure He had promised and planned for us.

Isn't it wonderful how *you* can change directions and move forward? *You* can actually begin correcting the problems that are destroying your marriage! For the first time you realize how one person can effect permanent changes in a relationship. You are now ready to join the thousands of other couples who learned the truth of I Corinthians 10:13, finding that there were answers, that you are able to face and conquer the problems that you feared the most. Isn't it great to know as you progress that you have the promise of God Almighty to constantly be with you, support you, lead you, and bless you? Christ didn't just offer Christians a "pie in the sky, bye and bye," but *real* answers, *real* solutions, to revolutionize their marriages right here and now!

Do you realize how far you have progressed in your thinking patterns in just the last few minutes? You are on the brink of discovery; *hope* is now yours. Those answers that have eluded you for so long are now in your hands. You aren't alone any more, you are traveling a well-worn path, and at the end you'll find the most beautiful reward of all, love renewed.

GOALS: Your goal at this moment is to realize that divorce *isn't* the answer that God would have you seek, nor is it the cure-all that the world has made it out to be. Your goal is to recognize that you are not alone in your problems, that thousands and thousands of others have walked this same way, and through the application of God concepts have changed hell into happiness. You have to understand moment by moment that you are not alone, that the power of God Almighty is always with you, always ready to support you, all that He asks is your availability. You are ready to become a survivor.

ASSIGNMENTS:

(1) Memorize Philippians 4:13, Luke 18:27.

(2) Begin to regularly study the Scriptures, beginning with I John. If you feel insecure in studying the Word, write me and I will put you in touch with a wonderful study ministry.

(3) Remove the word *divorce* from your vocabulary.

(4) Review your problems, and see which ones are molehills and which ones are mountains.

(5) Read Hebrews 10:23, and ponder Hebrews 11:1 and 6.

(6) Prepare yourself for a marvelous new experience, get rooted firmly in the Word, and then step back and let God take over!

(7) Make a list of six instances of loving behavior that you've made toward your mate in the last month. If your list is blank, begin today to correct that situation. Check yourself on a new list two weeks from today and see the marvelous improvement God has accomplished through you.

(8) For your own edification and encouragement make a list of all God's blessings in your life. You'll be amazed at all the things you actually have to be thankful for. When a blue

mood hits, just pull out your list and thank God for His many blessings.

(9) Quickly move on and read the miracles wrought in the marriage written about in Chapter 3.

CHAPTER 3

PROBLEM: MARRIAGE WITHOUT CHRIST

Symptoms

- Lives with constant problems and no solutions
- The Sunday Christians
- Intellectual understanding of Christ and God's purpose for Him with no personal relationship
- Lives which fail to produce the fruit of the Spirit: gentleness, peace, forgiving nature, kindness, etc.
- The Christianity and occult mixers
- A self righteous attitude
- General resentment against life
- Sensual attitudes
- Disdain for God and His Authority

Have you ever talked to God like this?

"Dear God, it hurts so bad, I'm so scared, I don't know where to turn. God, who can help? I've searched, I've read—where are the answers? I want to be Your child, but God, I don't know how, I'm confused, I want answers, but I don't want to be put down. If You can't bring me answers, if You don't care enough, if You can't get through, who can? Who can? I feel so alone, so isolated in my pain, my search, dear God. If You can't help me, reach me, I'll feel pushed to seek the world's answers. I don't want to, but I often question my own sanity. Maybe I'm crazy, maybe I'm praying to nothing. I don't want to believe that, but who's to say. I've pleaded and no answers. Why? Maybe fulfillment is only admitting my friends are right. Is it that I am all-important, that I'm all that is, that fulfillment and pleasure are life's ultimate reward?

"Sometimes I wonder if You're there. Why, oh why can't You hear my cry, see my pain? Where are all those promises, all those answers? Why don't they connect for me? Dear God, hear me, hear me!"

A blasphemous prayer? No! A prayer of one lost, searching, begging for answers from a God they don't truly know!

I was talking with a Christian counselor the other day, and I asked her, of those you counsel, approximately what percentage who feel they are Christians actually have a personal knowledge and relationship with Christ? I was astounded by her answer. "Anne," she said, "I would venture to say about seventy per cent!" Unfortunately, I've found the same problem. So many of those who plead with God for answers, intervention, blessings, don't know Him. Before we can learn and apply God's solutions to our lives, we need to be sure we know the One from Whom we seek help.

I talk with so many couples in counseling who *think* they are Christians because they were raised in the church, or their parents were Christians, because they try to observe the Ten Commandments, or they strive to live good lives, go to church on Sunday. Some have an intellectual understanding of Christ and His mission, without ever having accepted His work on the cross for themselves personally, but in each case the premise on which they base their Christianity is wrong.

Being raised in the church does not a Christian make. Nor is Christianity genetically passed down. Living a good life, going to church, having an emotional experience, even observing the Ten Commandments are fine, but they aren't the requirements for being God's child. John 14:6 (AMP) tells us: "Jesus said to him, I am the Way and the Truth and the Life; no one comes to the Father except by [through] Me."

Sadly many people rely on their supposed Christianity to get them through the rough times, and then, when it fails before their eyes, they become hostile and bitter. Many times these precious souls have never read the Bible, never learned God's Word, or applied it to their lives. They pray in traumatic situations, cry because they feel God has let them down, when actually they never knew Him. If you fall into this category, don't be ashamed; many of us have walked this way before you.

"But Anne, what has Christianity to do with my marriage?" *Everything*. But from the standpoint of statistics, in today's world you will find that one out of every three marriages ends in divorce. In Christian marriages, where the family has a regular time of Bible study, either personal or through tapes, and family prayer, the divorce rate drops to one in every 1,015.[1] Why? Because when Christ is controlling the life of both the wife and husband, harmony results. Christ does not war against Himself. (I Cor. 14:33)

Before we get into the how-to's, the concepts, I'd like to stop right here and share with you the *true* story of a couple, Melony and Todd Winters, whose marriage had reached the brink of divorce, but who, through the love and dedication of two lovely Christian women, discovered a new life. Melony and Todd's story isn't pretty, but often those who are searching have to reach the depths before they are open to Christ's message.

I recall many years ago when I first met Melony Winters; it was at Lake Junaluska, North Carolina. Her flashing green eyes were dramatically set off by her coal-black hair. Even through the teeming crowd, her radiant face stood out. We were both babes in Christ at the time and were there to attend a Lay Institute for Evangelism.

But Melony's story begins before that meeting of long ago. In the following pages she and her husband have opened their hearts, their lives; they have shared their joys and the transgressions which brought them to the brink of divorce. It wasn't easy for them to allow someone to probe and dissect their lives so that others might find permanent answers. There were many tears shed, but they felt that it was worth every reopened wound, if only one person found the hope, the solutions and the miracle which changed their pathetic lives.

TODD AND MELONY WINTERS' STORY

MELONY

Sitting, staring through a dirty window, I watched the grim crowd below, the prostitutes, perverts, dope pushers, and the addicts shuffling down the street. For a moment, I turned and surveyed the walls of the apartment I now called home. Faded roses dangled like wilted flowers from the paper which hung in strips on the wall. Spiders had happily made their home in each corner of the room. I glanced at the couch where Sherry had crashed the night before. As I turned again to the window, I wondered how Todd and the girls were doing without me. As I thought about them and the house in suburbia that I had run from, my mind went back to my illustrious beginning.

Who would have believed that the daughter of one of the wealthiest merchants in Houston would ever be living in such a place? Why, hadn't I been raised in the "Finger Bowl" district? Certainly, this wasn't the future that my parents had envisioned when I was born.

Of course, marriage hadn't been first on their list of accomplishments for me either. I had been raised (or should I say spoiled) to be a lady. I never learned how to cook, clean, or do anything that would have prepared me for marriage; we had maids to do such things. My parents provided me with schooling in the "right" private school in Houston. All my life I had been taught that accomplishment meant a proud career, graduation from the right college, and in time, if need be, marriage.

Jesus was a silent word in our home, although we went to church every Sunday, and I was properly sent to church camp each summer. At the age of eleven, I joined the church, not because I knew or wanted Jesus in my life, but because it was the proper thing to do. I presumed from that point forward that I was a Christian.

From my earliest years, I can remember feeling an emptiness in my heart, which I felt could only be filled by love. During my early teens in a search for fulfillment, I turned to promiscuity to fulfill my needs. I suppose, if I had sat down and thought about it, I would have realized I was taking the wrong road, but I never let thinking get in the way of my search for the one who would "love" me unconditionally and completely.

At the tender age of fourteen, I thought I had found my guy. Andy awakened deep feelings in me, and at long last I felt the search was ended. A short time after we met, we were making love on a regular basis. Confusion took root in my soul. No matter how much I thought I loved Andy, no matter how fulfilling our encounters were, after each I had such horrible feelings of guilt and remorse that I told myself that it would never happen again. Andy knew I was troubled about something, so I told him how I felt and he seemingly understood and promised that we'd never go all the way again. Naturally, the next time we were alone the tide of our emotion became so high that there was no stopping.

I don't recall knowing much about birth control, but even if I had, I wouldn't have used anything. You see, each and every time we had relations, I promised myself that that would be the last. I reasoned that if I started taking the pill, or using some other method of contraception, that would be admitting that I intended to do it again, and in my heart I really didn't.

We were playing the odds and finally our luck ran out. One period missed, then two. I was smart enough to realize that I was carrying Andy's baby inside me! I didn't know how to tell Andy, but I felt secure in his love. I knew he'd gladly marry me, considering the circumstances. As I talked with Andy, I began to slip into a state of shock. I couldn't believe the words I was hearing. Andy refused to marry me, and the final blow came when he questioned the fatherhood of my child!

I ached with fear and loneliness. I knew I had to tell my parents, but how? As time passed, I began to feel everyone was noticing my protruding abdomen. Day after day I put off the dreadful encounter—that moment of truth with Mother and Daddy.

Well, my fear was confirmed. I might as well have dropped a bomb between the great oaks which are nature's symbol for this socially prominent neighborhood. When my heart and soul were screaming for love, understanding, and guidance, I was met with accusations about my moral character, and comments about my thoughtlessness in not considering their social position. "Melony, do you realize the scandal that this can make?" Mother asked.

Like the matriarch she was, Mother assumed responsibility for the only option she felt was acceptable. Her decision: abortion! After the arrangements were made, she presented me with *my* choice—the choice was abortion or else. I was so confused, I really didn't know what to do. For one fleeting moment I sat down, put my hand on my stomach and felt the butterfly movements of the life within me. As I sat there feeling the life within, I wanted to run, to stop the abortion, but how could I? I'd made such a mess out of my life, I didn't dare defy my parents' wishes in such a serious matter. Of course, abortion was illegal then, but if you had enough money, knew the "right" people, all doors would open.

When it was all over, my parents tried to console me by saying, "Melony, it was only a mass you aborted; it wasn't a child. Honey, just think of it like having a tumor removed." I couldn't cope with the reality, so I pushed the dreadful incident to the back of my mind, and there the corrupting force silently ate on my subconscious for years.

Following proper tradition, I graduated from high school and was promptly enrolled in Sweet Briar, far from the "corrupting" atmosphere of my old friends.

Sweet Briar was a sister school to Washington and Lee, a well-known college for men, and on the weekends the guys would often host dances for the girls. It was at one of these first dances that I met Todd.

TODD

Every week or so, we would look forward to the Sweet Briar girls coming up to our campus for a dance. One particular evening I spotted the most beautiful woman I had ever seen. I asked Jody, "Who is the gal in the green dress?"

"I don't know, Todd, but if you are so interested, why don't you go over there, cut in and get acquainted?" That sounded like a logical suggestion to me, so I strolled across the floor, tapped her partner on the shoulder and cut in. "I'm Todd Winters," I said, "I don't believe I've seen you here before."

"I've never been here before. Oh, I'm sorry, my name is Melony Addair," she said. As we talked, we realized that we had a lot in common. She was an art major and I was studying journalism, quite compatible fields. Before the evening was over, I had asked her to come back the next weekend to a fraternity party. She was hesitant at first, but finally she agreed.

Melony confused me. To look at her, the way she filled out a dress, the sensuous way she moved, spelled "easy." But as we became better acquainted, another girl emerged—a rather shy, pious one. The combination fascinated me, and I was determined to get to know her better.

Getting to know her wasn't as easy as I had anticipated. I couldn't believe that after three or four dates she hadn't even let me kiss her. I guess perhaps she was checking me out too, because after a few more dates she slipped warmly into my arms, not like the pious, innocent façade she had presented, but like a woman who wanted and needed physical love.

She was full of surprises. As we lay in bed, I was astonished when Melony started crying and babbling something about the fact that I shouldn't get mixed up with her because she was "bad news." She told me about the abortion her parents had arranged and of the affairs before me. At first I was stunned by her outburst, but I consoled her by telling her, "Honey, all that is just past history." In reality, I just wanted to calm her down. I wasn't really interested in her past, and since I had no thought of marriage, the abortion and other indiscretions were of no interest to me.

MELONY

I remember how Todd was with me that first time. He was so gentle, so sweet. When I broke down and told him about the abortion, he took me in his arms and soothed the pain. Of course, none of my heartbreaking past kept him from taking me again.

TODD

As far as Melony was concerned, I thought, "Who am I to judge her?" I suppose, like most of the guys at college, I was mainly interested in a girl to sleep with, setting the highest score.

Melony and I continued dating throughout the school term. When summer came, we decided that we'd better cool it for a while. Melony was getting that dangerous look of love in her eyes, and I wasn't too secure in my ability to hold out.

MELONY

When the leaves began to turn and fall came, we resumed dating. Coming together with Todd after three months was like the cooling rain after a long drought. Considering my past experience, you would have thought that by this time in my life I would be using contraceptives, but I wasn't, so in January I discovered that I was pregnant.

I can't explain the panic that gripped my whole body at the thought of telling Todd about the baby, but I knew I couldn't hide the fact forever. Dear Todd, how precious he was. By this time, he too realized that we weren't a passing fling, that he actually loved me. He asked me to marry him.

But what about telling Mother and Daddy? I'd pick up the phone, start to dial, then hang up. What could I say? What words would open their hearts and make them understand? Finally, I gathered my strength and called. Daddy answered and I explained the situation to him. He said, "Melony, this is the last straw. As far as we are concerned, we don't even want to see you again. And young lady, I want you to understand this right now: I am going to my lawyer's tomorrow and disinherit you!"

Silent tears rolled down my face as I listened to his harsh words. When I hung up the phone, Todd didn't have to ask what they said. Gently he took me in his arms as I cried out all the pain and disappointment that filled me. When there were no more tears to weep, he wrapped me up in a blanket and I fell into an exhausted sleep.

TODD

As Melony slept, I walked over to her desk, picked up a pen and paper and wrote her parents a long letter. I told them that I planned to marry Melony immediately. I knew how badly Mr. Addair's words had hurt Melony, and I wanted to accept my responsibility, and perhaps build a bridge of understanding between Melony's parents and us. I told them that I truly loved her, cherished her, and that I was thrilled about the baby that we were going to have. I assured them that I was willing and able to support her.

MELONY

Todd's simple, open, honest letter seemed to melt my parents' hearts, but not their tongues. Their reply was: "Melony, you are a lucky girl; at least this time someone is willing to marry you!"

"Anne, I still cry when I tell this part of our story. It isn't a part that I share when I speak in public, because it still gets to me so bad," Melony said. "But Anne, you know, I *know* the scars that an abortion can leave. Whether it's legal or illegal isn't the issue. I know the wretched pain women will be going through in their spirits in years to come, so I tell you this in the hope that it will reach at least one girl, save one innocent baby."

Todd and I were married and the baby was already on its way. The whole time I was pregnant with Dina, I read all the material my obstetrician gave me. The books graphically described exactly how the baby was forming in my womb. Like a ton of bricks falling on me, I realized that when I had that teenage abortion, the child that was growing inside me wasn't a nothing—or a mass, as my parents had said. Dear God, by the time that abortion was performed my baby already had eyes, it had little feet, toes, and hands. Sometimes I'd sit feeling the movement of this new life and wonder what the child I'd aborted would have been like.

As my pregnancy progressed, the memories of that "lost" child haunted me more and more. I'd read Psalms 139 and my heart would break, as I wept for the child I would never know. I felt that I had committed murder. Sometimes I would wake up in the middle of the night screaming and crying, and Todd would have to hold me and soothe the pain and fear away. I'd just shake, believing that I was going to go to hell for murder. My mind could no longer deal with the grief and guilt I felt. It was at this point that I consciously quit thinking about God; I wanted to have nothing to do with Him, because I was so frightened of His wrath.

TODD

Melony was a wonderful mother when Dina was born. I can't say that she was any great shakes around the house; her pampered upbringing hadn't taught her a thing. But she was a real soldier during this time. She learned to sew, cook basic meals, and boil water without burning the bottom of the pot!

I know that this is hard to believe, but one day I came home from work, and Melony was sitting on the divan with our neighbor and they were laughing themselves silly. What happened was, Melony had been trying to clean house, and when she moved the divan she discovered all this gray fuzzy stuff under it. Frantic, she ran over to Linda's. She said, "Linda, you have got to come over—there is the oddest mass of stuff under my divan." Linda rushed over, looked under the divan, and collapsed in laughter. What Melony had discovered was dust, something she had never seen in her well-kept home.

MELONY

When Todd graduated from college he decided to accept an offer as an editorial assistant on one of the major newspapers in Houston. Personally, I didn't want to go back home, but Todd was firmly committed to starting out in Houston. So we moved back and rented a small apartment on Sage Road.

This was a traumatic time for me. We were just beginning and Todd wasn't making much money. Yet, here I was back in the city where I'd grown up, so socially prominent, living only a few miles from my original home. I felt like I'd gone from riches to rags. I couldn't afford a new dress. I desperately wanted to get ahead, back to the status to which I'd been accustomed. I began to push Todd. I wanted the "right" clothes, I wanted to travel, I wanted my own car, and most of all I wanted out of this apartment and into a respectable home.

One night I just came right out and asked him, "Why can't you make more money?"

Todd didn't answer. He had tried to explain to me before that it took time to become established as an editorial writer, but I couldn't or wouldn't understand. I was sick of living like everybody around me, so I went out and charged the clothes that I wanted. Naturally, Todd would get mad and say that we couldn't pay for them. I didn't care, I simply wasn't going to adjust to doing without.

Sometimes I hated myself for being so selfish; I hated myself for nagging Todd. Every week I'd make a new vow: "This week I'm not going to nag him. I am going to be the wife he wants and needs me to be." And every week I'd fail. I tried positive thinking. That worked until a problem arose; obviously I had no inner source of strength to draw on, and I'd fail. I simply couldn't get over being me, and I realized more and more what the real me was like. And I didn't like her.

TODD

Even with Melony's ups and downs, the first year in the apartment went pretty well. But by the second year, I was getting more and more involved in my writing, taking extra jobs at night, and Melony was getting lonely. I loved writing so much I was willing to work days, nights and weekends too. I was proud,

I was being the young, aggressive writer. I was having my ego fed, but my marriage was starving.

Oh, I did think about Melony and her desires. Who could overlook those charge accounts for long? Much of my overtime work went to help meet the bills that Melony was forever running up. I knew that I was doing the best I could, and it hurt me when Melony ranted and raved about our financial status. I resented her fits, but as soon as I got back to my typewriter I was able to put her voice out of my mind and peace again filled my being.

MELONY

With Todd working all the time, my loneliness and frustration grew. I thought perhaps I'd married too young. At other times, I thought what I needed to do was return to my art studies and have a career as my parents had planned. I wasn't sure what I did want, but I definitely knew that I didn't want to be stuck at home like my neighbors. I looked down on what I felt were dumpy housewives, tied down with four or five kids. To be sure I didn't get caught in that trap, I took up art again.

If it was going to be art, I was going to go the whole route. I let my hair grow real long, and dressed like an escapee from a hippy colony. I ran around and exhibited in art shows and, instead of cleaning the house, spent my time putting my creative genius on canvas.

Todd knew how miserable I was in the apartment, so as soon as possible we bought a house in Spring Branch, a suburb of Houston. He was so sweet, he went along with almost anything I wanted to do. He thought I had talent and he wanted me to be fulfilled. Ofttimes he'd go with me to the art shows and help me set up. The pictures I put on canvas were beautiful and sold well, but the one I was painting in our marriage was a living nightmare.

TODD

Even after I bought Melony a new house, the fights between us increased. Melony, bless her heart, was one heck of a rotten housekeeper. The home we'd purchased was deep in the woods and the trees kept it dark. I guess it was a bit depressing for her.

But daily when I'd come home she wouldn't have cleaned anything, the lunch plates were piled on top of the breakfast dishes, and naturally there was never a meal fixed. She would blame it on the house. "It's a dumpy house to begin with and cleaning it won't change anything, it would still look horrible," she complained. She could rationalize anything. Finally, I would get fed up with it, we'd fight, and then, mainly out of self-defense, I'd pitch in and help her clean up the mess. Thinking back, I believe now that what she was really looking for was a fight, because that was her way to get attention, the attention that I was spending on my work. When we fought, I was there, we were talking, and this seemed to satisfy her. Of course, after each fight there would be a passionate time of making up and then things would go fine again for a while. Melony was crying out for attention, but I was too consumed with myself to hear her.

MELONY

Occasionally I'd venture out of the "dump" and walk down to the neighborhood pool during the day. As if Todd and I didn't have enough problems, I injected a new and more devastating one into our lives. Sex became the big issue in our lives for years to come. It began one day when I was sitting around the pool talking with some women who were discussing their sex lives, likes and dislikes, etc. All of a sudden I began to realize that I'd never experienced an orgasm. I never knew what it was to relax in bed. I'd always been putting on a show, always faking it, just like I had done in the back seats of cars during high school.

Through all our hell, Todd and I never lost the ability to communicate, so as soon as I got home I told Todd that there had to be more in our sexual relationship for me.

TODD

I was taken back by Melony's declaration. I realized what Melony was talking about, but I had developed a pattern through many years of illicit relationships, and I actually didn't know how to make love and fulfill a woman. I suppose I was being selfish; I was mainly interested in my own gratification, and I really hadn't thought much about hers.

Naturally her put-down on my masculinity in the bedroom

didn't help our sex life at all. I recall thinking, "Yes, you may be missing out, but I guess that's *your* problem." I thought I was doing pretty good. You have to realize that I was pretty selfish myself, and I felt that if she wasn't being satisfied, it was because she was asking too much. I don't think at this time I ever seriously said to myself, "Todd, maybe you have a problem too." My opinion was, "I'm okay, the problem is hers." I just kind of passed the buck. We never sat down and faced it one on one and said, "Hey, let's look at this problem and do something about it." Oh, we talked about it occasionally, but nothing was ever resolved. And the problem lingered on and got bigger and bigger.

As time passed, Melony did her best to make a go of the wife and mother act. She tried to clean the house better, she joined the garden club and got in with all the ladies' coffee groups; in essence, she tried to become one of the girls, but it didn't work. Sitting around discussing their husbands, the baby's colic, or what floor wax did the best job, just wasn't her style, it wasn't enough.

MELONY

When I did go to have coffee with the girls, I felt a strange combination of envy that these women were satisfied with their lives, and at the same time, disgust because I felt they were selling themselves short. I kept looking at them and saying to myself, "What is it that makes you get up every morning, make your beds, change diapers, do the wash? How can that be enough?" I decided that the reason they did it was that they had a love for their husbands that was so great it made it all worthwhile. What drove them was love, and I didn't have that kind of love for Todd; we just didn't have that kind of marriage.

Obviously, Todd was wrong for me. From the moment that crossed my mind, every time we went out I began to look around the room for "Mr. Right." I thought, "You haven't found him yet, he's somewhere." You know how you go to parties and flirt around. Well, I became the talk of the town. I'd get crushes on, first, this man, then that. I'd think each time, "Maybe he's the one for me." But each encounter would end in disappointment.

Andy, who'd fathered the baby I'd aborted, also lived in Houston, and that didn't help matters at all. In my fits of rage, or fights about money or sex, I'd go off the deep end and drive around town looking for him!

I constantly confronted Todd with my sexual frustrations. I'd say, "I've never had an orgasm, and I know enough now to know that it's your fault, you are just too quick. You don't know how to make love to a woman." Then I'd go through a stage when I'd think it was my fault and cry, "Oh, Todd, I'm so messed up because of my past." Of course, the truth was we were both messed up because of all the illicit sexual relationships in our pasts.

Too many times I cruelly slashed at his male ego, so that our lovemaking became less and less, because it was so demeaning for both of us. By the latter part of our marriage, we were making love about once every two months. Naturally, we were both frustrated.

TODD

We became involved in an arty crowd that Melony knew, but one which appealed to me also, since there were a number of "writers" involved. Much of our get-together time was spent talking about depressing things like, Why are we here on earth? or the unfulfilled goals of our lives, or our current frustrations. Many of the group were into pot, acid and the like. "But you know, Anne, everybody in that group was searching for more in their lives, just like us. It was a false existence; our main goal was to out-art each other."

I wasn't assuming my masculine role as head of our home; both of us were just wandering in a daze, confused, searching, but so screwed up that we didn't know which way to turn. I encouraged Melony to dress in a seductive way. It was fun to have a wife who was so popular, who always got the most attention at parties.

MELONY

I did as Todd asked. I can't say I minded the attention at first, but deep down I felt that Todd was using me like an ornament in his life to attract people to him. If we were at a party and I danced on the piano, fine; he seemed to need this attention as much as I did.

Of course, my sensual actions did lead to some bad situations.

Men would make open advances to me right in front of Todd, and he'd stand there and do nothing! When we got home I'd scream, "How can you watch things like that happen to me if you love me?"

"Well, I just didn't want to cause a scene, and anyway, I thought you could take care of yourself," he'd reply.

When dancing on pianos didn't get a rise out of him, I sought out wilder schemes. It became a vicious circle. I wanted *his* attention so bad. My desire for him was almost a physical pain; I felt like I was starving for lack of love and affection. But Todd was never there. He was always working. The house started to close in around me. I resented it. By this time, we had a second daughter, and I even resented the time I had to spend caring for the girls.

When Todd got in from work, I'd scream at him for being late, or working such long hours. One weekend, to appease me, he brought his work home so he could spend some time with me. He still didn't understand it wasn't merely his presence I wanted, it was him. Him to talk with, share and love. But there he sat at the dining-room table typing, and I stood there hating him so much for being in there working instead of talking to me, that I ran into the dining room, picked up his manuscript and tore it to shreds. At this point in our lives, I would do just about anything to get him to respond to me. I was like the verse in Isaiah 57:20–21 (AMP): "But the wicked are like the troubled sea, for it cannot rest and its waters cast up mire and dirt. There is no peace, says my God, for the wicked."

TODD

Melony was becoming more and more nervous. She hardly ate, and she slept even less. I suggested that we see a marriage counselor and she finally agreed. We saw a non-Christian counselor, but after only three sessions the doctor threw up her hands and said that she couldn't help us. She said that Melony was too emotionally unstable. Privately she said, "Mr. Winters, I strongly suggest that you get your wife in the best sanitarium as soon as possible."

I couldn't accept the diagnosis of just one doctor, so I took Melony to three more. They all came to the same conclusion. I realized that I needed to talk with Melony's parents. They too agreed that Melony obviously needed confinement and help. Her mother said, "I've known all along that she was mentally unbalanced; that is why she has always been so promiscuous." I felt like saying, "If you've known this so long, why haven't you gotten her help before this?" But I didn't.

MELONY

Todd had just changed jobs and our insurance didn't go into effect for ninety days. I will always thank the Lord for that time. I had had enough of psychiatric sessions to feel that the answers for me didn't lie in their maze of questions. The psychiatrists would say, "You hate your mother." Well, I already knew that. Then they'd ask me, "Why do you feel this way about her?" and I would tell them the whole sordid story of the pregnancy and abortion and how often after that, when she would get mad, she'd slap me in the face and call me a whore. "Man, can't you see what that did to my spirit?"

"Then you have a problem with insecurity too," the psychiatrists would comment. They'd continue with their analysis by saying, "Melony, the problem is that you need love all the time, and that is why you've gone to bed with so many men." Big deal! I didn't need them to tell me that either. I would sit in their offices, begging and pleading for solutions, and their basic answer was that the solutions were within myself, and to come back next week to the tune of fifty dollars a session!

After a particularly trying session, in a daze, almost disconnected from reality, I drove home. Life had lost all its meaning; my body felt like a hollow shell and I could find nothing with which to fill it. I had no desire to continue in what people called life, nor could I see any reason for my children to have to cope with this grim, cruel world. At that moment, I seriously considered killing both myself and the girls!

Dina was asleep and I recall standing over Sharlene's crib, looking down at her, and falling to my knees in tears. I thought, "Oh my beautiful baby, sleep, sleep and enjoy this blessed time of innocence. Darling, I'm just messing you up, the way I didn't want to do. I'm doing everything wrong. I scream and call you names just like my mother did me. I know you don't understand why. Please believe me, I don't mean to, I really don't, I just can't help it. I had such plans for you, but they've crumbled into ashes. I'm not teaching you right and wrong, I'm failing all the way around."

By this time, I had become notorious in the neighborhood as the *femme fatale*. No one would have anything to do with me—at least not the women. I didn't have any real friends, and I was having an affair with Craig, a man who worked with Todd. Craig was more messed up than I was. I don't know now how I thought he could help me, but I did.

TODD

I had caught Melony out with Craig several times, and when she'd come home, I'm ashamed to say, I'd often scream, cuss, and occasionally hit her. For some reason I had a deep-seated belief that marriage was for keeps, so I didn't leave. A seed must have been planted long ago in my mind, because this was the only right way of thinking I seemed to possess. After their affair had been going on for some time, Melony finally came home one night and said, "If you're not going to leave, I'm going to, because I want out of this marriage!" There wasn't much I could say. I tried to stop her, but I was still waiting for an opening in the private sanitarium her parents and I had selected. I couldn't forcibly restrain her. The next morning she asked a neighbor to pick her up, and she left.

MELONY

Todd wasn't going to stop me, nobody was. Craig had offered to rent me an apartment, and made promises of financial support. I felt confident in leaving and having a place to go, and money to live on.

TODD

Strained almost to the breaking point, I made one more attempt to talk with Melony. I said, "Darn it, Melony, can't you even accept your responsibilities as a mother? Through our love we brought two precious children into this world. Dear God,

Melony, how can you leave them? They are a part of you, don't you understand?"

"Todd," she said, "I don't know when it started, maybe I've always been messed up, but I can't take this life one minute longer. I'm not asking for anything. I just want out."

MELONY

Behind me I left a house, a "marriage," a husband and two children. I couldn't cope with the life I'd chosen and my only thought was to run, and run I did.

TODD

With Melony gone, this was a hard time for me. Melony was living and mixing with a hippy colony which had sprung up in Houston. I knew, of course, that Craig was her steady companion and nightly lover. Make no mistake, I'm no saint. Often my mind would take trips of fantasy about what I was going to do to Craig, but then reality set in. I recognized that, as emotionally unstable as Melony was, if I did something wrong, there wouldn't be anyone to look after the girls. I kept telling myself, "I've got to be responsible about what I do." It was pure hell facing Craig at work every day. Horrid pictures of him and Melony together would constantly loom up in my mind.

Wifeless, I was faced with the total responsibility of the girls. Each day I farmed the children out with understanding neighbors so I could continue working. In the evening, tired from the day's pressures, I picked up the children, tried to fix a decent dinner and, if sleep didn't overtake me, I'd make vain attempts at cleaning the house.

During this time I had many hours to think and I realized that Melony was messed up, but that I wasn't the caring, thoughtful person I should have been either. I decided that perhaps the long hours that I had been putting in at the paper were part of our problem. I hoped my new job would give me more time at home.

Weeks passed, and occasionally I'd call and check to see that Melony was all right. Then my new company decided that I had to go to Detroit for a week to consult with a new author! I had to call Melony; someone had to keep the children.

MELONY

Todd called late one night. He told me about his new job and that his first assignment was going to take him to Detroit for a week. He *insisted* that I come home and take care of the children while he was away. My mind fought the idea of returning to that house for even a week, but Todd wasn't going to take no for an answer. I did tell him, if he made me do this, that probably by the time he got back I'd be dead and so would the girls! It scared him, but he still demanded that I come back and babysit.

Todd was gone, and the second day I was home one of my neighbors called and said that she had told her sister, Pat, about me. She said, "Melony, Pat is a true Christian, and has really been growing since she has been attending a ladies' Bible study in the neighborhood." I wasn't impressed with the glowing terms she used to describe Pat, nor was I interested in any God stuff. Not long after our conversation, Pat called and asked if she and a friend could drop by. She said, "I know some of the things you've been through and I wondered if I could come by and bring a friend who has had a similar experience."

I wasn't too polite. I said, "No, I know you are all involved in church and I don't want any part of that. I've tried that and it doesn't work."

"It's not really church that has meant so much," Pat replied. I was at a loss for words, I really didn't know how to say no, so I told her she could come over the next afternoon.

I didn't do anything special to get ready to meet my first Christians. In fact, all day I thought, "Oh, what have you gotten yourself into now?"

I heard the car pull in the drive and looked out as Pat and her friend came up the sidewalk. They were both carrying Bibles. That turned me off. What did impress me was how attractive they both were, not at all what I'd expected. They both seemed so full of life, so happy. We talked and talked for hours.

I let all the bitterness and poison in my soul spill out in the room that day. I shot all sorts of questions at them. Questions about God and the Bible. I'd ask, and in a minute they'd turn to the Scripture and give me the answer! These gals were the first people who had ever clearly answered questions and dealt with me directly from the Scripture. To my amazement, the answers were logical, even to my messed-up mind.

I finally spilled out the whole story about Todd and me, about how much we hated each other and how we couldn't live together. Finally, after all was said and done, I told them what it really came down to was my relationship with God. I couldn't believe what I was hearing coming out of my mouth. I blurted out the whole nightmare about the abortion. I said, "Look, I'll tell you what I've done that is so bad that God will never forgive me." With love glowing in her face, Pat said, "Melony, there is nothing, nothing that God does not forgive, and you can have that wiped clean from your slate forever. God has promised to forgive and forget it, never hold you accountable for it, at the moment you accept Christ's payment on the cross for you personally. Melony, the only unpardonable sin is personally rejecting Christ's reconciling death for you."

I could hardly believe that, my mind could barely take it in, I'd never heard that before. Then Pat shared a booket, called the "Four Spiritual Laws," with me and asked me if I'd ever prayed and accepted Jesus' payment on the cross for me personally. "Well, I joined the church," I said.

"That isn't what I'm talking about, Melony. I mean, have you personally asked Jesus into your life?"

"No," I replied.

"Melony, let me read something from the Scripture which I think may be meaningful to you," Pat said.

My heart broke as she read: "Come now, and let us reason together, says the Lord; though your sins be as scarlet, they shall be as white as snow; though they be red like crimson, they shall be as wool. If you are willing, obedient, you shall eat the good of the land." (Isa. 1:18–19 AMP) Then she read Isaiah 51:6 (AMP). I didn't hear the whole verse, but I clearly heard: ". . . but My salvation shall be forever, and My rightness and justice (and faithfully fulfilled promise) shall not be abolished."

"Melony," Pat said, "let's make this personal the way God intended for it to be, in John 3:16 (AMP): 'For God so greatly loved and dearly prized Melony that He (even) gave up His only begotten (unique Son) so that if Melony believes in (trusts, clings to, relies on) Him she shall not perish—come to destruction, be lost—but have eternal (everlasting) life.' That's God's personal message to you, Melony . . . that is exactly what He meant!"

"Melony, wouldn't you like to know the peace and forgiveness that Jesus offers?"

To myself I thought: "Why not? I've spent so much money on doctors, I'm so tired of running, I'm completely out of answers, out of places to hide. Lord, I'm turning this whole mess over to You."

With tears streaming down my face and with no embarrassment, I slipped off the couch and fell to my knees, knowing inside that at long last my internal war was over. I didn't know exactly what to say, how to pray, but Pat explained that prayer was simply talking to God, honestly. She graciously helped me as I confessed to my Savior the horrible mess I'd made of my life and all those around me. Then I simply shared with God the Father the pain and misery I felt, the lost hopelessness in my life. I thanked Him for already paying for all the rotten awful things I'd done, and for accepting me at that moment, just as I was. Then we all praised Him for loving me enough to bring me the answers when I needed them the most.

After Pat and her friend left, I sat thinking through my sordid life and glorying in the forgiveness Christ had given me. All of a sudden my twisted thinking began to clear. I realized that all that love that I'd been screaming about all those years, all the searching for a man, all the love that my hippy friends were talking about was in these two girls! I was overwhelmed that they loved *me* enough to come and talk to me . . . and they didn't even know me before. Tears came again when I grasped the wonder of the day, the fact that these gals didn't have to care about my life, but they did, they really did. I was so touched, so deeply moved.

My old nature didn't leave me alone too long. In an hour or so I felt a tremendous pull to call Craig, but I asked Christ to give me the strength to resist, and He did. That evening, I got up and fixed a dinner for my girls, which was an absolute miracle because I *never* cooked. They had practically been raised at the fast-food chains. Then I noticed that my house was filthy, so I cleaned it, and I recall thinking while I was cleaning, "Boy, is this different for me."

That night Todd called me from Detroit and I said, "Todd, I want to tell you something that has happened to me, and I want you to promise that you won't laugh, but these two girls have come and talked to me about Jesus, His love and His forgiveness, and I have asked Him to forgive me, and to come into my life. I want to ask you to try to somehow find a way in your heart to forgive me too, because I want to try again to make our marriage work."

TODD

As Melony spoke, I sensed a calm and peace in her voice that I'd never heard before. After she told me about accepting Christ, I was so surprised, all I could say was, "Honey, that's great."

MELONY

The next day I was invited to my first Bible class, and the Lord gave me a great sendoff. Just before I left home, I received a telegram from Todd and it contained a whole page of "I love you, I love you." Later he told me he had called Western Union and asked the operator, "How many times can I say I love you for five dollars?" As I held the telegram, I remember thinking, "You're a fool for trying to get rid of this man, he's so fabulous. You'd better try hard to straighten your marriage up."

When Todd came home, of course, everything didn't turn into Utopia overnight. In fact, the very next day we had a terrible fight because I wanted to go back to my apartment to get my clothes, when Todd and I both knew that I was going to see Craig one more time. I felt that I had to be certain, to make absolutely sure that I didn't want to stay with Craig. Todd let me go and God opened my eyes to the area where my apartment was located, and to the man I had left my marriage for. The area was filthy, smelly. Guys were riding around in cars shouting obscenities, and one man actually came up and tried to proposition me. He thought I was a prostitute! It was horrible, so ugly, and I thought, "How could I have lived here?" All I wanted to do was get back to my house in the suburbs.

TODD

When Melony came home, she immediately got fortified as she read the Bible, listened to tapes, and attended as many as four Bible studies a week. I could almost see an hourly change in her. I tried to go to every meeting that Melony heard about. In fact, in watching her and the changes I saw occurring, I became curious about Jesus also. (I Pet. 3:1)

Melony was really on fire and she grew. Then all of a sudden she decided that Jesus wasn't just for her, that I needed Him too. It just so happened that one of the men she had heard speak in North Carolina, Howard Ball, was going to be in town and she asked me to go. I don't know if I'd have gone, except I was daily seeing the Lord making tremendous changes in Melony's life. The house was always clean, the girls beautifully cared for, and mealtime was a pleasure. By this time I was even attending some night Bible classes with her. I wasn't a Christian, but I didn't want to do anything to discourage her. I was a little embarrassed about the open way her friends talked about Jesus; it didn't seem like the proper social thing to do.

Well, Melony convinced me to go hear Howard Ball. I liked the way he spoke and what he had to say. He went through the plan of salvation, step by step. For years I had been an intellectual Christian. I mean I knew who Christ was, what He had done, I thought I was a Christian, but I had never asked Christ into my life. I didn't feel that it had any personal relevance to me. All of a sudden, for the first time, while Howard was reviewing the "Four Spiritual Laws" I realized that Jesus Christ was actually the Son of the living God and that I, Todd, was a sinner separated from Him. For the first time, I prayed, confessing my sinful state to Christ, thanking Him for His payment on the cross for me personally, and I asked Him to come into my life and take control. Privately I thanked Him for the daily wonders He was performing in Melony's life and our marriage. From that moment on, I *knew* in my heart that I was now God's child.

On the way home, Melony said, "Well, how did you like Howard?"

"Fine," I said.

"Well, did you?" she asked.

"Did I what?"

"Did you pray with Howard?"

"Yes, I did."

She shrieked, grabbed me, and began crying because she was so happy.

I told Melony that night that I fully believed that this was the reason that we came to Houston. I believe now that we came to Houston to find the Lord, and Melony agrees with me.

We were both amazed at the people we met at many of the Bible classes. There were prominent businessmen, men who were successful, and just because they were Christians didn't mean they didn't or couldn't have financial success. We were invited into some of the most beautiful homes in River Oaks, where we were surprised to meet many people who had stories very similar to ours. They were open, they glowed with their new, born-again lives. This group had to have been the best-kept secret in Houston; here was a huge core of people who believed in Jesus right in Melony's old neighborhood, and she had never known it.

MELONY

Todd and I began to grow together. It wasn't easy, we weren't even starting at 0 but at minus 0, because not only did we not *feel* love for each other, but we had built up so much hurt, mistrust and scar tissue over the years. But with God, nothing is impossible.

The Lord provided a marvelous opportunity for me to visit some dear friends in Atlanta. When I arrived, they said, "Melony, I hope you don't mind, but we have been planning to attend a seminar on God's role for wives, and we'd love for you to join us, but if you don't care to, please feel free to stay home."

"You've got to be kidding. This is exactly what I am looking for. Of course I want to go," I replied.

You can't imagine the look on my face as we sat down in a lovely church in north Atlanta, and my old friend Anne Carroll, whom I'd met in North Carolina, stood up to speak. As I listened to Anne and Darien Cooper, I realized how I had undermined my husband's masculinity. My heart broke when I understood the pain it must have caused him because of my unfaithfulness.

But I learned, and I learned what God's role for a wife was, and it was exciting.

I talked to Anne after the class and said how much I wished we had something like this in Houston. Then she told me that the whole series of lessons was available on tape, and I could start sharing what I'd found in Atlanta with women in Houston by tape. I gathered up all the tapes I could take back, and began spreading the wonderful word, and women responded.

As I began to study, I began trying to be God's woman, to submit. It was so hard, it was so hard. I remember calling Pat one day and screaming, "How am I supposed to submit when I don't even love the creep?" Pat said, "Melony, you've got it backwards. The Lord says, 'Give first and love will come.'" That was my first realization of fact and action before feeling.

As we grew more in the Lord, I began to see first and foremost I was to be submissive because God told me to. (Eph. 5:22) But in being what was honoring to God, I was supplying what Todd needed. I began to pray, "Lord, show me the ways that I can meet the needs of this man."

That is when I really began to learn what submissive was. I then became his helpmate in a real way, and I began to fulfill him in ways where we were vastly different. Poor Todd was like the absent-minded professor, never on time. On the other hand, I couldn't stand to be late. Needless to say, this caused many fights. God began to show me that it was a need in Todd's life for me to let up the pressure of having dinner at certain hours. So I prayed that the Lord would cool me off in that area and that I wouldn't care so much about punctuality and, sure enough, my desire to gripe about Todd's lateness disappeared. I began to plan so I could fix foods that would stay warm, something that I could serve when he walked in the door on time or late. If he was late, I fed the girls first, and I waited and ate with him. There were a million little things around the house that I had always made a list for Todd to do. But now I thought, if I wanted more time with my husband, perhaps I could do some of these things myself. I knew my man and I knew he'd think it was neat that at long last I could get things done by myself. I just praised the Lord, because Todd's attitude began to change; he began to respond to me when I began to help him.

Sex was still a horrible experience for us. As I studied the Scriptures I realized (I Cor. 7:4–5) that it was wrong for me to withhold sexual pleasure from Todd, even though I still wasn't getting anything out of it. Of course, in the past I'd been *using* sex. In my B.C. (before Christ) days I felt that it was the greatest tool a woman had! Christ graciously changed my attitude in this area and gave me the insight to understand that until all the other areas of our life were in the right balance, my sexual fulfillment probably wouldn't change. Sex was going to be like the icing on the cake, and I realized that I had no right to expect this beautiful physical relationship until all the hurt and bitterness were healed.

TODD

In becoming a Christian, the first thing I had to learn was what love is. I always thought that love was sort of an emotional thing. Then as I studied the Scriptures I learned that love is an *action* word. Maybe another word for love is *do*. Once I learned that, I began saying to myself, "It's my responsibility to do for Melony, and even though I have hard feelings, I have to let Christ heal them." I had to reconcile with my soul through Christ to forgive her. Then I had to *learn* to love all over again. We've had our ups and downs since then, but when we look back we have come so far, it is incredible. I have to admit I'm much more in love with Melony this year than I was last, and last year I said the same thing.

The hardest thing for me to learn was to be a giving person, because I had always been a selfish person. Giving is something that I've always had to struggle with. In the past, when I became upset or discontent with Melony or the girls, I'd withdraw to my work and fulfill myself there. Now I recognize that I was causing many of our problems, I was actually robbing Melony and the girls of myself. I know now that I have to feed the fires of love around me, because like fire, love left untended slowly dwindles and burns out.

My mother told me something very wise when I was a little boy. I didn't understand it then, but now I know the deep meaning of her words. She said, "Todd, never date a girl that you wouldn't want to marry." Well, that sounded silly to me, but she continued by saying, "You see, Todd, once you develop a relationship with somebody, the relationship cannot stand still; it either has to grow or it dies . . ." Now I know you have to spend time to make a marriage work. Marriage and love are like a garden: they can be beautiful growing plants, or untended, be overtaken with the weeds of business, clubs, friends, TV, etc., and then wither and die.

MELONY

As time passed, I finally got down on my knees to my Lord, and said, "Lord, I don't care if Todd never responds to me physically as I wish. I don't care if he never remembers my birthday or our anniversary. I don't care if he is ever what I think he should be. I'm going to be what he needs, and I'm going to be Your woman." That was the turning point for me. God implanted a deep desire in my heart to be a better housekeeper. I searched for areas where I might be failing Todd. In a short time, the Lord gave Todd the desire and ability to be what I'd prayed he'd be, and it has been that way ever since.

I feel like I'm on a perpetual honeymoon. Honestly, I do. I can't wait until Todd gets home. I love for him to touch me, and I look at him and think he is the handsomest man on earth. The Lord has blessed our sexual life; it is so wonderful, nothing like I ever thought I could experience, and I feel like we're just starting. God has beautifully taught us the truth of Psalms 127:1 (AMP): "Except the Lord builds the house, they labor in vain who build it . . ."

Melony and Todd spent years searching for an answer to their torn lives. Perhaps you too have sought happiness and peace of mind in every outlet, pleasure, escape, indulgence, and illusion the world has to offer, yet that precious peace still eludes you, your marriage continues to crumble. Like Melony and Todd, you may have desperately tried to draw strength to face life's problems from within, from your mate, through positive thinking, transcendental meditation, etc., only to find that the reserves of these sources soon ran out.

Melony and Todd aren't isolated cases. The solution they found is available to each of you individually. What happened to

Melony and Todd was simply that they met the Master, they came to terms with God the Father and accepted His plan for them personally.

With the Holy Spirit at the controls of their lives, Melony and Todd were able to apply God's concepts. In their humanity neither was capable of being the kind of mate the other needed. As they began walking with Him, the Lord provided new soil for the sowing of a new life together and in Him. The self-centeredness which had dominated each of their lives now turned to other-centeredness.

The impossible, unconditional type of love which Melony had been searching for on a human level was fulfilled. She no longer made impossible demands on Todd, demands that only Christ could fill. Melony's view of herself changed her whole personality and her whole world. Instead of seeing a promiscuous, desperate failure, now in the center of His love she saw reflected a new woman, justified and acceptable to God through Jesus Christ. With His guidance she learned God's concepts for marriage, and in His strength she was able to apply them to their pathetic relationship. As she was open and available, He changed her wants, desires, her actions and reactions, so that in time she became the woman that Todd could truly love, the mother her girls needed and a person she could respect.

Instead of misunderstanding and condemnation for Melony, Todd saw that he too needed to accept God's plan for his life. As he came to know the Master, his demanding, selfish, critical nature mellowed. Through his study of the Scriptures, he realized that he hadn't been the kind of husband and father that he should have been. In time, Todd learned how to be the leader God created him to be, and as he took his right position, gently guiding, strengthening, leading, and protecting Melony, their home became a relaxed place, free from constant fights, criticism and unfulfilled expectations. As he allowed God to work in his life, he ultimately became the husband that Melony could respect and respond to with all her heart.

Each of them learned that as they began their new marital venture they must first accept each other, as Christ accepted them—just as they were. They learned that true love isn't a feeling trip; it is an action word!

THE AVAILABLE MIRACLE

Todd and Melony's personal unhappiness and marital discord were a reflection of what happened in the Garden of Eden. In the Garden, man chose to go his own independent way, to do his thing, not God's. At this point, man lost the power to live the life God had designed him to live. Romans 5:12 (AMP) describes how this nature is passed down from generation to generation: "Therefore as sin came into the world through one man and death as the result of sin, so death spread to all men, no one being able to stop it or to escape its power because all men sinned." Sin isn't only overt acts such as adultery, murder, lying, cheating, stealing, anger, jealousy, gossip, etc. These are simply sins which result from the sin nature inherent in every man. Sin is actually acting independently from God, choosing your way instead of His. The Scripture refers to this state as the "natural man," or non-Christian.

God, being merciful, looked down and said, in essence: "I love mankind. I designed them to have fellowship with Me, but in their sinful state I can't commune with them. My character of Justice and Righteousness demands that payment be made for their sins, and payment is death!" Then God, in His love, designed a plan whereby you might have this blessed fellowship restored. He did this without compromising His perfect character. About two thousand years ago, Jesus Christ, God's Son, in essence said: "I will leave the wonders of heaven, and I will become the God-Man. I will live a perfect, sinless life, and after living a perfect life I will willingly pay the price of death on the cross for each person *individually.*" And that is exactly what He did. While He was hanging there on the cross for a period of three hours, everything you have done that was wrong, thought about and hoped you could do, everything you will do wrong in the future, was poured out on Jesus. During that time, He suffered your hell for you! It was so excruciating that it caused Him to cry out, "My God, My God, why have You forsaken me?" (Ps. 22:1 AMP) Jesus Christ acted as your substitute; it took that to pay for your sin and mine. But at the end of those three hours,

Jesus said, "It is finished." (John 19:30 AMP) "Father, I have paid for every one of them."

The fact that Jesus Christ paid for your sins doesn't make salvation yours. "But to as many as did receive and welcome Him, He gave the authority (power, privilege, right) to become the children of God, that is to those who believe in (adhere to, trust in and rely on) His name." (John 1:12 AMP) You can only receive what He did for you with an act of your own will, personally.

If you haven't accepted Christ's payment for you personally, or if you are not sure that you are God's child, why don't you make sure. Right now, in the silence of your own heart, you can tell the Father that you do accept His perfect gift of salvation by receiving His Son as your personal Savior. Prayer is simply a talk with God the Father, so in your own words, share with Him your acceptance of His Son, your desire for Him to come into your life, and take the broken pieces to create a beautiful new vessel.

When you receive His payment for yourself, personally, then God credits to your account the righteousness of Jesus Christ, and at that moment you become God's child. If you just accepted Christ as your Savior, or if you have in the past, then Jesus Christ has come to dwell in you through the regenerating power of the Holy Spirit. (Col. 2:10) You now have the power to begin living the life that you always thought Christians were supposed to live, the life that God designed you to live from the beginning. You still have the sin nature, but as you allow Jesus Christ to handle the controls, through the Holy Spirit, then the Big "I," old sin nature, is rendered inactive and has no control over you.

As you allow God, through the power of the Holy Spirit, to relive Christ's life in and through you, He then will make the changes necessary in your life—curtail your sensual nature, cancel your jealousy, thwart depression before it comes, bind your ugly tongue, love others through you, and bring you to maturity in Jesus Christ. He'll be your power, as He was and is for Melony and Todd. He'll be whatever you need, whenever you need it. He is the life changer. (Eph. 2:10) All you have to do is let Him.

The Scripture also describes another type of Christian, a carnal

Christian, who is a person who has Christ in his life, but the Big "I" or self is in control. That can happen, and most likely will happen, as you begin your walk with Christ. Jesus Christ is a gentleman and He will never push Himself on you, so anytime you want to get back in control of your life, act independently, He moves right over and you are again sitting at the controls.

Of course, as soon as you do, you'll notice all your priorities will get lopsided and out of balance. You will probably begin thinking up rotten things to do to your mate because he or she hasn't acted exactly to suit you. As long as you want to control your own life, Christ will let you. Of course, He will never ever leave you (Heb. 13:5 AMP): ". . . for He (God) Himself has said, I will not in any way fail you nor give you up nor leave you without support, nor in any degree leave you helpless, nor forsake nor let (you) down (relax my hold on you). Assuredly not!"

"But Anne, what happens when I take over my life again? I mean, How do I get the Holy Spirit back in control?"

Good question. In I John 1:9 (AMP): "If we (freely) admit that we have sinned and confess our sins, He is faithful and just and will forgive our sins and continuously cleanse us from all unrighteousness—everything not in conformity to His will and purpose, thought and action." It is perfectly normal to feel that in the beginning all you are doing is confessing sins, but as you are obedient to do that, each time God makes you aware of an attitude or an action that is opposed to Him, then gradually your walk with Him will become more consistent, and less interrupted by having to stop and confess a sin every few minutes.

Isn't it great that you don't have to "feel" forgiven, that, just like when you became a Christian, you take God at His Word, when He said you become My child on the basis of believing in Christ. And the same is true for confession. You are back in fellowship and the Holy Spirit is controlling your life again, not because you may "feel" as though He is, any more than because you "feel" that you are a Christian. Your assurance of salvation, and being restored to fellowship when you have sinned, are both based on what God says, not how you "feel."

Christ is standing at the door of some of your lives right now, waiting for you to open it. He is the first step in saving your marriage from the brink of divorce. He is waiting; the choice is yours.

As you sit and think for a minute, recall what this one choice did in the lives of Melony and Todd. All the power and strength, peace and purpose they found are waiting for you!

GOALS: To come to a personal relationship with Jesus Christ and to learn to walk with Him daily, allowing Him to control your thoughts and your actions. Most important, allow Him to mold and change *you* into the kind of marriage partner who is pleasing to Him and fulfilling to your mate. In this you will find your ultimate peace and happiness.

ASSIGNMENTS:

(1) Read Romans 6 through 8; I John 1:1–10; Galatians 5:16–21; I Timothy 2:5; Proverbs 6:16–19; I Corinthians 2:14–3:3; and John 10:28.

(2) Memorize I John 1:9 and use it as often as necessary. Keep short accounts with God by confessing any sin, overt or mental attitude, the moment God makes you aware of it.

(3) Ask the Lord to make you vitally aware of areas in which you are displeasing your mate, and ask Christ to change *you* in these areas.

(4) If you aren't already in a Bible-teaching church, find one and try to attend regularly.

(5) Realize that your marriage didn't get to the brink overnight and that it will probably take some time to repair the damage that has been done. In the meantime, ask the Lord to show you new and exciting areas that would please your mate, perhaps remind you of things he or she has asked you to do and you've overlooked or forgotten.

(6) Begin to relate to your mate as Christ does to you, no matter how he or she reacts.

(7) Have a personal, regular time to study the Scriptures. Read constructive Christian books and have a quiet time with the Lord in prayer daily. A suggested list of books is in the back of this book.

(8) To learn fully how to discard unnecessary or sinful habits and replace them with those that will honor God, read *How to Overcome Evil,* by Dr. Jay E. Adams, Presbyterian and Reformed Publishing House, Box 185, Nutley, New Jersey 07110.

(9) Make a list of your current priorities (such as children, work, entertainment, prayer, fellowship, spouse, sleep, exercise, etc.), then make a list of what order they should be in. Now make notes on how you can rearrange your first list to bring it in line with God's divine order, and begin to put those notes into practice.

(10) In privacy, on a piece of paper write down every unconfessed sin in your life as the Lord brings it to your mind. When you've listed everything you can recall, bow your head, claim I John 1:9, and thank God that Jesus has paid for each and every one. After you pray, write "FORGIVEN," across your list, then throw it away, because God not only forgives but He forgets. Now you are facing life with a pure, clean slate.

(11) *Do your assignments.* Remember if you truly mean business with the Lord, if you sincerely want to save your marriage, reading alone won't bring changes. The assignments at the end of the chapters are designed for your benefit, to guide you into activity, putting into practice God's concepts. Without action little will be accomplished. Begin today to let God know you mean business.

CHAPTER 4

PROBLEM: POOR SELF-IMAGE = POOR MARRIAGE

Symptoms

Adultery
Suicidal tendencies
Physical sickness (at times)
Feelings of inferiority
Constant state of apology
Materialism
I-centered, instead of Christ-centered
Depression, fear, insecurity
Withdrawal
Spiritual sickness
Self-criticism
Constant search for approval
The perfectionist
Critical spirit
Inability to trust God

"If I were prettier, maybe he would love me."
"If I could only get a higher-paying job, I could provide my wife with more, and perhaps she'd respect me."
"No wonder my mate finds me boring—I don't like me either."
"If only I'd come from another background, everything about my life would be different."
"At least after a few pills, or a few drinks, I don't care what anyone else thinks about me."
"God, when it came to talents and abilities, you must have passed me by."
"Dear God, how I want to understand, like and enjoy me, but I don't know how."

I doubt that there is a person reading this who at one time or another hasn't had feelings such as those expressed above. Many of you have probably spent a lot of money and much time reading self-improvement books, taking positive-thinking courses; yet when the going got rough, when you'd drawn on all the inner resources you had, no matter how many times you told yourself you were adequate for the task, you finally fell on your face in defeat. Thinking on the bright side is wonderful, but it isn't the basis of a right self-image.

Some of you have been told so often that you were incapable, stupid, ugly, dull, or unlovable that you have come to the point of almost believing it yourself. You say to yourself, "I've heard it so many times, it must be true." Some of you are so down on yourselves that even when you are complimented, or when wonderful things happen in your life, you are suspicious, because you think: "There must be an angle to this. Why should they be so kind, why should I be loved? I'm not worthy, etc." Right now, some of you are facing marital failure because your wrong self-image doesn't trust or understand your mate's loving acceptance of you exactly as you are.

Others, instead of searching, have regressed. Tired of wondering why, you've chosen self-isolation. You want to be left alone; if you could, you would like to disappear from the face of the earth. Depression and despair seem to stalk your every step. Some of you feel the only relief left is found in a bottle of pills or the temporary escape alcohol brings; yet every time you open your mouth to down a pill, to swallow a drink, you hate yourself a little more, knowing that in that act itself you are admitting you can't cut it alone, that you are totally reliant on mind-twisting supports. Now you are facing the last straw in your precarious emotional balance, the breakdown of your marriage. Your mate has finally grown tired of shoring up your moodiness, your self-defacement; he or she is weary of the black cloud which seems to hover over your every action and word.

Every one of these areas, and many more, are symptoms of a wrong self-image.

Never a thing out of place in your house, you are the ultimate housekeeper, and you wonder why your husband isn't relaxed and happy at home. Your wrong self-image refuses to allow you to do or be anything but perfect. You are constantly having to prove to yourself and your mate, "I am somebody, see how perfectly I do everything." You live in fear, afraid that if you aren't always right, always dressed correctly, always on time, always seen in the right places with the right people, that you will lose your mate's acceptance of you. What a miserable way to live.

THE ETERNAL TRIANGLE

A right self-image is not found in the feelings another person gives you of yourself. Often a person who has been put down and torn apart by a sick marriage reaches out to someone beyond their turbulent situation. With their new "love," they again feel needed, admired, possibly even loved. This need to feel better about oneself, to feel appreciated, is the basis for most marital infidelity.

If all feelings could be removed from the "eternal triangle," most people would realize it isn't a matter of your caring for the new person in your life that has drawn you away from your mate, but your own feelings of insecurity; you desire to feel loved, appreciated, admired. In essence, you are looking to a new relationship to create a good self-image for you.

If you were able to unemotionally analyze your actions, you'd see that first and foremost they are self-centered; you aren't following Christ's example. If He hadn't put His love for you above Himself, He'd never have gone to the cross, nor defeated the Devil and provided eternal reconciliation for you. Secondly, the basis for what you feel is a good self-image is no more stable than your current marital relationship, because it is still founded on another human's evaluation, which in time can shift and change.

I realize if you are in the middle of such a situation, riding high on new "feelings," you're none too receptive to what I'm sharing with you. If you can reflect back, I imagine the feelings of importance, acceptability, desirability that your new "love" has given you are quite like those you had when you first met your mate. When you decided to marry, you swore that the deteriorating situation, your failing self-image could never happen, just as you're ready to vow about this new one. Under man's law you can change partners, but the self-esteem you're so desperately seeking is still going to be perched on a clay foundation, and adding marital failure to it isn't going to help.

In retrospect, I've analyzed some of the friendships I enjoyed when Jim and I were divorced and I was dating. I've discovered, with time, that the one man I was particularly drawn to attracted me because my feelings were based not on who and what he was, as much as on how I felt with him. I discovered his personality brought out traits, feelings and actions in me that I liked; therefore, I enjoyed being with him because of the "me" it created. In essence, his personality brought out a "me" I liked, and that was the basis of my feelings for him. I'm not saying that that's wrong. That certainly is what marriage partners should do for one another, but like all estimates of self based on others, sooner or later there is pain and disappointment because the keystone that your self-image is built upon is faulty. Today the world may love you, tomorrow it may turn like a wild animal and attack.

Only the value God places on you is stable. It's the value He places on you that never changes, and when you anchor your identity firmly in Him you're ready to deal correctly with whatever the world, your children, or your mate may say. You'll know who you are by the standards of the King; all other scales or criticisms can be accepted, evaluated, appreciated if they're right, but that right self-image erected on the Rock will stand, unwavering—your search will be over.

THROWING IN THE TOWEL

Your self-image has hit rock-bottom, you feel that you have searched everywhere, explored every way out of the pit your life has fallen into; now, in that bottle of pills beside your bed, you seem to see the sweet choice of escape. Think for a minute. Do you realize that suicide is the height of self-centeredness, formed on the basis of a wrong self-image! A friend who'd tried this approach to problem-solving cried: "Anne, I wasn't thinking about myself, really; it was simply that there was no more meaning, no usefulness to my life, no answers. I'd gotten tired of trying." Sounds logical, doesn't it? But the girl in question in her emotional turmoil hadn't taken an assessment of the assets in her life. She is a pretty young woman, with a lovely home, three beautiful children, no major financial problems, yet she felt rotten about herself. Her act was the climax of a self-centered attitude;

she was only thinking of Margaret. She failed to consider the traumatic impact her actions would have on her children, her friends, or on those with whom she'd shared her Christian testimony. Margaret was only concerned with Margaret's marital disappointment, Margaret's feelings of being unloved, rejected, a failure, and divorced. Margaret became consumed with Margaret, basing her total worth as a person on her ex-husband Dirk's scale of values, so she overdosed. Fortunately, she failed in her attempt, which in itself is embarrassing—to find you can't even kill yourself.

When Margaret was released from the hospital, we spent many hours talking, redirecting Margaret's thinking. Finally, she realized that her every action, thought, and feeling about herself were based on Dirk's actions and reactions toward her. She was a slave to Dirk's opinions, constantly up and down as his moods changed. In time she understood that she'd placed Dirk's evaluation of her above Christ's. As she learned how much Christ loved her, that in His eyes she was a unique creation for whom He had special plans and a special ministry, Margaret began to see herself through His eyes, and the vision was clear and beautiful. As Margaret's self-image found its right foundation, she was able to relate to life, the children and Dirk in a loving, interested manner. No longer do those around her determine her self-esteem. Margaret now knows who she is. Although the future isn't crystal-clear before her, she intimately knows the One who holds it in His hands, and she approaches each day reaching out to others, bringing light and hope into their lives and leaving her fulfillment as a woman in Christ's hands. Dirk is beginning to notice the new quiet, contented spirit in Margaret, and I feel that by the time I write a sequel to this book, they will be reunited, having a beautiful story to tell about the healing power of Christ Jesus.

It doesn't matter whether your wrong self-image is expressed through a sense of inferiority, being a perfectionist, a materialist, having a critical spirit, spiritual sickness, self-centeredness, or even in suicide attempts, the root problem remains the same!

Believe it or not, God didn't create you to be the miserable, unhappy, frustrated person you are. More than anything, He desires that you be a happy, fulfilled human being with a zest for life, a love for others, and a deep inner contentment. You were designed to be a person loved by others and one who can enjoy and respect yourself!

WHAT HAPPENED TO GOD'S PLAN?

"Well if that is what God had in mind, He must have been out to lunch when I was created," you are thinking? No, God wasn't out to lunch, nor did He decide that you were to be doomed to a life of frustration and inner despair.

In the beginning, Adam and Eve never faced an identity crisis. They were happy, emotionally free to be exactly as they were created. They were contented, enjoying fellowship with God and each other. Then Eve decided she knew a better way, and sin entered the picture. When sin entered, human beings could no longer live and relate to themselves and each other as they were originally created. Our old sin nature, that nature like unto Satan, destroys and distorts everything, including our self-evaluation.

This plague called sin separated us from God and prevents us from living as we were created to live—Christ-centered and Spirit-controlled. When we are in right relationship to God, controlled by His Spirit, then and only then are we free to be ourselves, happy, and fulfilled. When sin is in control, we leave God out of our lives and become bound and controlled by our old sin nature. When this happens, all types of problems develop. Trying to live life like this is comparable to demanding that a man off the street compete in an Olympic race. He may begin the race, but in a short time he will be huffing, puffing, dizzy, stumbling, and will finally collapse on the track. He didn't have the inner power source, correct training, and although he tried, he failed. Just as the inexperienced runner wasn't designed to be on an Olympic track, we are not designed to face, adjust and relate to life, marriage and our mate while controlled by the old sin nature. The results of approaching life's situations under its control produce a distorted thinking of God, a warped self-image, and our responses toward our mate and others often hurt them and ourselves.

THE IMITATORS

Some of you have tried to become a person you can like by attempting to model yourself, your thinking, or your actions after others. No one could have tried this method more than I did. Many years ago, I tried to become a Christian this way. I thought I would do everything I thought a Christian should do, and refrain from doing things I felt they shouldn't do. I may have fooled some people for a while, but inside I was the same old miserable me.

The world values youth, looks, and personality very highly, but the world is very fickle. Years ago, when I discovered that I was accepted in many groups and functions simply on my looks, I thought, "There is the answer." But what is "in" today is "out" tomorrow. One day the world exalts the Sophia Loren-type figure; tomorrow, Twiggy—and no one can be both. Even if you or I could keep up with the changing fads, time has a way of catching up with all beauty based on the purely physical. Another dead-end street.

If you have ever taken a quiet moment to give serious thought to the concept of solving your problems by imitating others, you realize how futile this approach is. If you pattern your behavior, looks, actions, thoughts, or opinions after others, you are simply copying those who are also distorted by sin. Instead of correcting your problems, you increase them. The Word shares how foolish this is in II Corinthians 10:12 (Beck): ". . . But they do not show good sense, because they do continue measuring themselves with one another and comparing themselves with one another."

A right self-image is never achieved by mimicking another. The image that you seek is achieved only by reflecting your Creator, in whose image you were created. Christ explains it this way: "You shall love the Lord your God with all your heart, and with all your soul, and with all your mind." (Matt. 22:37 AMP) When you accepted Jesus Christ as your personal Savior, He wiped you clean of sin. As you become Christ-centered (seeing yourself and others from His viewpoint), Spirit-controlled (no unconfessed sins), and obedient to His Word, the confused, distorted image begins to be corrected. Like the cleansing of a spring rain, you are washed and released from the confines of sin and free to develop real maturity. The real you begins to emerge, the beautiful person God originally designed you to be. You truly become a new creature, the one, *original you.* "Therefore, if any man be in Christ, he is a new creature." (II Cor. 5:17 KJV) Having a personal relationship with Jesus Christ gives birth to a new person inside! Your future has just begun. This person that God foresaw in eternity past can now emerge, a person that you'll like, a person your mate and friends will respond and thrill to.

"Well, how do I carry out the command to love God with all my heart, mind and soul?" To learn to love somebody, even God, it takes getting to know Him. You can't love someone, even God, unless you know Him. Once you have come to know Him, you will be so overwhelmed with His love and care for you that you cannot help but respond with all the love humanly possible. But the only way you can come to this intimate knowledge of Him is through His Word and prayer. As you search through the wonders of the Bible, you'll find: "In Him lie hidden all the mighty, untapped treasures of wisdom and knowledge." (Col. 2:3 LVB) Daily studying His Word should be a wonderful expedition as you find the treasures and riches He has waiting for you. Your heart will sing as you realize the boundless love He has for you, the provisions He's made, the eternal desires and plans He has for your happiness.

His Word is like an iron which straightens out the twisted, wrinkled, crushed thinking we have of ourselves. "The entrance and unfolding of your Words gives light; it gives understanding . . ." (Ps. 119:130 AMP) God reminds us in Isaiah 55:8–9 that our thought patterns are not His, and our actions are not His. "For My thoughts are not your thoughts, neither are your ways My ways, says the Lord. For as the heavens are higher than the earth, so are My ways higher than your ways and My thoughts than your thoughts." (Berkley) Our view, our thinking, our feelings about ourselves begin to be revised, renewed, rewarding, when we see ourselves from His perspective. How wonderful it is to learn what God has to say about us, and begin to see ourselves through His eyes!

YOU ARE LOVED JUST AS YOU ARE!

"But God proves His own love for us by Christ dying for us when we were still sinners." (Rom. 5:8 Berkley) Here you were, rotten, filled with sin, and yet a holy, perfect, sinless God loves you! That is exactly the message. He loved you so completely that He made it possible for you to rise above the sin, corruption, and distortions of this world. That's tough love, real love, love that gives itself for another. God provided this gift in the person of His beloved and only begotten son, Jesus Christ.

I imagine you are thinking: "I am such a mess, I cursed my wife out this morning because I couldn't find the car keys. Sometimes I'm so hateful I can hardly believe the words that come from my mouth. Or I hate me because I constantly resent having to do, to pick up behind the kids. I don't know how anyone could love me, especially if they knew the me I know." Ephesians 1:6 (LVB) explains this: "Now all praise to God for His wonderful kindness to us and His favor that He has poured out upon us, because we belong to His dearly loved son." God sees you, loves you, and accepts you exactly as you are because you belong to Christ. When you accepted Christ as your Savior, you were placed in eternal union with Him. In this state the Father sees you as a new creature, a new being, the one you are becoming as you allow Christ to work in and through you. If God Almighty loves and cares for you this much, why should you concern yourself about what mere man thinks?

God knows you as you are, you can remove the mask, drop the façade, and begin to become the real you, the one He wants to mold if only you will let Him. When you accepted Jesus Christ, God put His eternal stamp of approval on you, you are now free, there is nothing to prove ever again. Of course, you will blow it from time to time, but as you commit yourself to the creative skill of the Master's hands, you can relax, knowing He can be totally trusted to fashion a beautiful new you.

ACCEPTING YOURSELF

Since God accepts you just as you are, you certainly should. That means that you don't feel like God was busy on another project the day you were created. Maybe you do have a big nose, you're too skinny, your legs are paralyzed, or your back twisted. If you aren't perfect you can't blame God for imperfections, pain or suffering. "Every good gift and every perfect gift is from above." (James 1:17 KJV) When God created Adam and Eve they were physically perfect in every detail. When sin entered the cosmos, by man's disobedience to God, with it came sickness, defective genes, and all the pain and suffering of this world. God is not responsible for the mating of defective genes, sickness, or disease. For instance, two diabetic parents can hardly expect to produce nondiabetic children. Even in those areas of physiology which we do not understand, God seldom violates physical laws. God wants to use whatever your physical imperfection is to do a greater work, to make a more wonderful person than you could have ever been otherwise.

God can use physical imperfections for your happiness and to His glory. Perhaps if your body were physically perfect, you would never seek God, but spend your life in total self-reliance. Sometimes those who are perfect physically never find a desire in their lives for God. They are self-reliant, never realizing the need you know so well. Perhaps you are truly the fortunate one. There are so many examples of those who we all thought had everything—a beautiful body, popularity—like Marilyn Monroe, Freddie Prinze, and over 27,000 other Americans each year who find that no matter what their situation, rich, poor, handsome, or plain, they lack the inner happiness, contentment, and acceptance of themselves to face another day on planet earth.

If you want true inner happiness, a fulfilled, useful life, draw close to Christ and a much greater, more beautiful work will be accomplished than that of physical perfection. Through Christ the real you will develop and mature. Your body is simply the house that you abide in; it lives for a short time, then goes back to the dust from which it came, but the real you will live forever, and in eternity there awaits a perfect, whole body for your soul to dwell in forever.

The Devil loves it when we become totally preoccupied with ourselves, when we should be occupied with the image of Christ developing within us. You are probably thinking, "This sounds good on paper, but I bet it is about as practical as diapers on a donkey . . . I mean, what about my looks, my background, etc.?"

God wants to deal with you right where you are *this* moment. So you had a rotten childhood, missed many of the "American advantages"; so did Nicky Cruz, a gang leader from the streets of New York who found Jesus Christ in the slums. The Son of God, born almost 2,000 years before Nicky Cruz, turned this young man's life around, lifted him above his "background," and now Nicky is sharing the transforming power of Jesus with thousands all over the world.

Perhaps you are dealing with a serious physical handicap; you feel totally useless, depressed, and unneeded by a world which seems to be rushing able-bodiedly past you. STOP. God may have such plans for you as you never dreamed possible. Ephesians 3:20 (LVB): "Now glory be to God who by His mighty power at work within us is able to do far more than we would ever dare to ask or even dream of—infinitely beyond our highest prayers, desires, thoughts, or hopes." If you want to be used, God has a place for you, no matter what your physical condition may be! There are hundreds of stories of those who have turned their impairments and handicaps over to the Lord, and through them He was able to work wonders and draw many people to Jesus Christ. Are you interested? Think for a moment of Joni Eareckson, the quadriplegic, who has become a wonderful artist, painting pictures with a pen in her mouth, and sharing the wonders of her Savior's love. Now her life story is being made into a major motion picture which will reach millions for the Lord. What about Fanny Crosby, the blind composer who gave Christianity over 6,000 hymns praising her Lord? Imagine the number of hearts they have touched and brought into the Kingdom. Then I recall recently reading in Corrie ten Boom's book *Tramp for the Lord* of a woman in Russia who was totally twisted and deformed by multiple sclerosis. Miss ten Boom said the woman could only move the index finger of one hand, but by typing with that one finger, she had translated portions of the Bible and other Christian books into Russian, Latvian and other languages, a peck at a time! Only in heaven will this blessed woman know and meet all the souls she reached, one finger at a time.

It is almost needless to mention the tremendous impact Helen Keller had on the world. Henry Viscardi, Jr., born without legs, has a lovely family, and children who adore him. Beyond that, he is the author of eight books and Assistant Professor of Clinical Rehabilitation Medicine at New York University Medical Center. He recently said, "Being handicapped is a state of mind rather than a state of body." The real difference comes in whether you let your background, upbringing, physical impairments, looks, etc. control you, or whether you, through the grace and power of God, learn to control them and use them to the utmost for the glory of God and true inner peace and happiness.

God is capable of using you in whatever situation you are in. Often He can use our weaknesses for His glory. It says in II Corinthians 12:9 (AMP): "But He said to me, My grace, My favor and lovingkindness are enough for you, for My strength and power are made perfect and complete and show themselves most effective in *your weakness* . . ."

If you happen to have nice physical features, appreciate them; there is no need to feel guilty. God can do a mighty work through you, just as He can others. Just be careful that you keep your eyes on Him, your dependence on Him and not on you. Ask Him to help you concentrate on developing the inner qualities that will shine through and reach out to others.

You can't sit around meditating on self. You have to begin to obey God in terms of loving others around you, your neighbors, your mate, children, into that ever-widening circle, realizing that everyone you will ever meet is someone whom the Son of God loves and died for, whether or not they have accepted His gift. If you are radiating His love, you may be the turning point in many lives. That will not only bring to your life happiness for today, but in eternity when you meet the souls your life testified to here on earth!

Self-image in the life of a Christian, then, is a false issue! Before you get confused here and stop to write me a long, heated letter, reread this. The *real* issue is God's acceptance of me, not my acceptance of myself. When you get your issues in their right order, then the Christian life becomes the pursuit of Godliness, not self. As you seek to be more and more conformed to the image of Jesus Christ, seriously studying the Word of God on a daily basis, then this beautiful love which only the Spirit of God can create in your heart begins to grow and begins to express itself in a precious way to others, especially the Lord. Then and only then will you know the quiet contentment of liking the you God created.

SELF-LOVE

In the past, writers, psychologists, and psychiatrists have promoted the view that before you can relate correctly to others, before you can even love another person, you must first love yourself. In time, this thinking has penetrated the Christian world. I have no argument with psychology, etc., as long as it is biblically oriented. I think one of the problems we face is that many are taking their preconceived psychological ideas, then going to the Scriptures trying to find a substantiation for the presuppositions they have found elsewhere. I believe that, as Christians, we'd better study the Word first, then be sure that the concepts and theories we read square with them. There is a danger that we take the "world's" thinking and try to read it into the Word.

If your marriage is crumbling and you are floundering between man's psychology and God's Word, confused and frustrated, the basic confusion that you are facing is that man is saying that you must first love yourself before you can love, give, care, or accept your mate. On the other side, God's Word, when studied in totality, says the opposite! In your dazed state you are finding some Christian writers who are trying to mesh the two concepts, which only adds to your frustration.

I realize that this is a traumatic point in your life, that if you didn't have self-image problems before, they are certainly cropping up now. As a mere human I can't answer your questions or solve your problems any better than you, but I know someone who can, and He has left us His Holy Word, and in it we will find the answers that you are so desperately seeking.

I imagine that after reading and searching source after source, these questions are foremost in your minds: "Are we commanded to love ourselves?" "Is self-esteem to be sought first before I can love my mate?" "Do I need to have a proper self-image before I can reach out, obey, and provide what my mate needs?" These are legitimate questions that demand answers from God's Word.

AM I COMMANDED TO LOVE MYSELF?

This is the biggest question to a Christian. To reply to it, we have to return to the Scriptures. You see in Matthew 22:36–40 (also in Mark 12, and Luke 10) that a particular incident in Christ's life is repeatedly told. In this, Christ is being tempted, He is being asked to tell which is the greatest of the commandments. In Matthew 22:36, a young Jewish lawyer, from a background of Jewish law (knowing there were over 613 laws, 365 negative ones and 248 positive commandments) asks Jesus: "Teacher, which kind of commandment is great and important, the principal kind, in the Law?" In verses 37–39 Christ answers: "You shall love the Lord your God with all your heart, and with all your soul, and with all your mind (intellect), this is the first great commandment. And a second is like it: You shall love your neighbor as (you) do yourself."

What Christ did here was to summarize man's total duty to God and man's total duty to man. The total of the laws is summarized in two commandments.

"Wait a minute," you say. What about "Love thy neighbor as thyself"? Wouldn't it be great if the first commandment got as much attention as the second? But we humans seem to be more interested in whether we need to love ourselves before we can love others.

While you are still reading, let me say that this verse does not say that we are to love ourselves. It does *not* command us to love ourselves!

There are only two great commandments! "Love God, love yourself, love your neighbor." "Wait a minute, that isn't how it reads," you may be saying. No, it isn't, and if loving yourself had been a prerequisite to loving your neighbor, it would have superseded the second commandment. It then would become the second, and loving your neighbor would become the third. The fact is that there are not three great commandments; there are only two.

But what about the "as yourself" part? The Greek word is a simple little conjunction, *hos,* used here to point out the degree. *Hos* is used here to point out the degree to which something happens; it is pointing out "love your neighbor to the same degree or extent that you love yourself." The emphasis is on intensity.

The Bible, then, uses a parallelism, quite frequently used in Scripture. The first line is, "Love God with this intensity, with *all* of this"; and line two, "Love your neighbor with the intensity of this." So you see the parallelism. Here are two great commandments, not three. Christ was talking about the quantity of our love, not the quality. The issue here is not content. Those with a psychologizing approach when they come to this Scripture have tried to make the *hos* mean, "I'd better find out what loving myself is. Then I can go on to loving my neighbor." They have made the content of love for myself the prerequisite to my love for others. But here Christ is speaking of quantity, not quality. As a Christian, your first obligation is to love God, your second obligation is to love your neighbor, your mate. (Love means sacrificing oneself, giving to others, thinking of others first. The prerequisite, positive steps of self-sacrifice are to be the order; that is where the emphasis should be placed.) Self-esteem will come in its proper place. Remember that the Scripture says, "It is more blessed to give than to receive."

God created you and me so that when we respond wrongly, fail to rightly handle our responsibilities, an inner alarm goes off, and our consciences let down a floodgate of rotten feelings. Therefore, to begin, use the keys to developing a healthy self-image, an image you will rejoice in, one that your mate will respond to.

GOD'S FIRST KEY

To open the door to that beautiful new self-image, you must begin by turning your back on old ways of reacting to life, your mate, your marriage, and form new reaction patterns. I realize that this is a difficult proposition to put into action, but you now know the One from Whom you can draw the strength; He is waiting for you to give Him the go ahead. To begin, I believe if we had to choose only one of God's keys for living, it would be the principle expressed in I Thessalonians 5:18 (AMP): "Thank (God) in everything—no matter what the circumstances may be, be thankful and give thanks; for this is the will of God for you . . ."

"Anne, you have got to be kidding. My marriage is falling apart. Our children are rebellious, and you are telling me to thank God for this situation. You must be crazy." That is just about the reaction that I had when I first read this concept in God's Word. Of course, like you, I was used to thanking God for the good things which came into our lives, but to thank Him for a broken heart, a crumbling marriage, that seemed to be a little far-fetched to me. But I got to thinking, If God's Word says to do something, there has to be a good reason, even if at this time it makes no sense to me. As time passed, I began to learn what the Scripture expressed in this verse.

Naturally, the verse doesn't mean, If your marriage is headed for the divorce court, you are to clap your hands and go out and celebrate. That would be ridiculous.

What the verse does mean is to thank God no matter what is currently happening in your life, knowing and recognizing that He is sovereign. He never allows anything to happen to His children that He cannot work out for their good. (Rom. 8:28) God is a loving, caring God. He isn't sitting up in heaven playing games with our lives. Whatever situation you are in right this moment, it *can* ultimately be for your total benefit. God is all-powerful. He can take your broken, torn marriage, even if you created the disintegrating situation yourself, and turn it around to be good for all concerned.

Thanking Him in your situation is simply saying, "Father, I thank you that I can trust you through this situation to make me more like Jesus. I know that You love me even more than I do myself, and that You are vitally concerned with our marriage. I am trusting you to use these tragic circumstances to draw us both closer to Christ and to teach us valuable lessons which we may not have had the opportunity to learn any other way. I know that if I learn and apply your concepts to my marriage, that if there is any way possible, You will work on and with both of us to reunite us, rekindle the love we once had, and restore the home I so dearly love." Your praise and trust tells Christ that you are putting yourself, your mate, your marriage and all its complications in His hands. You are letting Him know that you are willing for Him to do whatever He wants, however He wants, in your life and marriage, in His way and in His time. You may not totally understand why you are having to face the heartbreak you are now enduring, but in the future you may reflect back and see the good, the positive changes that were created through this experience, not only in your life, but in your mate's and in your marriage.

Ask God to continually remind you to have a thankful spirit regardless of what the future holds, knowing that He is constantly concerned and caring for your welfare.

GOD'S SECOND KEY

When you come into a personal relationship with Jesus Christ you know that at that moment Christ totally cleanses you from all past sin. From this point on you are filled with the Holy Spirit, but whether or not He is controlling and directing your life depends on *you*. When you sin again, and you will, the Lord has given you I John 1:9 to claim, confessing your sin, whether overt or mental to the Lord, simply agreeing with Him that it was sin, turning from it, and moving on. As you begin to use the keys to a good self-image, you may have to take steps to restore relationships with your mate, children or friends which have been crushed and damaged in the past. This may mean saying, "I'm sorry that I was so short with you yesterday" or "I apologize for not being the mate I should have been in the past. Please forgive me."

In other instances, it may involve some form of restitution. The restitution doesn't necessarily involve sin on your part, unless it isn't handled correctly. For instance, I was at the grocery store the other day. I didn't have very much cash with me, and when I went through the check-out line I was surprised that I even had enough to pay for the groceries I'd selected. I had mentally figured about what my bill should be, but to my astonishment it was about five dollars lower! When I got home I checked out my purchases, then realized that when I began unloading my cart, I had a large package of chicken which was dripping all over the counter. The clerk had stopped, placed it in a plastic bag and laid it to one side. That was it. When she put it to the side she forgot to charge me for it; it came to five dollars! Well, my old mind rationalized, it wasn't my fault I wasn't charged. My mind continued down that wrong-road thinking, That store is overpriced on almost everything anyway; I'm sure they have made a lot more than five dollars overcharging me on their products. Pretty good rationalization, right? But, I knew in my soul that if I went to a store whose prices were high, that was my choice. If I didn't go back and tell them, it would be my wrong, and those rotten feelings would swell up in my heart and I wouldn't like me much. So I returned to the store, told them and paid for the chicken. You have never seen such surprised faces. I didn't return to pay for the chicken for the store's sake. They would never have known the difference. I returned for my sake, because I did know the difference. There may be areas of your life in which you need to make restitution. Whether your act was innocent or direct, no one else may know, but you and the Lord, and that's what makes the difference. Keep the slate clean with Him.

As you are working on restoring your torn and wounded relationship, next you need to give the rights, the privileges, the desires, plans, expectations you have to the Lord. After all, you really belong to Him, don't you? I Peter 1:18–23 says that He has paid the total price for you. If He has paid for you, saved you, if you belong to Him, all your rights, dreams, hopes, and desires do too. Give God your right to a happy marriage. Dedicate your position as a Christian husband or wife to Him. Relinquish your right to play golf on Saturday, your Tuesday night with the boys, your lunches with the girls, or even your position as head of the women's circle at church. Whatever the source of strife in your relationship, place it in the hands of God Almighty. Then, thank God for whatever He allows to happen! Trust Him to give you back the things which will enrich and fulfill your life, knowing He is most interested in your happiness—not just today, but for all your life on this earth. Realize that He sees the future; you can only visualize the present. What seems like an important right, privilege or desire today, will seem small and of little importance in the light of a lifetime. When you turn your rights over to Christ, your attitude toward Him is right, then it is easier for you to see your marital relationship in the right perspective.

Your new attitude will reflect through your actions and words, releasing your mate from former sources of irritation, and allowing God to work in his or her life to help them see areas which they also need to change.

When you begin to feel or think, "I've given up this and this for my marriage, and look at my mate—he's done nothing," when hostility rears its ugly head, before you open your mouth in anger, open your heart in prayer, consciously saying, "Lord, I don't clearly know what You are doing in our lives. At the moment I feel cheated, I feel like this is a one-way street. I give, I obey, and my mate just takes advantage and moves on like nothing has changed. Lord, it doesn't seem fair, but I know that whether or not I can see You in action, I know You are working on both of us for our ultimate good, so right now I am trusting You for me. You are going to have to be my patience, my self-control. I don't feel like responding in love, but I'm trusting to reflect Your love through me right now." Then know that God is true to His Word, and respond to your mate as you would Christ! "Keep putting into practice all you learned from me and saw me doing, and the God of peace will be with you." (Phil. 4:9 LVB) This approach won't become habit overnight. Keep using it, mentally going through the steps, until it becomes as natural as breathing. When you learn to respond in this manner, you will be filled with peace because you know that you have obeyed the Lord. There will be peace in your home because you haven't lashed out, and you will feel good about *you* because you can daily see the Lord maturing you, changing you, and His peace will fill your heart. In your soul you will feel good about *you,* because for the first time you gave the control of a heated situation to Christ, and in doing so your relationship was saved from one more life-sapping stab wound.

GOD'S THIRD KEY

Oddly, the more we try to build ourselves up by putting others down, the more *we* hurt. Did you ever notice that? For instance, ladies, perhaps you have been invited to a particularly important party, but you weren't able to get the new dress you wanted. When you arrive, there is Susan wearing "your" dress. A friend comments on how pretty the dress is, and you reply, "Oh yes, it is a beautiful dress, but it certainly would look better if Susan would lose about ten pounds. Have you noticed how much weight she has gained?" Slash, slash, cut, cut. Men, I overheard a conversation the other day where a couple of guys were commenting on the golf game of another man. One said, "Joe has really smoothed out his game. Man, isn't he playing great?" One of the other men chimed in, saying, "Yeah, he's hitting the ball well. Who wouldn't if they were on the tees as often as he is, when his company thinks he's working?" Never a kind word, always building yourself up by putting the other guy down. This is another dead-end road on the way to a right self-image.

For some of you, "cut down" is your favorite indoor sport. Romans 2:1 (Williams) says: "Therefore, you have no excuse, whoever you are, who pose as a judge of others, for when you pose judgment on another, you condemn yourself, for you who pose as a judge are practicing the very same sins yourself." Zap! That gets you where you live, doesn't it? Maybe after serious thought, you will want to rid yourself of that critical spirit, since you have just realized that when you are criticizing you are saying more about yourself than about the other person.

When you put Susan down, you are actually flaunting your own pride. You are placing yourself above the one whom you are judging. When you implied that the golfer was "stealing" time from his company, you stole the right to judge, which belongs only to Jesus Christ. (John 5:22, 27) Making a practice of pointing out others' failures doesn't build you up in the minds of those you are talking to. It only isolates you, which ultimately lowers your own self-image. You see, while you are vividly describing everything that is wrong with so and so, your listeners are mentally thinking, "I wonder what he says about me when I'm not here." Next time you get the urge to get the old knife out and stab someone with your mouth, reflect on Romans 2:1, and see the knife turn toward you. Ask the Lord to reveal to you the fault you were starting to criticize in another. Then open your heart and ask Him to search it, and change this cruel desire of yours.

As you close your mouth to criticism and open it to praise, you'll be amazed at the warmth and love that you will attract.

To begin with, make a mental note to make a habit of saying something nice about the person you were about to cut down. "Wow, Anne, that's a hard one." Yes, I know, but if you scan through everything you know about them, and still fail to think of anything kind or good, you certainly can say, "Well, Susan is certainly an interesting person, isn't she?" This is another area where you might best ask the Lord to help in making your mind and eyes more conscious of a person's attributes instead of his liabilities. You can become a magnet of joy and happiness in the lives of others, a person everyone is drawn to, if you will leave the judging to the Lord, and let the praises flow. Again, when this happens, you are the benefactor, and there is a warmth and peace when you have uplifted another.

On the other hand, being too self-critical is just as wrong as being critical of others, and just as disgusting and boring to have to live with or be around. When I was a teen-ager I knew a girl who was the all-time queen of self-deprecators. Dina was attractive, extremely talented; yet she would describe herself as ugly, a physical tragedy, stupid, and totally unable to do anything. The longer Dina held on to this attitude the worse she got; depression was her constant companion. Finally only those who really loved her dared to call her. Most of her friends learned that trying to argue with her, telling her that she was pretty and talented, was like whistling in the wind. In time she became a lonely woman; few called on her any longer because they knew exactly the line of put-downs and self-complaints she would deliver during the conversation. Dina used her self-created image to avoid circumstances and situations she didn't want to deal with. In the end, the love she sought through pity withered and died. She put herself down once too often, and finally there was no one left to build her up. What she first appeared to be was extremely humble; what she was practicing was inverted pride. This is where many people fail in their search for a good self-image. They view humility as synonymous with self-deprecation, and pride as the opposite of humility. They carry this conclusion to the extreme, making themselves something they are not, which ends up being inverted pride.

Maybe you have fallen into this inverted-pride trap. You can readily recognize the symptoms: apologizing for what you have, trying to speak humbly by putting yourself down, making issues over your lack of ability, or doing your best to look as dowdy as possible. This is inverted pride. "I can't do this, I can't do that." That's false humility. The Scripture says you can do all things through Him who strengthens you. Self-deprecation then becomes an inverted form of pride. Why? Because it is an unrealistic view of yourself; it's not God's view of you.

GOD'S FOURTH KEY

Loneliness cripples even those who are not facing the brink of divorce. Marriages that aren't based on God's concepts, marriages that are being held together because of the children, the church, or other reasons can be as lonely as being by yourself. Loneliness isn't just the companion of the single person; it stalks many homes, many streets. Loneliness is not having anyone to share your plans, your dreams, your ideas, your happiness, or your heartbreak. Loneliness may be just not being asked to join the local garden club, or it may be found right in your own bedroom.

Loneliness is another block in the road to a good self-image. "But Anne, I'm so bashful, so shy, I can't change." God says you can, and beyond that He has commanded you to love your neighbor with the same intensity you love and care for yourself! Are you obeying Him? If not, then you are suffering from a poor self-image, and loneliness which is self-inflicted. Don't blame anyone but yourself. Deep down you probably have needs you want met, but you are afraid to chance being misunderstood, rejected, etc. In such a situation you can easily slip into a vicious circle of *self-centeredness*. The issue actually becomes nothing more than me, me, me, and my needs.

Share your situation with God. Tell Him you are scared, that you resent being left out, uninvited; then confess your loneliness by its real name—selfishness or self-centeredness. Ask God to heal your fear. II Timothy 1:7 (LVB) says: "For the Holy Spirit, God's gift, does not want you to be afraid of people, but to be wise and strong, and to love them and enjoy being with them."

Everyone needs someone else. Romans 1:12 (LVB): ". . . Then, too, I need your help, for I want not only to share my faith with you but to be encouraged by yours: Each of us will be a blessing to the other." Everyone has this need. Who do you think spoke the above verse—some weak, lonely Christian crying out for friends? No, it was Paul! Not only do you need others, but they need you, yes *you*. If you isolate yourself, you are robbing your mate and your friends of the gift God has given you. "Gift?" Yes, gift. God has given you at least one gift with which you are to serve others. "As each of you has received a gift (a particular spiritual talent, a gracious divine endowment), employ it for one another as (benefits) good trustees of God's many-sided grace—faithful stewards of the extremely diverse (powers and gifts granted to Christians by) unmerited favor." (I Peter 4:10 AMP)

Instead of concentrating on *your* needs, *your* wants, *your* desires, become absorbed in the needs and desires of others, then you will be using your gift, whether you are aware of what it is or not. You aren't alone on an island of loneliness; there are a heap of people sitting on that same island. You just haven't taken your eyes off yourself long enough to notice them. Galatians 6:2 (NEB): "Help one another to carry these heavy loads, and in this way you will fulfill the law of Christ." Open your eyes and look around you; you can help others, and in doing so, help yourself by reaching out and taking the first step. I know the first step is always the hardest, but know that Christ is right there with you; rely on Him for your strength. Begin at home; reach out to those you love. If the first time you stretch out your hand, you're rebuffed, just realize that your mate is probably acting in such a manner because of a similar deep need, and simply doesn't know how to respond to this open, loving change in you. Don't revert, crawl back into your shell saying, "Well, I tried, and it didn't work." Realize that the stronger the rebuff, usually the more need is hidden behind it. Keep loving, keep reaching until you have nurtured that wounded mate back to emotional and spiritual health. Don't sit around in the meantime waiting. Begin to reach out to others. As you are obedient to Christ's command, those old feelings of uselessness and loneliness will vanish, and a glow of inner peace and satisfaction with the real you will emerge.

Beware. Don't ever expect relationships and involvements with others to meet the deep inner needs that only Christ can fill.

Learn the beauty and fulfillment of being totally alone with Christ. Mature in this personal relationship with Him by meditating on His Word, and sharing your thoughts, feelings, and needs with Him through prayer. Be sure that your feet are firmly planted on the Rock (Christ). He is the basis for all stability. Remember, no matter how much others may care, they are only human and at some point will disappoint you, fail you. But He promised in Hebrews 13:5 (AMP): ". . . I will not in any way fail you nor give you up nor leave you without support. I will not in any degree leave you helpless, nor forsake nor let (you) down (relax My hold on you). Assuredly not!"

GOD'S FIFTH KEY

If you learn to view yourself the way God does, then this will eliminate pretentiousness. "Let's pretend" has its place in fairy tales, but when it comes to life and marriage, pretending can be fatal. It is disastrous to pretend that a marriage relationship is stable when both of you know deep down that the foundation is about to crack. Quit faking. You aren't kidding anyone but yourself. Some of you have been faking so long you have forgotten what the real you is like. In James 4:13–17 some businessmen were boasting about the future and they were rebuked by James because they failed to acknowledge God and His plan. They had tomorrow in a bottle with the lid screwed on tight.

When you pull the mask off, reveal yourself to yourself, acknowledge to God your true situation—He already knows anyway—you are on the road to repair. Nobody likes a phony, not even the pretender. As you learn to accept God's assessment of you, as you begin to respond to your mate and others as the real you, you will have taken great strides on the road to a strong self-image.

GOD'S SIXTH KEY

Christlike humility enables the believer to understand and give God the credit for strength and accomplishments. Humility doesn't say you have to play down your strengths. Humility is rightly expressed when you are able to take genuine assessment of your strength and accomplishments. You know exactly what you can do. If you are good in your work, when someone compliments you on your job, you don't say, "Oh, I don't do very well." You don't have to play the game of, "If you say something nice about me, I have to put it down." That's not humility. Paul said in I Corinthians 3:10 (KJV): "I am a wise master builder." He knew what gifts he had, what position he had, he wasn't intimidated by the other apostles, he ascribes the gifts to the giver. "But by the grace of God, I am what I am." (I Cor. 15:10 AMP) Paul gave God the credit. In this way you can accept your strengths and accomplishments. Notice that Paul never claims personal credit for any virtue or any talent. God gets the credit. Giving God the credit isn't putting yourself down. If you can do a good job, if you make a big sale in business, accept the compliments and move on. If you are a good interior decorator and are known for the attractive way you arrange your home, or the dinners you create, don't knock yourself out to be humble. Pride can take genuine account of that, and humility can keep it under control.

GOD'S SEVENTH KEY

Self-evaluation based on God's value system enables Christians to accept their weaknesses and failures also. How? Because you can get a realistic view of those. If you blew half your life before you came to know Christ, so what? That is in the past, forgiven forever. Move on. You, through God's grace, realize that whatever you are, God has an eternal love and an eternal plan for your life, and the things that you once saw as deficits can be turned into assets through His power working in you. You realize that those things you can't change aren't important in God's value system.

GOD'S EIGHTH KEY

God's eighth key to a right self-image is knowing who you are. Do you know who you are?

You get your identity and meaning and definition in life because you are identified with Jesus Christ; that gives you the total basis for your identity. Philippians 4:13 (AMP): "I have strength for all things in Christ Who empowers me—I am ready for anything and equal to anything through Him Who infuses inner strength into me (that is, I am self-sufficient in Christ's sufficiency)."

Secondly, you are *royalty!* Have you ever dreamed of being a member of a royal family? Actually, you have much greater nobility than any the world has to offer. You, the precious child of the King of Kings and Lord of Lords—you should be standing tall, with your head high, walking with a new and secure confidence. You are a child of the King!

As you begin to realize what being a child of the King means, you will realize that with the help of your Father, you will never have to say, "I can't." Remember who you are. The Mighty God of heaven and earth resides within you, and for Him *nothing* is impossible. "For nothing is ever impossible with God." (Luke 1:37 Berkley) Anything that is profitable for you, important to you, as long as it is right, He's promised to do in and through you! (Phil. 4:13) God delights in making the weak strong, the shy bold, the inadequate adequate.

Thirdly, you are a *priest!* "Anne, this is getting to be too much, I didn't realize the resources that were mine in Christ."

"I told you so. Aren't you proud?"

"Proud—I just can't believe it! Look who I am! Look!" Yes, and I was saying, look at I Peter 2:9 (AMP): "But you are a chosen race, a royal priesthood, a dedicated nation, (God's) own purchased, special people, that you may set forth the wonderful deeds and display the virtues and perfections of Him Who called you out of darkness into His marvelous light." Just think, you have a straight line to God, you can converse with Him anywhere, in any position, always knowing that He is listening. "And this is the confidence—the assurance, the (privilege of) boldness—which we have in Him: (we are sure) that if we ask anything (make any request) according to His will (in agreement with His own plan) He listens to and hears us." (I John 5:14 AMP)

See how very special you are. This direct line wasn't available to Old Testament believers. You don't have to ask anyone to intercede for you; it's just you and God, and His line is *never* busy.

The only time you have phone problems between heaven and

earth is when there is unconfessed sin in your life. The moment you confess your sin, agreeing with God (I John 1:9), you are reconnected, and the conversation can flow. God longs to talk with you, to have fellowship with you. Make frequent use of this unique opportunity we call prayer.

Fourthly, you are *Christ's official ambassador* here on earth. "So we are Christ's ambassadors, God making His appeal as it were through us." (II Cor. 5:20 AMP) What this verse is saying is that you aren't a "lay person"; you are a commissioned, twenty-four-hour ambassador for the Kingdom of Heaven, at home, in the office, on the golf course, at social functions, wherever; you are representing Him. There is no vacation time, no off hours on this job, but you have the unique privilege of representing the King of Kings! You represent Him by what you say, where you go, how you look, what you do, and who you associate with. In this position, you are to be a reflection of the One you represent, radiating His love, His care, sharing His eternal message through your life.

This is who you are; this is the image God has of you. How can you have any less? You are somebody, somebody special, somebody with abilities, gifts, a purpose. You are somebody with a unique source of power that will never fail.

SELF-IMAGE AND YOUR MARRIAGE

Perhaps in the past your rotten self-image was one of the basic causes of your marital problems. Now that you realize who you are, what value you have, what a constant source of strength you have to draw on, you can begin to apply this new you to your marriage. Now that you know who you are, you have the confidence as a child of the King to take His concepts and moment by moment apply them.

As your new self-image reflects its creator, Jesus Christ, you will have the stability to rightly respond to the upsetting situations which exist in your marriage. The hostility or moodiness which used to toss your marriage back and forth on a stormy sea can cease.

As you are being His ambassador, you should begin to praise, support, and undergird your mate. "Anne, you don't know my mate. She or he already thinks she or he is God's gift to the world. You should just hear her or him talk."

From lots of experience, it is usually the ones who talk the loudest who (beneath the talk) need the most praise and support. They usually mouth-off about themselves because no one else does. They are begging for confirmation of their own self-esteem. "But Anne, I can't think of a thing to compliment my mate about." Well, I realize sometimes it is hard. I suggest you think back to the time you were dating. What initially attracted you? Perhaps it was lovely eyes, a nice voice, broad shoulders, her talent for creating her own dresses, his sense of humor. Most of those qualities are still there. They may be a bit hidden, but if you think, I'm sure you can come up with some. Be honest. For instance, don't tell your wife she looks beautiful when she has her hair up in curlers and an old bathrobe on. No one's self-image is improved with lies.

As you are secure in yourself, you will have the God-given patience to understand the wrong or cruel actions of your mate which may be leading you to the brink of divorce. As you studied in Chapter 2 the action-reaction process, you will have the inner ability, sufficient in His strength, to begin to relate differently to your mate, and in time the love that gleams from your face (Christ's love), the calm that surrounds your presence, will create an atmosphere that will require a different reaction from your wife or husband.

As they see a stable, happy, secure you, you will be sharing a silent witness of Christ to them, giving God all the room possible to work in their lives and your marriage. Never forget who you are when a case of the downs attacks, and since you are human, they probably will. Just reread this chapter. *You* are somebody, *you* are an original, *you* have a purpose, a divine destiny, *you* have a unique opportunity to have a dramatic effect not only in your marriage but on the world!

> I sought (inquired of) for the Lord, and required Him (of necessity, and on the authority of His Word), and He heard me, and delivered me from all my fears. They looked to Him, and *were radiant; their faces shall never blush for shame or be confused.* (Ps. 34:4–5 AMP)

GOALS: The goal of this chapter is to give you a real understanding of exactly who you are on God's terms of reference. It is my prayer that you will clearly understand that you can't have a stable identity when it is based on any thing or anyone's approval or opinions. Hopefully, you will realize that as long as you allow others to establish who you are, you are going to be on a constant roller coaster emotionally. When you have read and digested God's view of you, then you will be ready to correctly view yourself as the special, important, unique creation for which He died.

If you keep your eyes focused on God, His Grace, His blessings, and realize that His gifts to you are not dependent on who and what you are, but who and what He is, then you will be well on your way to a healthy new life, a bright, exciting new you!

ASSIGNMENTS:

(1) Memorize II Corinthians 10:12, II Corinthians 5:17, Philippians 4:9.

(2) Recall daily that self-image in the life of a Christian is a false issue. The *real* issue is God's acceptance of you, not your acceptance of yourself.

(3) When you feel down, reread Paul's dissertation in Romans 7:8–25.

(4) Be sure that you make use of I John 1:9 as often as needed. Guilt is the enemy of a right self-image.

(5) Learn patience as God changes you, and step back so He can have a straight line to your mate.

(6) Begin today to put God's first key into action. Next week, add key two, and so on, remembering that what you are feeding your mind on is what you are going to reflect in your heart and life!

(7) Remember who you are. Make a list and place it somewhere to constantly remind yourself that you are a child of the King, royalty, a priest, and God's ambassador!

(8) You have two choices. You can accept the world's evaluation of you, or God's. If God is Who He says He is, then aren't you foolish to allow anyone else's value to affect you, degrade you? You know who you are now; God has told you. Either it is true, or God is a liar—that is the choice!

(9) Improving one's self-worth may be done by reaching objectives, overcoming obstacles, and expressing your special talents and abilities. To begin to develop self-control and discipline, daily make a list of your responsibilities in

God's order of importance, then no matter how you "feel" get to work. Mark off each job when it is completed.

(10) For one week keep a running diary of all your activities, work, play, etc. After a week you'll probably be amazed to see how spasmodic and disorganized your life actually is. With your list in hand you can better see how to organize your time in the future. Compare this list with the list of God-given priorities you made and make the necessary corrections in your use of time. Perhaps for a while you might keep a notebook in your purse or pocket as a helpful reminder of your right priorities.

CHAPTER 5

PROBLEM: GOD ACCEPTS YOUR MATE. WHY CAN'T YOU?

Symptoms

Critical attitudes of mate and/or others

Rebellion

Constantly comparing one's mate to someone else

Adultery

Alcoholism or use of legal or illegal drugs

Withdrawn personality of unaccepted mate

Sexual failure

Communication breakdown

Superior or self-righteous attitude

This chapter, dealing with the third of the concepts, has opened with a checklist of symptoms which are usually present when you are *not* accepting your mate as he or she is but are trying through various methods to change him or her to fit your idea of the ideal mate, to conform to your social standards, your religious beliefs, etc.

Beyond God's concept of coming to know Jesus Christ as your personal Savior, this is probably one of the most important concepts, and the one which causes more marital breakups than any other.

Lois Wyse did a beautiful job of explaining this concept in her poem "Heart to Heart."

HEART TO HEART

There is a cord
Unseen
That binds us heart-to-heart.
The surest way
For me to shorten the cord
Is to let you choose the length.
For if I choose to tighten

That unseen cord
By poking,
Prying,
Wondering,
Why?ing,
You will dissolve the cord
And create
An unseen wall
For both of us to see.

And that, my beloved,
Would be the tragedy
Of this
Or any
Marriage.[1]

Those words really sum this concept up. Have you ever thought about the many ways you tell your mate that you do not approve of him/her, or you wish he or she would change? Sometimes you do it by making comparisons to someone else's husband or wife; sometimes through constant criticism, or by trying to make him/her fit into your unfulfilled expectations of a marriage partner. Whatever is your personal mode of destruction, *you are killing your mate. Killing love and destroying your marriage.* Strong words, yes, but true.

Let's review how some of these symptoms occur when you aren't accepting your mate as he or she is. Certainly you can quickly understand how a critical attitude would cause a person to withdraw from you. If your marriage is suffering because of a lack of communication, remember that no one is very inclined to have depth-level talks, to really have a soul communication with a mate who has a disapproving spirit. *I sincerely believe that more adultery occurs because of nonacceptance in the home than for any other one reason.* I have talked to the hurt wives, the crushed husbands, and yes, to the other women and men in their lives too. You'd be amazed that at least 80 per cent of the time the cause is the same. The other woman, or the other man, gave the wandering mate the love, attention, praise, etc., that was missing at home. Particularly men who have been involved in adultery have said to me: "Anne, it wasn't so much that I didn't love my wife, but there was never any peace at home. She was always pushing, always trying to change me, put me into a mold. I didn't intend to get involved in an affair, it just happened. You see the woman I'm involved with makes no demands, she takes me like I am, and although I know it is wrong, *I feel free* for the first time in years, *I feel accepted, I feel loved for me.*" Most wandering wives say the same!

If your mate doesn't know Christ, or is a carnal Christian, and is at a period in life where for some reason—business, home, children, whatever—he or she is having to face failure or disappointment, believe me, he or she is all too aware of the failure. He or she doesn't need you to point it out. Sometimes your criticism is the final push that he or she needs to run to the bottle, or to pills, and just drown the whole thing—in essence, to escape the reality that he or she feels unable to deal with.

You may not have realized what an influence you have in the life of your mate; you may still not believe it, particularly you women. Take a minute and turn to the third chapter of Genesis. As you begin reading, you will see that it took Satan almost six verses to persuade Eve to disobey God. In the closing sentence of verse 6 (AMP) it says: "and she gave some also to her husband and he ate." What influence! Ever think about it that way?

IN THE BEGINNING

When you walked down the aisle, you were probably full of dreams, Hollywood ideas, but few concepts of the reality of day-to-day married life. After you stepped through the door of that vine-covered cottage you discovered that the white knight snores, doesn't put his clothes away, never gets to the table on time, and obviously was born in a barn. Likewise, your fairy princess wears cold cream, curlers, she's gained weight, and often prefers soap operas or talking on the phone to cleaning the house or conversation with you.

In reality, you both brought many different ideas and attitudes, actions, likes, thoughts, and manners into the marriage. Constantly discovering and enjoying these differences, these interests, and exploring them together is what continues to make marriage a growing, exciting experience.

On the other hand, when you try to fit your mate into the ideal you had, the dream you thought up as a kid, or perhaps what your parents told you a marriage partner should be like, then you are tampering with destruction. Maybe you are so disappointed that you feel you *certainly* must have gotten the wrong mate, this couldn't be the one God had planned for you.

Did you ever realize how God can use just those traits that you find so offensive to mold and conform you more to His image? You know, if we married someone just like ourselves, instead of fitting and complementing each other, like a lock and key, we would be like two keys or two locks, unworkable and bored stiff.

Often the Lord uses the traits we find most offensive in our mates to fashion us more to His image. If our mates are irritable, perhaps the Lord would have us learn patience; if they are demanding, He would teach us to give, and give again; if they are depressed or withdrawn, perhaps through our example they will learn their true worth, that of one who was so important that the Son of God died especially for them. If they are unaffectionate, unloving, through the examples He gives us in I Corinthians, we can share through our lives what "real" love is.

Ephesians 3:20 tells us that God has something wonderful, more than we could ever hope for or desire, planned for us, so begin learning His concepts, begin allowing Him to conform *you* to His image, and the rewards will be beyond your wildest dreams.

Marriage in God's eyes isn't just a piece of paper, a civil contract; it is a sacred vow made between you and your mate before God Almighty. Remember in John 10:10 (AMP) it says: ". . . I came that they may have and enjoy life, and have it in abundance to the full, till it overflows." You say that doesn't sound much like the life that you are experiencing with your mate. You don't see how that is possible. Well, turn back and reread Romans 8:28.

FREE LOVE

Sounds racy, right? Don't get excited. Free love is what Jesus Christ offers us—that is, unconditional love as expressed in Romans 5:8 (AMP): "But God shows and clearly proves His (own) love for us by the fact that while we were still sinners Christ, the Messiah, the Anointed One, died for us."

God loved us, sent His Son to die for us when we were unlovable. After we become His children He continues to love and care for us, when we're in fellowship or when we fail. This is free love, love without conditions. Just as Christ loved us and died for us when we were sinners, so are we to respond to our mates!

"Impossible. No one could love someone like I'm married to," you say.

Impossible isn't in the Christian dictionary. The Scriptures say that through Christ all things are possible. (Mark 9:23, Luke 18:27) Most of us get so wrapped up in our own desires, our own selfishness, that we begin to erect barriers around our mates —maybe not actual ones, but unspoken lists of do's and don'ts. They know, and if you are honest with yourself, you'll admit that when they transgress these barriers all hell breaks loose.

Don't you realize what you are doing? Slowly but surely you are binding them, limb by limb, like a prisoner. You are saying, I don't trust you, I don't approve of you, I want you to change. If you will think for a minute, I imagine you will realize what type of response this is building up in your mate. No one wants to be caged. The harder you try to possess, the more rebellious they become. Proverbs 25:23–25 expresses the disgust and rebellion this brings out in the heart of man.

Remember Proverbs 16:25 (AMP): "There is a way that seems right to a man and appears straight before him, but at the end of it are the ways of death." This is exactly what happens when you refuse to accept your mate as he or she is. When you have erected the fences, set the standards, it is as if you have confined a beautiful tree. You want it to grow tall and straight, but it needs room, freedom, space to branch out and to reach up. When we allow our mates true freedom to be the persons God created them to be, the miracles that begin to happen are amazing.

Think about it this way: as long as you have barriers, fences, standards, no-no's, etc., you, in essence, have a robot responding to you. Just as God created you with a free volition, to be and do as you choose, you must give your mate the same right. Do you really want actions, presents, forced endearments that are produced because your mate has no other choice? Or would you prefer the freedom, the spontaneity of love as it was when you met, love that wasn't demanded, love that was given freely because you are who you are? The choice is yours. You can exist in a house with someone who acts and reacts out of fear, intimidation, like a slave to his master, usually obedient, but with bitterness and rebellion in his/her heart, or you can let go and learn what real love is as it blossoms and grows in the free light of the Son.

BUT MY MATE NEEDS TO CHANGE

"Anne, you don't understand. My mate needs to change for his/her own good." I have heard these words often enough, and ofttimes the complaining partner is right. Perhaps the mate is degenerating with drugs or alcohol. But, all the good intentions of the marriage partner—and direct action trying to effect a change—won't work. No matter how a person may be destroying his/her life, hurting you, etc., when you start communicating your desire for change, he or she is hearing, "I don't approve of you. I don't love you. I want you to be different."

Proverbs are full of wonderful words of wisdom on keeping your critical thoughts to yourself, like Proverbs 21:23 (AMP): "He who guards his mouth and his tongue keeps himself from troubles." And Proverbs 21:9 (AMP) really says a lot: "It is better to dwell in a corner of the housetop (on the flat oriental roof, exposed to all kinds of weather) than in a house shared with a nagging, quarrelsome and fault-finding woman!"

"Well, if I'm not supposed to change my mate, who is?" God! God is the life changer, and *only God*. Most of the time we only slow down the process of God's work in the lives of our mates by our nagging, criticizing, comparing, and complaining. God did not put you here on earth to do the work of the Holy Spirit. You can talk until you are blue in the face, but John 6:44 (AMP) reminds you: "No one is able to come to Me unless the Father Who sent Me attracts and draws him and gives him the desire to come to Me . . ." Read I Thessalonians 5:19, and don't be guilty of quenching the Spirit's work in the life of your mate.

WHAT DO I DO IN THE MEANTIME?

Good question. The answer is, Take inventory of your life! Ask God to show you areas that are antagonizing your mate, causing him/her to rebel, or possibly supporting problems in his/her life such as alcoholism, drugs, or adultery. "I'm not the one who needs to change; it's my mate." Yes, but you see, as we have discussed before, when you become what God wants you to be, when you get out of the way long enough for God to go into action, then change will occur.

I don't want to get too preachy on you, but it might be well to stop here and reread Matthew 7:1–5 (LVB): "Don't criticize, and then you won't be criticized! For others will treat you as you treat them. And why worry about a speck in the eye of a brother when you have a board in your own? Should you say, 'Friend, let me help you get that speck out of your eye,' when you can't even see because of the board in your own? Hypocrite! First get rid of the board. Then you can see to help your brother."

THE CHANGE MAKERS

You may have succeeded for a long time in demanding your own way. Perhaps your mate is the type who prefers peace at any price, but the estrangement and communication blackout that ultimately occur will not be the reward you are seeking.

Some of you are "comparers." Have you ever given your husband what you believe is a polite hint, by pointing out the good qualities of a friend's husband . . . the thoughtful things he does for her . . . how much money he allows her for clothes . . . or the affection he shows her? Whatever the comparison, the message is, "I wish that you were like him. I want you to change. I don't approve of you." This is a form of manipulation used mainly by women, but some of you men are guilty too, and believe me it won't encourage your mate to be the loving, responsive, thoughtful person you want at all.

If you think you are acting in love in your desire to change your mate, reread I Corinthians 13:4–8 and see what true love is from God's point of view.

Before we discuss God's formula for letting go and loving freely, let me share the following story with you, and perhaps you can better see how disastrous our attempts at changing our mates are, but how beautiful God's ways always are. I don't usually title these stories, but when this particular one was shared with me, the woman had already titled it "The Miracle of the Night-blooming Cereus." An unusual title, but I am sure by the time you review their lives you'll understand the title.

"Anne, you know when God starts His chain of events it is like the blooming of the Night-blooming Cereus. It begins unnoticed but unfolds in full view for us to see. This is what happened in our lives," Pamela said.

PAMELA AND HOWARD PHILLIPS' STORY

PAMELA

Howard and I had been married nineteen years when I first began to realize that there was something missing in our lives. Although I had been brought up in a Christian home, with a Christian mom and dad, I never came to know Jesus Christ personally. Oh, I guess to the rest of the world, Howard and I looked like we had it made. Howard had a good job with Lockheed in Burbank. We had a lovely home, a boat, a beach house, healthy children, plenty of money, everything. Yet, like the song, I felt, "Is That All There Is?" Something deep down told me that there was something more we needed in our lives. Howard and I would talk about trivial things, but our souls never seemed to communicate on a deep spiritual level.

Howard seemed to be happy. He told me on numerous occasions that if he died tomorrow he wouldn't have felt that he'd missed a thing. Howard had been raised in quite a different atmosphere from me. His parents didn't go to church. His mother had to work because his stepfather was an alcoholic; his real father deserted them when Howard was three months old. He was brought up with nothing. He had to work all through high school and college to pay for his own clothes, books and tuition. So his main desire was to have material things, and he told me once that he hoped to have his first million by the time he was forty.

The nagging fear that something was missing in our lives turned into a real problem during the next year.

Howard began staying after work and going to a nearby bar with some of the men from the office. Sometimes he'd get too drunk to come home and would stay over at a friend's apartment. (And sometimes, he said later, he could have made it home but didn't want to listen to my sermons or face the condemnation in my eyes.)

He quit his well-paying position with Lockheed and began selling real estate in California. With no one to account to for his time or his whereabouts, and with all forms of discipline gone, he gradually went from bad to worse.

Real estate wasn't the gold mine he'd thought it would be, and between the lack of income and the bills piling up, he turned more and more to the bottle.

He began not coming home on time, sometimes not coming home at all. When he would get in, he'd say he'd been off somewhere looking at real estate. He actually called me one morning at 2 A.M. and said that he and another real estate man were in Nevada looking at property!

I was so mad, it's a wonder the words didn't burn the phone wires up between us. When he got home, I told him in no uncertain terms what a rotten, thoughtless, disgusting husband he was. I hated him for what I felt he was doing to me, to the family. I even hated him because he wouldn't fight back. He usually ignored me.

HOWARD

Like most alcoholics, I don't know when I crossed that invisible line from a social drinker to an alcoholic, but it didn't happen overnight.

My heavy drinking began two years before I left Lockheed.

Time was passing and I wasn't reaching the financial goals I had set—and Pamela was always home keeping an eye on everything I did.

PAMELA

As things got worse, I had a friend who kept telling me about Al-Anon meetings, but at this time I felt I could handle the situation myself. Besides, I didn't want to go down there to one of those meetings and let everybody see me and let everyone know we had this horrible problem. The whole idea was too embarrassing. Dear God, I learned what real embarrassment was like as Howard continued to slip deeper and deeper into the bottle.

I was desperate, but I kept my desperation to myself. I tried praying. Even though I didn't know Christ, I prayed that God would put a stop to Howard's drinking. I felt if Howard would stop drinking, all our problems would be solved.

Why, I asked myself, was I having to live like this? I didn't have any idea that I could possibly be a contributing factor, not then. I felt so alone, so depressed. Resentment and hostility built up in my soul because I felt I was being put in a situation I didn't deserve.

I continued to try to get through to Howard. I constantly reminded him of what he used to be, and what a "sorry no good" he was becoming. "You could quit if you really wanted to . . . it is just that you are so weak. Howard, are you listening to me? I said, If you cared anything about me or the children, you would quit."

Silence. The more I fussed and nagged, the more he retreated. On one occasion when I was going through my speech of "If you cared about me or the kids you'd quit," he responded.

"Pamela, my dear, I don't give a damn about you or the kids!"

I had forced an answer, hadn't I? Now, could I live with it? Was that actually how Howard felt or was it the liquor talking?

I pressed Howard hard, stayed on his back night and day. In my mind I rationalized that *I* had to straighten him up for the children's sakes! I realize now that most of the problems with the children occurred because I was always steamed up and stewing around the house. When he wasn't home on time, I'd fuss and say, "I guess he's out drinking, that no good." Occasionally I'd even put the kids in the car and go out and look for him, no matter what time of night it was.

Our oldest child, Betsey, finally couldn't take the nightmarish situation at home any longer, and when she graduated from high school she moved out. I thought it was a good thing because she said to me, "Momma, if I keep staying here I'm going to begin to hate him. I hate seeing what he's becoming and I'm going to get to where I hate my daddy." So she left. Occasionally she'd drop by, but only when she was sure that he wasn't at home.

The boys felt the same way, but they weren't old enough to leave, so they had their own ways of avoiding him. When he came home on time, they'd leave the house. If he came in drunk, they'd retreat to their rooms, or to a friend's house.

One night, Howard got dead drunk and had a bad wreck in the car. He was pinned in, but fortunately some passers-by pulled him out because they thought that the car was going to blow up. They took him to a nearby hospital. He called me, and I could tell that he was drunk. He said, "I've had a little accident over here, and I need you to come over."

"No, I'm not coming. You can call some of your drinking buddies to come and get you" was my answer and I hung up on him.

My sons were standing there, and I could tell they were disappointed with me. Sam said, "Mother, I'd be ashamed. He may be hurt."

I thought for a moment, then called the hospital. When a nurse answered, I asked her what shape Howard was in. She said, "He has a deep cut over one eye."

"How bad is the drinking?" I asked. She kind of laughed and said, "Pretty bad."

"Well," I lied, "my children are in bed asleep and I can't leave. I'll have to send somebody else over there."

I called my daughter and told her that her daddy was in the hospital. "If you want to go to see about him, you can," I said. "I'm not going."

When Betsey and her fiancé, Jack, got there, they found that the policemen had handcuffed Howard to a table, and he was ranting and raving that he wanted a plastic surgeon. "No intern is going to sew up my eye," he hollered. The nurse tried to find a specialist, but none was available at that late hour.

The policemen told my daughter that they were going to have to take him to the charity hospital, so Betsey and Jack followed them over. When they got there, Howard was still in handcuffs.

Betsey went all to pieces. "Take those handcuffs off of him," she cried. "He isn't a criminal." One of the officers felt sorry for her and told her, "Well, ma'am, the hospital is awfully crowded. If you can handle him, we'll turn him over to your custody. But get that cut sewn up and get him home."

Bless their hearts, Betsey and Jack got him back to the other hospital, got the eye sewed up, and brought him home.

He was the most pitiful-looking human being I have ever seen. He was so ashamed. I just stood there and looked at him. I didn't say a word, just shook my head, and he went to bed. He had totaled his car, one that he had only had a week, and we'd have to pay for two ambulance rides, a hospital bill, a fine, and lawyers' fees to get his license back.

I didn't know what to do when I realized that Howard had a problem bigger than either of us could handle. We made the rounds of psychiatrists and counselors, but the drinking continued.

One psychiatrist believed that Howard was deeply depressed, had a low opinion of himself, and recommended tranquilizers three times a day! Tranquilizers—just exchanging one problem for another. Besides, the mixture could have been deadly. *This is why I feel all physicians should have a real working knowledge of alcoholism.*

When Howard came home with the pills, he threw them across the room. "I have one problem already," he said. "I'm not going to get hung up on another." I didn't know anything then, so I tried to get him to take them. Here again, I was trying to run his life for him, thinking, Anything is better than alcohol. I realize now that that isn't true. In fact, I understand from some of the doctors at the Drug Rehabilitation Center that often drugs are harder to get off of than alcohol!

Then a friend told us about a "Christian psychiatrist" who was supposed to be very good, so reluctantly we went. Of course, Howard only went because I pushed him. At the first meeting, Howard sat there like a knot on a log. I knew he was resentful, and he let me know that he wasn't going to tell her anything.

She needled him a bit, but he didn't respond. She suggested we come back to group therapy sessions. Howard was to go to one, and I to another. *I think that was one of the biggest mistakes we ever made.* I have never heard such filthy talk. They were a collection of mixed-up people trying to analyze each other's problems. "I wouldn't put up with that . . . I'd leave him," was their answer for my particular problem. They were mainly "group pity sessions," which could easily have led me down the road to depression.

HOWARD

I went to three of those meetings and then decided that I wasn't going to any more. I told Pamela, "My problem right now is that we're in debt, and you're just adding to my problems with all of these extra doctor bills. That woman is charging us too much money, and right now what I need is to get out from under these debts."

PAMELA

We did have financial problems. Howard had been trying to make it in real estate for five years and little money was coming in, and with all our expenses, we'd gotten in a mess.

I called the doctor and told her what Howard had said, and also what I thought of the group sessions. Her reply was huffy to say the least: "You don't love him as much as you say you do because you are letting him kill himself. It is my advice that you leave him." Some Christian advice!

It left me feeling mighty low.

Then, one July night, God's plan began to unfold. I have this old Night-blooming Cereus, which you probably know is an ugly plant that you keep hidden all year until the one night when it blooms. The bloom is the most beautiful thing you have ever seen. Its flower resembles the Christ child in the manger, and the five-pronged tassels look like a star. It is breathtaking in detail and the fragrance is so sweet, you can smell it all over the neighborhood. It opens at midnight, and when the morning sun hits it, it closes, turns brown and drops off.

This night, while I was waiting for my Cereus to come out,

had started like many others, but I would remember it as a turning point in our lives.

Howard had come in that night drunk as usual and had crashed on the living-room couch. The boys had gone into another room to watch television.

Around midnight, my Cereus had opened fully, and it was so exciting to see this miracle once more that I wanted to share it with someone. I remembered that my neighbor had said that she had never seen one, so I called her and offered to bring it over for her family to see.

Kay and I had talked a few times and kept each other's boys on occasions, but we were not what you would call close friends. I don't know why we began to talk that night. I know I was terribly depressed, and I really didn't want to go back home and see Howard passed out on the couch.

Kay mentioned a Bible study class she was going to, and asked if I'd like to join her.

"I'm not going anywhere," I said. "Those Bible studies aren't for me. I've tried them and they haven't worked." Then I blurted out, "Kay, I guess you know about Howard and his drinking problem."

She said, "Well, I sort of thought he drank." Her quiet manner brought out my need to confide in somebody. "Well, Kay, I have had it," I said. "I am seriously considering divorcing him."

Her answer wasn't what I had expected. "Pamela," she said, "I know you will think this crazy, but do me a favor and don't do anything until I get a book to you tomorrow morning." Then she suggested that *I might have a problem*, too, or at least I might be contributing to Howard's problem! I didn't understand what she meant about my having a problem. The only problem I had was a problem living with the problem named Howard.

Bright and early the next morning she brought me a copy of *We Became Wives of Happy Husbands*. It was a lovely summer day, so I got my tea and went out on the patio and read the whole book that day. It was like one woman sat down on that patio, and another one got up. What I learned were God's concepts, my responsibilities as a wife, similar to what you are reading in this book right now.

I saw myself for the first time in my life. Here I was judging

Howard, when God said a wife's role was to be submissive, to pray to God *not* to try to change my mate, but to let God change *me!* The more I read, the more I realized, here I'd been trying to do it myself. I wasn't accepting Howard as he was, as Christ accepts us; I was trying to manipulate him, change him. I had never seen my faults before, and all of a sudden I realized the many things I did that provoked him, especially trying to get him to quit drinking. I realized for the first time that you can't change another human being; all you can do is pray for that person and ask God to do the changing, and get out of the way.

I realized that changes would only occur when I allowed God to change *me*, that this was the secret to God's being able to work directly in and on Howard.

All along I had been getting between God and Howard. When I pushed, complained, nagged, tried to change Howard, I was actually getting between Howard and God and shortcircuiting God's work.

I realized that I had not fulfilled my responsibilities as a wife; I had just been living for my children. I put a meal on the table for Howard and that was it. He wasn't first in my life as the Scriptures said he should be. (I Cor. 7:34b) My children came first. I had really gotten God's line of authority messed up. That book brought on my search for Christ, to know Him personally, and for Christ's will in my life.

The next day, another friend dropped by, and I excitedly told her all about what I'd been reading. She said, "I have a book in the car I want you to read." She brought me a copy of Tim LaHaye's *How To Be Happy Though Married.*

God was really getting busy in my life. You see *who He* wanted to work on first—not the person we would have thought needed to be straightened up first, *but me.*

That morning I had an interview for a job. I was going back to work to make my own money and leave Howard. I went to the interview, but when I got there the man I was supposed to talk with was out, so I told his secretary that I'd just wait in the car until he got back from lunch.

When I went back to the car, I began reading Tim LaHaye's book. I'd never known how simple it was to accept Christ and what He'd done. I didn't realize His forgiveness and love was available if only I'd ask. (John 3:16–18) Sitting in the car, I prayed and asked Christ to come into my life, to forgive my sins, and to begin to lead and teach me how to be the helpmate that Howard needed. I thanked Him for filling me with His Spirit. I read Colossians 2:9–10 (AMP) over and over: "For in Him the whole fullness of Deity (the Godhead) continues to dwell in bodily form—giving complete expression of the divine nature. And you are in Him, made full and have come to fullness of life —in Christ you too are filled with the Godhead: Father, Son and Holy Spirit, and reach full spiritual stature." I thanked Him for filling me with His Spirit, which would provide the power to live the Christian life, my life, even the one I had with Howard.

I left without interviewing for the job. The Lord had a job already cut out for me, and that was my home. A couple of nights later there was a program on TV called, "Drink, Drank, Drunk," and I watched that. And when it was over, I got up and said to myself, "That's it, I'm going to A.A." I went the very next night.

I know I'd never have gone to Al-Anon if I hadn't realized my responsibilities and God's concepts for marriage. I know it was Christ who gave me the strength to take that first step. (II Tim. 1:7)

In the past, when I had prayed that God would make Howard quit drinking, I'd say, "If You are as loving a God as they say You are, all You have to do is take the desire away from him, and he won't even want another drink, and all our problems will be solved." Of course, that isn't the way God works, and it wasn't His plan for us. But at that time, when nothing changed, I simply got fatalistic about it and decided, "What will be will be." I hate to say this now, but sometimes we would be lying in bed, and I would look over at him lying in the bed drunk and wish that he would die and get out of my life. At the same time, I'd say to the Lord, "Why are you leaving him here to torment me this way? I haven't done anything to deserve this."

Christ is so beautiful, He works in our lives exactly where we need Him, when we need Him, but most of all when we are ready. It's just sad that most of us have to hit rock bottom before we look up.

I began to regularly attend Al-Anon meetings, and I was learning and beginning to understand the problem of living and helping an alcoholic. Funny, their answers were the same messages I read in God's concepts and His Word. The first thing I learned was that the alcoholic must face up to the fact that without self-discipline, without being honest about his problem, he cannot survive. They told me that all my threats, tantrums, tears, etc., would do nothing but add to the guilt he already carried, and send him even faster back to the bottle. I learned that I must accept him just as he was.

After I had been attending Al-Anon awhile and putting God's concepts into practice, Howard noticed a change in me. I wasn't acting the same, and just like Anne says, a vacuum was created, and it demanded a change from him. To begin with, it wasn't a good one. He resented me. I became a threat because he saw that I was getting help, that I was coping, and it quietly condemned him.

But my life did change. When he'd call and say he'd be home in a few minutes, and hours passed, and bedtime came, I just put Howard in the Lord's hands, and the children and I would go to bed. If he came in, I thanked the Lord that he was all right. If he didn't, I knew that the Lord was quite capable of caring for him wherever he was. I relied constantly on Philippians 4:6–9.

Sometime in November 1972, Howard called and said he was going to election headquarters. About 2 A.M. he called from jail; he was drunk and had been driving on the wrong side of the street. The police had picked him up and put him in jail. I went and got him, and he was crying like a baby. He said, "I've got to do something about this problem." I took his hand, and said, "Yes, I know you do. You know that I've been going to Al-Anon, and, honey, I think if you really want help A.A. is the place. But, Howard, this is something you will have to do yourself, if you want it bad enough." He just sat quietly and thought. He wasn't quite ready yet.

God continued to give me strength to deal with our daily lives. (II Corinthians 2:9) Now, instead of hating him and wishing him dead, I prayed for him. I felt for him. I realized that it was his problem, and although I had contributed to it, he was the only one who could bring himself out of it, by wanting to. I still loved him, and I helped him all I could, but I had to stop being a crutch for him. So when he would come in drinking, I would have his supper ready, no matter what time it was. Or, if he didn't want to eat and wanted to go to bed, I would let him. I didn't say anything to him about the problem. I could see that he was having a struggle within himself, that he was struggling to get the strength to do something about his drinking.

I encouraged the children to pray for him. After I learned more about alcoholism, I talked with the children, and we discussed ways in which we could help him. The boys did their best to acknowledge his presence in the house, and tried not to avoid him as much.

Bible verses that I had read in *We Became Wives of Happy Husbands* kept running through my mind: "Confess your sins, He will forgive you and cleanse you from all unrighteousness." (I John 1:9) "By faith you are filled with the Holy Spirit." (Col. 2:10) "He promises to never leave you." (Matt. 28:20) "He will take all things and work them out for your good." (Rom. 8:28) Christ says you should tell Him about your problems, then let Him work them out. Trust Him for the solutions. "He waits for you to come to Him and share with Him and ask for His help." (II Cor. 12:9) Over and over, these thoughts ran through my mind.

I began to experience God's peace and for the first time in my life I had a deep inner quietness that I still cannot understand. I knew that I must accept Howard as he was, and daily that took some doing. But I relied on Jesus one day at a time to get us through. (Matt. 6:34)

The night of December 23, I was busy cooking our Christmas dinner. It was an awful night, pouring rain and foggy. Howard called at 10:30 P.M. and he was so drunk he didn't even know where he was. All he said was, "I'm on my way home," and hung up.

I went to my room and got down on my knees by the bed. I prayed harder than I had ever prayed in my life that God's will be done where Howard was concerned. "Please, God, if it's Your will, please don't let him get killed or kill or hurt anyone else. I know You love him more than I do. Thank You, Lord, for loving me, saving me, teaching me Your concepts. Now, Lord, I will commit Howard to Your care." In my prayer I was claiming the promise of John 14:13–14 (AMP): "And I will do—I Myself will grant—whatever you ask in My name so that the Father may be glorified and extolled in (through) the Son. (Yes) I will grant—will do for you—whatever you shall ask in My name."

Then I relaxed in His peace. (John 14:27)

At 4 A.M. on Christmas Eve, Howard called and said he was in jail. He had gotten in touch with a lawyer friend who was sending someone down to pay his bail and he would be straight home. I called the jail and they said no one had come to get Howard out. I called the lawyer and he said he couldn't find anyone with the money but that he was still working on it. It was noon before Howard came home. The rest of the day was spent getting his car, which had been impounded. He was so ashamed. He couldn't look me in the face. He said, "I know you won't believe me, but I've made up my mind. I am going to A.A."

HOWARD

Boy, that first A.A. meeting was something. I was scared, embarrassed—all sorts of mixed feelings were running around inside of me. But a little after eight o'clock the chairman called the meeting to order. The group, which had been mingling and talking, took their seats; there were about ninety of them. They ranged in age from the very young to grandfathers. The chairman began by stating the purpose of A.A., which he said was a group of people who shared their strength, hope, and experience with each other so that they could solve their common problems and help others to overcome alcoholism.

A speaker then introduced himself. He said, "I'm Roger D. and I'm an alcoholic, it's good to be here tonight, and it's great to be sober!"

Another member then rose and gave his name, then shared the tormented story of his downhill fight with the bottle. Every word was my story!

When the meeting was over, I realized here were people who actually knew what I was going through, they'd experienced it all, yet they stood tonight, sober, happy, with families reunited. "Dear God, maybe there is hope for me," I thought.

I realized I had to take the first step. I had to admit I was an alcoholic. At my second meeting, with trembling knees I stood up and said, "I'm Howard and I'm an alcoholic!" Tears started running down my face as everyone applauded. They knew how hard those words were for me. I felt strength pouring into me from these people, and with God's help and their human support, for the first time I believed I could make it.

PAMELA

Not long after that first A.A. meeting, Howard started going to church with us. Oh Lord, what a wonderful feeling it was to be in the house of the Lord together, to be a family again. As I continued to be the wife God created me to be, Howard continued to change. Then one Sunday he too came to know Jesus Christ as his personal Savior! The Lord had performed the miracle I'd prayed for all these years. He just did it His way instead of mine, and I was reminded of Isaiah 55:8–9 (AMP): "For My thoughts are not your thoughts, neither are your ways My ways, says the Lord. For as the heavens are higher than the earth, so are My ways higher than your ways, and My thoughts than your thoughts." How true those words were.

Money was still a problem, but Howard realized that the material things which had been so important in the past weren't the fulfillment that he desired any longer, he had learned the truth of Matthew 6:21 (AMP): "For where your treasure is, there will your heart be also." I noticed one evening that he was reading and rereading Matthew 6:19–34. Not long after that, Howard left real estate and returned to Lockheed. It took some time to straighten up our finances, but the Lord was gracious and blessed, and today we are happily debt-free.

HOWARD

The Lord didn't just restore our family. He renewed our love, both emotional and physical. Jesus changed Pamela, then He made me into a different person. He gave me the ability and the desire to be the head of my home. He also gave me the desire to be the spiritual leader of my home, which was a switch for us. It is so beautiful, so natural for Pam and me to have our souls communing with Jesus together.

PAMELA

God works in mysterious ways to bring us to Him. It has been four years since that dark night I took the Night-blooming Cereus over to Kay's. Four years and Howard hasn't had a drink in the last three! God may be waiting right now to be the answer in your life to your problems, to your broken marriage. All you have to be is willing. He may not work through a flower as He did in my life, but I will always call my flower the miracle flower.

This story, as told by Pamela and Howard, illustrates a point that I would like to make clear.

If the problem in your home is alcohol, remember that all your problems won't disappear when the bottle does. Your problems weren't born in that bottle. Your drinking mate needs to be accepted as he or she is—and allowed to assume his or her rightful role and responsibility. Take a deep inventory of all the areas of your lives compared to God's concepts, because herein lies the root from which the bottle grew.

I know right now some of you are thinking, "That's a great story, but if I really let out all the reins and turned my mate free, no telling what he or she would do." Right? Most of us feel that way. I know I certainly did. If you will recall, I held on to Jim, watched him, checked on him, kept the leash short. Also, recall the result. The shorter the leash, the more rebellious he became. Change only began when I was willing to use God's formula, which is shared in Philippians 4:4, 6–9 (AMP): "Rejoice in the Lord always—delight, gladden yourselves in Him; again I say, Rejoice! Do not fret or have any anxiety about anything, but in every circumstance and in everything by prayer and petition (definite requests) with thanksgiving continue to make your wants known to God. And God's peace (be yours that tranquil state of a soul assured of its salvation through Christ, and so, fearing nothing from God and content with its earthly lot of whatever sort that is, that peace) which transcends all understanding, shall garrison and mount guard over your hearts and minds in Christ Jesus. For the rest, brethren, whatever is true, whatever is worthy of reverence and is honorable and seemly, whatever is just, whatever is pure, whatever is lovely and lovable, whatever is kind and winsome and gracious, if there is any virtue and excellence, if there is anything worthy of praise, think on and weigh and take account of these things—fix your minds on them. Practice what you have learned and received and heard and seen in Me, and model your way of living on it, and the God of peace—of untroubled, undisturbed well-being—will be with you."

God says, To get with My plan the first thing you are to do is just dump the whole mess in My hands. He promises us that He is not only capable, but He is reliable to handle the situation if we will just trust Him. We trust Him by first coming to know Him personally, then by sharing with Him the needs of our hearts, the problems in our lives, and then step back and leave it in His adequate hands. "I'm not sure I understand, Anne. How do I give Christ my burdens?" You commit your every burden, your every care, to Jesus through prayer, simply talking with God. God understands your situation. He knows every pain, mental and emotional, that you are feeling. He is capable of carrying the load. The question is, Will you let Him?

Now, don't fall into the trap I initially did, which was sharing with the Lord the needs and desires of my life, but in the process I also told Him the best way to correct each problem and approximately when it should be done! We humans have a habit of thinking we need to let the Lord know how to handle our lives. Someone once gave the illustration, and it is a good one, that our lives are like a beautiful needlework picture; the problem is we are only seeing the underneath side and it always looks like a mess, but our Heavenly Father sees the finished picture, from the top side, and He knows where each finishing thread should go.

LOOKING ON THE TOP SIDE

After you have given God your cares, problems, worries, etc., then begin to look at the picture as if you could already see the top side of it. Remember in Philippians 4:8 it says to set your mind on whatever is kind, lovely, winsome, virtuous, etc. Well, that is the beginning.

I'll tell you a little secret, and *believe me it works.* The Scriptures share it in Proverbs 16:24 (AMP): "Pleasant words are as a honeycomb, sweet to the mind and healing to the body!" Begin to look for areas in your mate that you can praise. "Anne, you have got to be kidding. There is nothing about my mate that I can praise." Well, I am sure if you think about it you can think of something. For instance, instead of looking at your mate's negative traits, reverse them in your mind, and share that reversal with him. For instance, if he is stubborn, realize that that can also be considered perseverance, and compliment him on that. If his conversation is inconsiderate, or too direct, consider the fact that he is open and frank. Look for the good.

Tolstoy, in *The Kingdom of God Is Within You,* makes this approach very clear when he says: "It seems to me that love, if it is fine, is essentially a discipline . . . In wise love each divines the high secret self of the other, and refusing to believe in the mere daily self creates a mirror where the lover or the beloved sees an image to copy in daily life."[2]

GOALS: To turn your mate over to the Lord, and learn to accept him/her exactly as the Lord accepted you, unconditionally. You might apologize for your past mistakes in this area, mistakes which included not trusting him/her, being his/her Holy Spirit, making unrealistic demands, and not being the loving mate God intended you to be. Begin to apply Philippians 4:4, 6–9. Caution: Do not confess past immoralities in your life; it may make you feel better, but it may plant deep seeds of hurt and mistrust that may take years to correct. If you have made morality mistakes yourself, confess these to your Father in Heaven, claim I John 1:9 and get going. Your main goal is to learn that true love can only grow and develop in an atmosphere of acceptance and freedom, and that if you want to save that marriage on the brink, you are going to have to risk enough, trust God enough to let go, and let God!

ASSIGNMENTS:

(1) Memorize Philippians 4:4, 6–9.
(2) Take your problems and anxieties to the Lord daily in prayer, and leave them there.
(3) Begin to look on the positive side of your mate, begin to praise him/her, build up instead of tearing down.
(4) Learn to guard your tongue. (Prov. 21:23, James 3:5–9)

(5) Change your prayers from, "Lord, please change my mate," to, "Lord, please change me, and make me into the kind of marriage partner who will be honoring to you, and a magnet to my mate."

(6) If alcohol is a problem in your marriage, get in touch with Alcoholics Anonymous or Al-Anon immediately. Check your phone book for the phone number and address.

(7) If the abuse of illegal or legal drugs is affecting your relationship, you will find trained persons ready to help you in this field, at your local drug rehabilitation center. Consult your phone book or check with A.A.

(8) Make a list of the things about your mate which you appreciate. Then, beginning today, compliment him or her on these areas.

CHAPTER 6

PROBLEM: THE COMMUNICATION BLACKOUT

Symptoms

Constant misunderstandings
Singular or mutual distrust
Mates who never listen
Marital infidelity
Resentment
Game-playing
Marriages that involve those "certain subjects" that we can't discuss
Mask-wearing
Mates who talk too much
Continual superficial conversation
Frustration, and tension buildup
Emotional divorce
Feelings of alienation on one or both sides
Occasional physical brutality

Marriage counselors report that nearly half of all the couples they see have serious problems in the area of communication.

Communication is necessary in almost every area of life, but in the intimate state of marriage it is vital. Unfortunately, you can sit in almost any public place and pick out the married from the unmarried. The unmarried girl is looking directly in her escort's eyes, obviously listening, clinging to every word. She is interested in his every thought, idea, dream, and plan. He, in turn, obviously values her thoughts and ideas, and readily responds to them. On the other hand, the married woman is too often looking at what other women are wearing, who is with whom, wondering if she can make her beauty appointment and still keep that tennis date with her friends—all this, while her husband is trying to communicate. While the wife is talking, expressing her excitement in areas the husband is not interested in, or knowledgeable about, his mind wanders off to replay Sunday's football game, or to wonder why he missed that putt on the eighth hole. His disinterested responses let her know he isn't listening. It is sad how quickly some couples move from the attentive unmarrieds to the preoccupied marrieds. Marriage grows and blossoms, or withers and dies, almost in proportion to the kind of communication involved.

Before we get into the right and wrong ways to communicate, I'd like to share with you the story of a couple whose major marital problem lay in their inability and lack of development in the area of communication.

R.D. AND BETTY JO TAYLOR'S STORY

BETTY

It was a beautiful, sunny day in July when I left my home in Charlotte, North Carolina, to visit my cousin, Beth Ann. The farthest thing from my mind was that in the next few days I would meet my future husband.

Beth Ann is the perfect picture of a true southern hostess. I had hardly arrived when she told me that she had planned a get-together for me and some of her friends. We went to a lovely supper club for dinner and a "Welcome to Jacksonville" party. The club had a super band and it was jam-packed with couples, plus many Marines from nearby Camp LeJeune.

I danced with a number of the young men Beth Ann had invited, but as the evening progressed, an attractive young Marine, all decked out in a uniform which looked as if it would stand up by itself from all the starch it appeared to contain, approached our table and asked if I would like to dance. I was a bit hesitant, but Beth Ann said, "Oh, Betty Jo, go ahead." So I thanked him and walked out to the floor as the band began playing "The Shadow of Your Smile."

This tall, sun-darkened Marine seemed quite polite as he introduced himself. "I'm R. D. Taylor and I am stationed at Camp LeJeune."

I wanted to say, "That's obvious"—I have a problem with a mouth that likes quick comebacks—but this time I held my tongue and tried to display some of my southern breeding. I replied, "Well, it's a pleasure to meet you, R.D. I'm Betty Jo Wilkins. I'm in Jacksonville visiting my cousin Beth Ann Owens."

"Will you be in Jacksonville long?" he asked.

"Only a couple of days. Beth Ann and I plan to go over to the Outer Banks to catch some sun and relax before she goes back to work, and I have to return to college."

"Gee, I'm sorry to hear that. I'd really like to see you again. Do you think you might be able to get away from Beth Ann and drive down to West Onslow Beach tomorrow?"

"I don't know. Let me think about it and I'll let you know before the evening is over."

When I returned to the table, I told Beth Ann how impressed I was with R.D., and that he had asked me to drive down to West Onslow Beach with him the following day. "But you know, Beth Ann, I just got here, and it simply wouldn't be fitting for me to run out on you like that." I think deep down I was hoping that she'd give me an excuse to do just that.

"Don't be silly, Betty Jo, go right ahead. I have some shopping to do tomorrow before we leave, and I have a sneaky idea that you'd have a better time with your Marine than spending the day following me around all over town while I do errands."

"Oh, thanks, Beth Ann, I really hoped you'd feel that way."

I spent what was left of the evening dancing and talking with R.D. I was surprised to find that he was from Charlotte also. I was thoroughly impressed when he told me his parents lived in the Eastover area, one of Charlotte's best and definitely not exactly the side of town in which I had been raised.

The next morning I got up early, fried chicken, and packed a picnic lunch, so we could eat on the beach, watch the water and just be alone. About nine o'clock, R.D. drove up in this terrific little red Fiat convertible, and off we went. As we drove, we talked, laughed, and swapped high school stories. The day was perfect, the sun made the waves look like glimmering stones as we swam and played like two kids.

On the way back to Jacksonville we had long silences, listening to mood music on the radio, and I suppose reviewing the day in our own minds. I silently dreaded the thought of not seeing R.D. again. I quietly wished that Beth Ann and I weren't going off. But what the heck, I had no idea how he really felt.

When we pulled up in front of Beth Ann's, R.D. gently pulled me over to him, kissed me in the most tender way, then said,

"Betty Jo, I want to see more of you; can't you postpone your trip just one more day?"

I knew Beth Ann had planned our outing around her work schedule, and I felt that it would be terribly thoughtless and selfish of me to try to make any changes.

"R.D.," I said, "I'd like to stay over another day too, but Beth Ann only has a set time off from work, and I just can't ask her to waste her vacation time for me. Perhaps I can stay a couple of days when we get back from the beach."

"That's my girl," he said. Then he reached in his pocket and pulled out a pen and notepad and wrote down his address and a phone number where he said I could leave messages for him. "You let me know as soon as you all get back in town. Promise?"

"Yes, I promise."

The next morning Beth Ann and I took off for the sun and sand, but my mind stayed behind. Those next two weeks seemed like months. I felt like we were never going to get back to Jacksonville. As soon as I got in the house, I called the number R.D. had given me and left him a message saying that I had returned.

You would have thought I was homesteading the chair beside the phone as I waited hour after hour for his call. Finally, six hours later, he called.

"I'm sorry it took me so long to return your call, Betty, but we were out on maneuvers, and I just got back in. I have a pass for this evening. Can you make it for dinner?"

Could I make it! I was half undressed as I ran up the stairs to bathe and dress.

R.D. kept asking me out, and I kept staying in Jacksonville. Mom and Dad were getting a bit concerned and asked me to come home, but each time I'd beg and plead and say it would be just a few more days. Finally, time caught up with us. I almost missed registering for my fall classes at the University of North Carolina at Charlotte because I continued to stall.

On our last night together, we returned to the supper club where we had met, and spent a lovely but rather sad evening. There were promises of writing, talk of love, but I'm not sure that either of us realized at that time that we were serious. I do recall we stayed until the last dance. The band was playing

"More," and I felt so torn inside, I wanted R.D.'s arms around me always. I didn't want to leave.

R.D.

Betty Jo was in college and I seldom got passes long enough to drive to Charlotte to visit her, so for nine months the U.S. Mail carried most of our messages.

My first extended leave was in June 1968, the same time Betty Jo was to graduate from college. My first impulse was to surprise her and just show up at the graduation ceremonies. But then I decided that two June ceremonies would make our lives complete, and I wrote Betty Jo asking her to marry me. We really didn't know each other, but I thought we did, and she agreed. You know you can put so many things in letters, but it is nothing like the day-in-day-out living and communicating with someone . . . nothing!

BETTY

June was a busy month. I had finals, but more pressing in my mind was my forthcoming wedding. I was thrilled that R.D. had planned for us to be married in a church near his home. I must admit I was impressed with the beauty and what I felt was "prestige" in having our wedding there.

Our wedding was beautiful. Mom and Dad had done everything possible to provide me with the appropriate wedding dress. Dad even suggested that Mom and I drive down to Atlanta to look for a dress, but we assured him that we could find just what I needed in Charlotte.

As I finished dressing in the bride's room at the church, I was almost moved to tears, because R.D. had remembered something special between us, something dear to me—the song we had last heard when we met. As Beth Ann handed me the penny for my shoe, I heard the strains of "More" being sung. It was going to be perfect, our whole life was going to be this way, I just knew it.

After the wedding, R.D. and I boarded a flight to Miami for a short but beautifully fulfilling honeymoon. I have often read how the honeymoon isn't all that a couple expects, but for R.D. and me it was more.

We only had a week in Miami before we had to return to Charlotte and look for an apartment prior to R.D.'s return to camp. We found a nice duplex and began our married life there.

A few months after R.D. left, I discovered that I was pregnant! I was thrilled and unhappy at the same time. I would have liked to have had more time with R.D. alone, time for us, time to get better acquainted, but babies don't wait.

R.D.

I was discharged six months after we were married and I returned to Charlotte. Betty Jo was already showing her pregnancy. I was really so happy to be home, I truly looked forward to the birth of our child.

I had been in the food brokerage business before I went into the service, so when I came home I returned to the only business I knew. For a time our marital life went smoothly. Naturally, there were adjustments to be made on both sides, but I felt that as soon as the baby was born, Betty Jo wouldn't be so moody and things would return to normal.

Return to normal. What was normal? We didn't know each other; we really didn't have any idea what to expect when we began living together. For a time our lives seemed to go well, but after a few months our strong independent personalities began to clash.

BETTY

It was an adjustment for me when R.D. did come home for good. I had been used to doing things my way, answering to no one, and the change was difficult. R.D. was rather chauvinistic in his ideas about family structure, whereas I believed in a fifty-fifty relationship; you have your money, I have mine, and no one accounts to anyone. We argued over everything, from who was going to pay the bills, to what kind of baby food to buy. From R.D.'s standpoint, the bills were his responsibility; from mine, it was an equal responsibility. I felt I was as capable of earning as good a living as he was. My basic nature caused continual problems. I am innately jealous, suspicious, and I fell into the destructive trap of constantly questioning R.D. when he wasn't home at the exact moment I thought he should be. Dear God, where had all the love, the romance, the tender moments gone? In only a few weeks we were about to rip each other apart.

About eight months after our wedding, R.D. began his first affair! At the time, I wasn't aware of it. I sensed that we had serious problems, but I just discounted it as the clash of two strong temperaments. The duplex was too cramped for the forthcoming baby, so we decided that we needed our own home. In the process of moving I knocked off his tennis gear and out fell a bundle of notes that a girl at his office had written him! I sank to the floor, shocked, and weeping as I read through the descriptive, wanton language. My mind didn't want to believe it, not R.D.! But the facts lay in a wadded heap in my lap, a silent witness to the devastating truth. I don't know how long I sat, stunned, thumbing through, reading another woman's expressions of desire for my husband. I could hardly think, but inside a desire to confront him began to swell in my heart.

"You rat, you rotten, no good, cheating creep! Look at these notes, just look. R.D., how could you? How could you?" I screamed when he came in. He almost turned white, and for a moment I thought I saw a look of pain cross his face, like this discovery was hurting him as much as it was me. But I was so wrapped up in my own feelings I dismissed it. He became very humble. He knelt down beside where I sat crying and said, "Betty Jo, please, please don't leave me."

"Why shouldn't I? Just give me one good reason," I cried.

"It was a mistake, Betty Jo. I promise it will never happen again. Honey, it was just the pressure of adjusting to marriage, the realization that I would soon be responsible for a child, just settling down in general. Baby, she meant nothing to me, honestly. Please believe me, please forgive me."

The pleading and begging broke my heart. I couldn't stand to see R.D. so broken, so humble. Inside I wanted to believe him. I didn't understand, but I wasn't willing to give up this soon.

We moved into the new house. Relations weren't easy. At first things were very strained between us. We were afraid to communicate, afraid of setting off an argument that would throw us over the brink. There became more and more "subjects" that were off limits, because when they were brought up, only hostility and fights followed. The words we'd said so easily in letters didn't seem to flow when we were actually together.

It seemed everything that I was interested in—good books, social causes and music—R.D. knew nothing about. Everything he thought was stimulating, such as politics, camping and sports, were either superficial or dull to me. There were few words shared and fewer listened to in our "home." I had a college degree; he didn't. Oh, the degree really didn't matter. R.D. made excellent money, but our interests were in opposite directions, and neither of us was willing to give an inch to change the situation.

R.D. was in a business that I didn't really understand. Not only did I not understand its workings, I didn't want to. It irritated me when he came home complaining about customers, late shipments, bad product, or tried to use me as a verbal sounding board for his plans to get new customers. I figured that that stuff was his business and it belonged at the office, not at home, and certainly not where I had to be bored stiff listening to it.

After our baby, Matthew, was born, things seemed to improve for a while. I was teaching full time and found my work extremely stimulating. I was able to again interrelate with people who were interested in the same things as I. I imposed on my mother to take care of the baby and, to further fulfill myself, I began taking night courses at the university. Perhaps, in retrospect, this time in our relationship seemed better because I was wrapped up again in myself, escaping for a while the problems at home. R.D., his business, and interests didn't have the power to invade this artificial world I had created.

A year passed and, lo and behold, I was pregnant again! I continued to teach until the baby was born. Isolated inside my cloistered world, I still felt things at home were fine. I was accomplishing what I had set out for myself in life, and I presumed R.D. was doing the same.

Oh, there were still fights over my lack of interest in R.D.'s business. By this time he had opened his own food-brokerage house, with financial backing from his father. Our main area of stress came because he was constantly pressing me to entertain more and more. I found many of the customers he wanted to court brash, boorish, uneducated, or downright "red necky." I saw no reason why I should have to spend time smiling, being polite, or playing up to people I was totally disinterested in. R.D., on the other hand, felt it was my responsibility as his wife to help him. I just felt his chauvinism was cropping up again, that he was trying to "use" me, and I refused as often as possible to co-operate. I told him, "Now, look, R.D., I don't ask you to teach my classes, to get me promotions or raises. I don't expect you to go to school to further my education, do my homework, or take my tests, right?"

"Right, but what's the point?"

"The point is, if I am capable of taking care of my job without your help, then I should think a grown man could take care of his without his wife's help. Now do you understand me?"

"I understand you, Betty Jo, but babe, you are out in left field. There are very, very few successful men who don't have a helpful, interested wife somewhere in the background. With all your education, you should know from history, if nothing else, that behind most successful men is a supportive, loving wife. My dear, if you haven't learned that, maybe you have wasted a lot of years in school. You may know a lot from books, but you don't know anything about the real world, about life, about what makes for success."

The discussion ended in a draw. No one won, no one lost, we just remained in our normal "Mexican stand-off" position.

R.D.

There was no understanding, no support, no love or care at home, and again I began to look for an interest in me as a person, as a man, beyond my own doorstep. Betty Jo seemed to have her own thing going, and she had built such high walls, such ridiculous social standards, that it was easier to wander into "greener pastures" than to fight the endless war at home.

BETTY

Eight weeks after our second child was born, R.D. came to me and said he was in love with someone else and wanted a divorce! I couldn't believe it. Before we could make any definite moves or decisions, I discovered I was already pregnant again! I couldn't stand the stress, the infidelity, plus another child. I totally broke down and had to quit work.

Again R.D. had become involved with a woman who worked in his office. Still the secret to the problem hadn't sunk in. Every affair R.D. had was with someone he either worked with, or someone who was in a like business. Now I realize he'd told me verbally, over and over, but I never heard him. I wasn't listening, not really. Not until I learned God's concepts and seriously thought through our lives did I realize that what R.D. was doing in the eyes of the world were the overt no-no's. But I was the one pushing him out the door. He was finding with other women the understanding, the interest in what he was doing, what he was, something he didn't find at home. I was always too busy advancing myself, considering my career. In essence, I was just too busy for him.

R.D.

When Betty Jo told me she was pregnant again, I felt like a man caught between a rock and a hard place. Respectability deemed I couldn't forsake her while she was pregnant. I knew, since I had told her about Wanda, that I would have to break off that affair. Now what would I do? We were back to the same old games, faking out everyone with our "happy little family" while the fires of dissension and hostility grew and grew inside.

I never really took time to examine the ramifications of the high cost of my affairs—I mean in terms of feelings, the possibility of permanently losing my wife and children. I just didn't think. What I found beyond home and didn't find with Betty Jo was an acceptance of me, just plain ole R.D.; there weren't any pressures and there was an interest, a oneness of minds which I could never seem to create with Betty Jo.

It is one thing to "listen" to what one is sharing, but it is another thing to understand. Most of the time, when I honestly tried to communicate with Betty Jo, she would already have her mind made up, interrupt me before I finished, trying to state for me what I was saying. I felt I was continually being prejudged, that no matter what I said, she had her thoughts preset, and that would be it. Finally I just retreated and turned to someone who did seem to care, who did know how to listen, turned to someone who understood my pressures, my business, and could at least help me sound out all the problems and anxieties I faced.

BETTY

Well, here I was pregnant again, and here came R.D. saying that he loved me, and that he was sorry. I started to tell him that he should have just made a recording of that speech so he could have it on hand to play at the appropriate times. We could never seem to get beyond that point. The why's and wherefore's of the situation, the reasons for his wanderings, were *never* discussed. We had always had a perfect sexual relationship, and instead of talking out a problem we tried to dismiss it with a romp in the bed. Sex is beautiful in the context in which God created it, but when it is *used* as an escape for serious problems, sooner or later the bedroom door can't hold back the flood of undealt-with bitterness, anxiety, frustration, hostility and jealousy.

R.D.

The communication brownout was turning into a blackout. I recall one day I came home so excited I was about to burst at the seams. I rushed in the door, threw my arms around Betty Jo, and said, "Baby, guess what happened today?" Without even raising her eyes from the book she was reading, she disinterestedly asked, "What?" Her blank look, her detached response, made me feel like cold water had just been thrown in my face. Sharing the triumph of the day just drained out of me. It didn't seem to matter any more. I silently walked out of the room, went into the den and flopped down in front of the boob tube. You know, the whole evening passed and she never even asked what had happened. I got the message loud and clear: "I don't care what is happening in your life. If it is convenient I might give you the pleasure of my attention, but if it interferes with my interests, then forget it." She didn't say that, but that is what I heard from her actions and her silence.

BETTY

The communication breakdown was a two-way street. R.D. reacted to my accomplishments with about as much enthusiasm as I did his. I recall I came in from night school, right after finals, grinning from ear to ear. When I entered, R.D. was sitting at his desk working on some business papers. "Guess what I did on my finals?" I yelled excitedly.

"What?" he asked, hardly looking up to notice me.

"I made a ninety-three on my literature test, and a ninety-six on my grammar exam. Isn't that terrific?"

"Uh-huh, that's nice."

Some response! I had worked like a dog studying for those finals, and I was so thrilled, I certainly expected a more interested, involved reply than, "That's nice."

Well, baby number three finally arrived, but baby didn't cure our marital strain, although with two under two, silence wasn't a problem! I became more bitter, more jealous, more possessive than before. My artificial world had been crushed, and now I was again facing and having to deal with the reality of our relationship. R.D. said he felt responsible for my horrible attitude, but that didn't change anything between us. I pouted much of the time. I felt trapped, and it wasn't fair, I thought. I continually checked up on him, followed him, searched through his wallet, all those things that a scared, insecure, jealous woman does. Of course, it accomplished nothing, only added to my angry feelings and drove us further apart.

There were two more affairs. I found out about the last one when I borrowed R.D.'s car one day and opened the glove compartment and discovered a charm bracelet that didn't belong to me. It was obvious that subconsciously R.D. was leaving things around all through the years; he seemingly wanted to get caught, either in an attempt to force me to leave, or as a silent plea for me to stop him. Neither of us has ever figured out which.

R.D.

I had become a Christian when I was a young teen-age boy, but through the years I had gotten away from God's teachings and was as carnal as a Christian could be. Betty Jo became a Christian right after we were married, but neither of us had any deep foundation in God's Word, we didn't rely on it, make decisions by it, or study anything it had to say about God's position on marriage or His concepts for family living.

BETTY

We always attended church, even through the heartbreak, infidelity, bitterness, etc. We were right there, I suppose, because it was the "proper" thing to do. R.D. was even a Sunday-school teacher, a dynamic one. Every Sunday I would sit and listen to him teach, at the same time seething inside because I knew he was sleeping around. We never opened the Bible at home. His Sunday-school teaching was just a façade.

R.D.

I knew Betty Jo was sitting in Sunday-school class listening, knowing what she did and judging me. I knew she resented my not taking the spiritual leadership in our home. But she was so strong-willed herself. I felt it would put me in the position of being either put down by her, or criticized by her, and I didn't care to take the risk.

BETTY

R.D. was right. I thought, "If you are such a big Christian, how can you be doing all of this?" Of course, I realize now that a carnal Christian can be as rotten as the lowest thing that walks the earth, but I didn't understand that then. Because my sins were either verbal, or mental, neither of which I really knew or considered to be sin at the time, and since I had never been physically unfaithful to R.D., I held this up to him like a banner.

As this last affair progressed, R.D. finally came to me and said, "This time I am serious. I love this girl, and I want a divorce." I hired a detective and he supplied me with everything I could want to hang R.D. Again, the girl was one who worked in a similar business.

R.D.

I was serious this time. I had had it with Betty Jo, her lack of care and interest in me. I felt I had found a woman who really loved me, who understood me, and would be the wife I needed. So after I told Betty Jo I wanted a divorce, I made provisions for her to live *very* comfortably, and moved out.

BETTY

R.D. hadn't been gone but a few weeks when Matthew became quite ill with an undiagnosed disease. R.D. realized the strain on me, and my need to be at the hospital with Matthew, so he returned home, with the understanding that as soon as school was out, he would leave again. In my mind, this was my "last chance," so to speak. I had to make whatever move, whatever power play I had while R.D. was still under our own roof. My mixed-up mind came up with one sure way to keep him. I deliberately got pregnant! This would save our marriage—I just knew it would. I was so desperate. I didn't want a divorce, yet I didn't want things to stay as they had been in the past. I don't know what I had planned if my scheme worked. I just thought getting pregnant would keep him home a while longer, and maybe we would have time to work things out.

R.D.

When Betty Jo told me she was pregnant again, I hit the roof. "You stupid b----. If you think you are going to keep me trapped in this marriage because you deliberately got yourself pregnant again, you are sadly mistaken," I yelled. Shock shot across her face; she couldn't believe her plan wasn't working. When we both calmed down a bit, we tried to talk it out. It's odd, I guess because of our ultimate decision; I suppose both of us have blocked out the memory of that conversation. Honestly, neither of us recalls how we reached our solution, or why. But we decided to abort the child!

BETTY

As soon as the abortion was over, R.D. left. That wasn't in my plan. Somewhere in my mind, I thought if I went through with the abortion, he'd stay. I finally filed for a divorce on the grounds of adultery. As soon as I filed, I let everyone in Charlotte know exactly what kind of a man R. D. Taylor really was. I told everyone and anyone who would listen what I had put up with for years.

R.D.

I was surprised when I was served with the divorce papers. I hadn't thought Betty Jo would rush to court so fast. But I was in no hurry. It was my thought that perhaps after a time apart we might begin to see the basis of our problems, and perhaps work them out. Then Betty Jo started blabbing and slandering my name all over town. That did it. I wasn't going to put up with that kind of defamation, so I countersued.

BETTY

I hadn't intended to go through with the divorce; I just wanted to scare R.D. real good. It was too late when I discovered that the stories I was spreading had ruined our chances for a reconciliation. I hadn't counted on R.D. taking any action. In reality, I had filed only intending to let the proceedings drag on and on, postpone them over and over, thinking that during this time he might get his head on straight. But when he countersued, that forced the case to court.

R.D.

When we got to court, we just looked at each other, almost like strangers. There was nothing left to say. Of course, that was the problem. We had never really learned how to say, how to talk, how to share; we only knew how to act and react according to our feelings and emotions, and that is what kept us in a constant turmoil.

BETTY

We were both so immature. I used the children against R.D. as a punishment. I wouldn't let him see them. He loved them very much, and this tore him up. Finally, the court stepped in and said that he was to have the children on alternate weekends, and that he would be able to keep them from 6 P.M. on Friday to 6 P.M. on Sunday.

One Sunday when I got in from church, he was there early with the kids. I went to the kitchen, fixed lunch, and he sat down with us, like nothing had changed. I couldn't stand it, sitting there at the table, playing like a family. I got up and ran into the bathroom, tears streaming down my cheeks. I still loved him, and the whole phony scene just broke my heart. R.D. followed me into the bathroom, grabbed me, kissed me, and said, "I still love you! I know you have been seeing other guys since we have been divorced, and I can't stand it."

We began to talk that afternoon, really talk for the first time in our lives. After that, we would occasionally see each other, although we both continued to date other people. R.D. was still seriously involved with the girl he had left us for, and I was enjoying the attention and stimulation of dating and being back in circulation.

R.D.

Divorce certainly did something for Betty Jo. Obviously, the interest of other men was more important to her than I had ever been because she lost thirty pounds, restyled her hair, and changed her makeup and wardrobe. What a doll, and I wondered why she'd let herself go, why she hadn't cared enough to do that for me.

BETTY

By the end of the year, I had made application to teach at a private school in Colorado. I put the house up for sale. I realized that R.D. and I were never going to get our lives straightened out while we were living so close together. After R.D. found out about my decision and then discovered that I had a buyer for the house, he was around all the time. He said that he wanted us to try to work something out, to remarry!

I told him, "You have got to make up your mind one way or the other, because I have got to let this buyer know about the house, and the school know if I am definitely going to teach in the fall."

"Betty Jo, I just want to come home, I want to try again."

"R.D., I think that I would too. But what makes you presume anything will be different?"

"I don't know. There has to be a better way; maybe the Lord will show us how."

I couldn't believe those words. He had never before said anything about Christ leading our lives. I thought, "I don't know how things can be different. We are the same people, we have the same problems, but maybe he is right, maybe the Lord will honor our recommitment to each other and send us some insight, some help."

We were remarried about a year after our divorce. It wasn't easy, and it still isn't perfect, but I know that in this life nothing will ever be perfect. But, praise the Lord, just a few weeks after we remarried the Lord let me meet a fantastic Christian woman. I shared with her how I felt, the problems we faced, and she suggested that I read, *We Became Wives of Happy Husbands.*

I sat down and cried when I saw, through God's Word, how out of line I had been. I realized I had been judging R.D., yet I personally had distorted and broken almost every concept God has for a wife. I saw myself for what I really was—a selfish woman who had belittled her husband, isolated him, failed to listen and respond to him, and certainly *never* followed his leading.

Then one day, I found out how to get in touch with Anne Carroll and we had the most tremendous discussion. As we talked, I realized that in my marriage I had *talked* too much and *listened* too little. She made me realize the importance of being interested and helping my husband in his business. I picked Anne's brain trying to learn how to begin this process of communication, and I learned. I learned exactly what you are now reading in this chapter. I wanted so much to be the wife God created me to be, and through the door of help He opened, as I was willing and obedient, our relationship began growing and developing a communication not just verbal, but of the soul too. I warned Anne that I'd be calling again. There is still so much I have to learn, and this time, with God's help, I'm not going to blow it.

R.D.

Bless her heart, Betty Jo really had a hard time at first in learning to back off and let me lead in the home. She had been deeply infected by the doctrine of the Women's Liberation movement, but with Christ's help she is changing, not just for me, not just for herself, but for the woman she knows Christ would have her be.

Betty Jo has shared much of the information Anne gave her on communication, and slowly we are learning to talk; but more important, we are actually learning how to listen, with our minds and our hearts. Now when there is a victory in either of our lives, there is excitement and sharing, and rejoicing in our home. No one is ignored any more.

I wish I could undo all the mistakes I made in our first marriage, particularly allowing Betty Jo to have the abortion. Of course, I know they can't be undone, the baby can't be brought back, but I just thank God that His grace is sufficient to forgive even tragic mistakes like that. Betty Jo and I are both back in church now, but this time a Bible-teaching church where we can learn the Word, a church where we are hearing God's viewpoint, not man's. We are doing our best through His strength to walk in His steps so that our relationship, our marriage, will be an example to others.

It is often easy to communicate on what you feel is a deep, meaningful level through letters. Many romances have begun that way, only to disintegrate when the couple has the opportunity to interact on a direct and personal level. Betty Jo and R.D. didn't take the time to make this vital discovery. Two strong personalities met head on, each desiring their own way and neither having the zeal, knowledge, or ability to change.

The beginning of love is based on the Greek word *eros*, which is a sexual, physically expressed love. In a healthy relationship, that love should progress to *philia*, a more mature love, where deep friendship, companionship and self-giving result. Of course, this type of love finds its roots in open, free, caring interchange between mates. R.D. and Betty Jo never had this. Ultimately, marital love can evolve to *agape*, a love for one's mate which is similar to that which the Lord has for us. During their first marriage, Betty Jo and R.D. never progressed beyond the *eros* stage.

Although R.D. and Betty Jo were both Christians, neither had ever intently studied the Scriptures, so they failed to learn and apply God's concepts to their lives or marriage. They were operating in a total state of carnality, controlling their own lives, and they quickly steered the ship of matrimony onto the rocks.

It was a difficult struggle for them to openly face each other and begin to rebuild the shattered pieces of a shallow relationship. But they began by getting the ship on the right heading. Before remarriage, they came to the conclusion that they personally did not possess the capability to change themselves or salvage their marriage. As with so many couples, they didn't have the slightest idea of how to begin repairing the damage or break down the walls, but they finally realized that they knew

One Who did, and in prayer they asked God for guidance, for answers, and He led them. (Prov. 3:5–6)

As they searched the Word, they became intimately acquainted with Jesus Christ, and recognized that He was the supreme example of love, and that the example which He set was in giving. As they allowed the Holy Spirit to control their lives, patience, care, and kindness entered their relationship. The cold, forbidding walls of strife began to crumble. (Gal. 5:16) Slowly at first, Betty Jo and R.D. began all over; just like children, taking the steps you will read about later in the chapter, applying them diligently and daily to their union. When a question arose in either of their minds as to what the other meant during a conversation, they immediately repeated what they thought they heard, and to their amazement, they discovered that most of the time what was about to offend them wasn't what their mate had meant to convey at all.

Seriously understanding that love was giving, Betty Jo saw how selfish she'd been in not being the wife R.D. needed in business. She began to make special efforts to plan entertaining get-togethers for his customers and clients. To her surprise, not only did R.D. respond with deep warmth, affection and gratitude, but she began to really enjoy her new expression of love. In time, she learned the importance of becoming a part of R.D.'s interests and discovered, as she was open for the Lord to work in her life, that He changed her likes and dislikes. Now she is an ardent football fan, loves tennis, and often you'll find her getting up early to pack the camper for a weekend outing! Sometimes she laughs at herself. Now she loves every minute of doing exactly the things she hated during marriage number one!

R.D. saw that much of his dislike for books, music, and the like were based on his feelings of inadequacy because Betty Jo had a degree and he didn't. He started expressing love by reaching out to become what she needed. He read, not enjoying all she suggested at first, but he read, listened to music, and in time found what wonderful hours of togetherness they were experiencing. Both of them are so immersed in the other's interests, activities, and careers, that the topics of conversation are endless.

Now the ears in the Taylor household are open, the faces and eyes radiate interest and care in the other's comments, burdens, discussions, suggestions and triumphs. When God's concepts came in, when caring and giving became the motivating force in their home, the Holy Spirit was able to put their ship on a new heading, where the waters were calm, and the harbor safe from the storms that had crushed them before.

THE "OTHER WOMAN" SYNDROME

If you women think that knowing your man and being able to discuss his goals, desires, plans, and business aren't important, then I imagine some of you already have an "other woman" problem. Far from being the sexy blonde he met at last year's convention, the other woman is usually knowledgeable in his field of interest, either because she happens to work in the same field, or because she wanted your man enough to learn what he cared about, enough to discuss it intelligently; and beyond that, she has learned the secret of communication—*she has learned how to listen,* she's taken the time to *hear* what he says verbally and nonverbally.

In discussing the "other woman" syndrome I'd like to briefly share with you something that through heartbreak I discovered and that many other women have discovered about their men. There is one aspect of men few wives seem to realize, and that is the difference between the man he is and the one he wishes to be, or in some cases imagines himself to be. He likes to think of himself as the world's greatest lover, a success in business, a fascinating conversationalist, the lighthearted, unrestricted young man you probably met ten or twenty years ago. In most instances, we women fail to recognize this. We let him know exactly what he is, we ignore him instead of giving him the attention he so dearly needs and seeks; we fail to praise him in the lovemaking category. All he either wishes to be, or thinks he is, is crushed the moment he looks at us.

He may choose to have innocent relationships at the local bars just to satisfy his ego; he may go there so he can again be the man he "thinks" or "wants" to be; or he may become seriously involved with someone who is wise enough to realize that he isn't exactly what he wants to be, but who doesn't remind him of that: a woman who is long on praise, and acts as though he is the most fascinating, irresistible man she has ever met.

The other day, a young girl called me about the marital problems she and her husband were having. She vividly shared with me his constant infidelity, but said their main problem was that they simply couldn't communicate. She asked me whether I would talk with her husband if she could get him to call. I told her I normally don't counsel men, but she was so persistent that I said if *he called* me, we'd discuss their problems. Surprisingly, the next day the phone rang, and a male voice said, "This is Joel Maxwell, Lana's husband."

I must admit, after hearing all about Joel and his indiscretions the day before, I had a hard time fighting my preconceived ideas of what type of man I was dealing with. But when we really got down to the nitty-gritty, he too confirmed that communication was their major problem. I discussed his infidelity with him, but I felt that they both might be right, so I just let him talk for a while. During his complaints about Lana, he said: "You wouldn't believe how immature she is. All she talks about is movie stars. The other day, when Burt Reynolds was down here shooting a new picture, she was over near the set all the time, trying to get a look at him."

I laughed and jokingly replied: "The only personality that I ever went to that much trouble to see close up was Bart Starr!" That did it. Joel opened up like a book. "Do you like football, Anne?" he asked excitedly.

"Love it, but I'll have to admit I didn't always. My husband, who is from Green Bay, brought me up on the Packers of the 1960s."

From the Packers, we discussed the stock market, international politics, economics, and more. All of a sudden I realized that we had been talking almost two hours about everything under the sun but their marital problems, and from long experience I could see that Joel was ripe pickings for any woman who could and would communicate with him about anything but her own feminine interests. Joel had been wrong in trying to find someone else to relate to, but Lana had opened the door and pushed him out because she was too self-centered to meet his verbal needs and interests.

THE "OTHER MAN" SYNDROME

The "other man" syndrome occurs less frequently than the "other woman" does, but it occurs just the same, and from recent surveys and studies it seems to be on the increase. Women who once were willing to accept their lot in life, even some Christian women, have been tainted by the new mores introduced by Women's Lib and are becoming impatient with a life which they've been told doesn't give total, personal expression and fulfillment.

Women look to other men for the same reasons that men are attracted to other women. But men, let me share this with you, if your wife still stays home, takes care of the house, the children, etc., she will have *more* need for communication than the working wife. You see, while you have been out in the adult world all day, no matter how much pressure you have faced, you have had people of your own age and educational level to converse with. Meanwhile, your wife, in many instances, has interacted with "Puff, Spot, Dick, and Jane," vacuum cleaners, stopped-up toilets, and boiling-over dinner pots. After a few years of this same routine, she has probably begun to feel that "glamor" and "romance" have gone out of her life. When she has had time to stop and relax for a minute, she probably has picked up some woman's magazine, which tells her in essence that she doesn't have to live like this, that there is more to life, and that she should demand her rights, her own fulfillment, etc. If you husbands don't step in before she buys the whole feminist program, you are going to have massive disruptive problems on your hands and in your home.

What she is looking for, what most women are looking for in the way of satisfaction, is appreciation, a reaffirmation of herself as a woman, not as the children's mother, but as your woman, personally, as a living, breathing female. If she isn't reassured *verbally, and nonverbally,* she will find that in time appreciative looks from other men become more and more appealing. She may try to shake the feeling off, but if she is continually ignored, if her feminine needs for appreciation, affection, romance, quiet talks, etc., aren't met, she may in time secretly turn to that man who has noticed her *as a woman,* who has reminded her that she is attractive, who perhaps flirts with her, letting her forget for a time that her teen-age years are long past.

No, she probably won't go to the local bar to find the feminine reassurance she needs, although more and more modern women do. Most starved housewives run into an appreciative man accidentally—perhaps the insurance agent who drops by with the new policy, the tennis or golf pro she is taking lessons from, the man at the service station, perhaps the guy who fixes the furnace. But sooner or later, if she is hungry to feel feminine, and you aren't fulfilling your God-given position to "love, cherish, and make her happy," then some man is going to pick up the signals, and if you are smart, it had better be you.

HAPPINESS IS "WORKING AT IT"

When the wedding bouquet has withered a bit, and the day-to-day routine has set in, you begin to learn the differences in the male and female needs for communication (particularly if the wife doesn't work). You also begin to learn that years of conditioning have probably brought the male to the point that, because of his male ego, he won't converse or communicate on a subject with which he isn't acquainted. This is the reason that only about three or four men out of every hundred will seek counseling when their marriage "is on the rocks." Men feel that admitting that there are problems they can't solve, emotions they can't cope with, is a direct threat to their self-identity, their masculinity. It isn't that he doesn't want to share, want to let it "all hang out," take his mask off; it is a matter of conditioning. But a wise woman can learn to bring her man out, help him across the walls, and with the Lord's help create the kind of man God intended him to be in the first place.

Just as men often build walls of defense, refusing to talk to their wives about any matter with which they are not knowledgeable or for which they have no solution, women usually go the other way, nagging and talking their men right out the door and into someone else's arms.

DO'S OF COMMUNICATION

(1) Speak only for yourself, and be direct, clear, and, if necessary, descriptive in your statements.

RIGHT

Husband: "I sure would like to go to a movie tonight."
Wife: "I certainly would too."

This situation was handled correctly. The husband stated clearly what he wanted to do for the evening, and the wife clearly stated that she would also enjoy a movie.

WRONG

Husband: "I sure would like to go to a movie tonight."
Wife: "Whatever you say, dear."

This situation doesn't express the wife's real feelings, her preferences, and it leaves the conversation on a closed basis. The husband is probably confused as to whether she really wants to go out, and is most likely irritated about the martyr-type answer she gave.

(2) It is risky, but use the *first person* in speaking, because it is honest, reveals your true feelings, and is the best way to establish clear communication.

(3) Make your statements and comments *concise,* and state your desires *clearly*.

Wife: "I am *tired of discussing* whether or not we are going to the beach, or going to the mountains. You are so busy pushing the beach idea that you probably haven't heard a word I have said."

Husband: "I thought you were primarily interested in discussing this vacation until you got your way."

Wife: "*What I am really interested in is being with you.* Whether we are on top of a mountain, or lying in the sand isn't the issue with me."

Husband: "I didn't understand you felt that way. Honey, you are wonderful."

Do you see in this discussion, first the wife made a clear statement that she was tired of the discussion. She added that she thought she wasn't being listened to, probably from past experience, since they were new at this type of clear talk. Next the wife stated concisely what she truly cared about, which was being with him; the place wasn't the issue with her. The husband *openly admitted* that he hadn't understood, but because both had been clear and concise, the discussion turned out to be a sweet time of coming together, of knowing that being together mattered more than where they were.

(4) *Please* learn to listen carefully to your mate. Listening is as important in communication as talking. (James 1:19 and Prov. 18:13)

(5) If you have something important to discuss with your mate, certainly, if the subject is a controversial one, *don't* just open your mouth and let the words begin to flow. Spend time thinking out exactly what you want to say, or ask. Consider the words you will want to use, words that will best express how you *feel*, what you *desire*, or what the *problem* or *situation* is as *you* see it. Run your side of the conversation through your mind to see how it sounds, to be sure it is *clear*, and certainly to eliminate any type of blame or abusive language. "Have you seen a man of hasty words? There is more hope for a fool than for him." (Prov. 29:20 Berkley)

(6) Carefully select the correct time to open an important discussion. The moment a man walks in the house from work, tired, hungry, and bushed from the five o'clock traffic is not a smart time to begin any type of discussion. If your wife is in the middle of fixing dinner, or the children are crying and calling for her, and obviously she is harried and tired, again wait. Get to know your mate well enough that you know when it is best to approach him/her. *Don't* make the bedroom the room of problem-solving—*never*. Problems, discussions, children, etc., are always to be left outside the bedroom door. Later you will learn about the table of harmony; it may be your solution to a time of sharing. But if it isn't a workable solution for your personal circumstances, then at least don't approach your mate in a negative

form, or when he/she is tired, emotionally upset, hurried, hungry, or preoccupied with another problem. *Wait.*

You can share with your mate that you have something you need and would like to discuss with him/her, and ask when it would be convenient for the two of you to have a time of sharing. Be sure that you agree on a specific time; *don't* leave the subject with a vague "later." This leaves both of you uncertain as to when you may engage in the conversation and can cause conflict. Proverbs 15:23 (AMP): "A man has joy in making an apt answer, and a word spoken at the *right* moment, how good it is!" Keep in mind, if at all possible, Paul's advice in Ephesians 4:26.

(7) When you feel there is a problem in your home, or in your relationship, remember that most problems are created by more than one person. And even if this problem is one you feel you have no direct part in, if it is upsetting you, then *you* are the one who needs to bring up the conversation. The best method to approach your mate at such a time is by saying, "We have a problem," or "I have a problem," since it is *you* who are upset. Your mate may have no idea he has done something to offend you, so if you are disturbed, it is also *your* problem, and the Scripture in Matthew says you are to go to him and correct the discontent. When you use the right approach, your mate is not likely to feel you are blaming him for the situation.

(8) There is a system which you might find very helpful. I like to call it "statement-restatement." Many disagreements, arguments, and the like begin because what you are saying and what your mate is hearing are *two different things.* To begin the "what I hear you saying" approach may sound and feel a bit silly, but it will help clear up many misunderstandings. The statement-restatement is approached this way. John says, "I really am tired tonight."

WRONG

Carol: "Do I understand you to say that you are too tired to go to Nancy's party?"

John: "No, that isn't what I said. What I said was, I am tired. Period."

Carol: "Then, what I hear you saying is that you are tired, but you still plan to attend Nancy's party, right?"

John: "Right."

Carol and John were trying statement-restatement for the first time and they forgot some of the rules, and almost had a misunderstanding. Statement-restatement is used to make sure that you are hearing exactly what the other person is communicating. Carol in her first try was constantly *adding* to what John said, which is a *no-no*. So let's let them do it over and see if they have learned how to deal with it correctly.

RIGHT

John: "I really am tired tonight."

Carol: "Do I understand you to say that you are tired?"

John: "Yes."

Carol: "Does that mean that you would prefer not to go to Nancy's party?"

John: "No, that is not what I meant. I still intend for us to go to Nancy's party."

Now both John and Carol are completely clear on how John feels, and also on what their plans for the evening are.

(9) Be aware of your mate. *Listen* to what he/she has to say. Check yourself out:

(a) Am I *really* interested in what he/she is saying?

(b) Do I honestly value his/her opinion, feelings, or wishes?

(c) Am I honestly encouraging him/her to be more open and free in his or her communication with me?

(d) Am I being self-centered or other-centered?

(e) Do my actions express love, giving of myself, or mere toleration of my mate?

(f) Who is in control of my life? If I am, before we proceed to converse I should use I John 1:9 and get back into fellowship with the Lord.

THE BASIC DON'TS OF COMMUNICATION

(1) To begin with, in communication, conversation and discussion, don't approach these matters with the mental attitude that

each time there has to be a winner and a loser. Communication *shouldn't* involve competition. You are trying to share, to get to know your mate—his feelings, desires, wants and interests—not beat him at a verbal game. When competition enters in, then normally self-centeredness enters with it.

(2) Don't be a *blabbermouth.* In other words, don't try to dominate every conversation. Studies prove that more marriages fail where there is too much talk instead of too little. "Self-control means controlling the tongue! A quick retort can ruin everything." (Prov. 3:13 LVB)

(3) Even if you are a "true" Southerner, don't drawl out your story, situation, problem, etc., so slowly that your mate goes to sleep before you get to the point. Nothing is as boring as listening to every minute detail of something as you anxiously await the "punch line" or the point. Be sure you have thought through your conversation, have eliminated the needless details, because the longer you talk, the less intently your mate will be listening.

(4) Don't speak like a 33 rpm playing at 78, your mate will probably not understand a word you are saying. It is obviously a sign of anxiety, insecurity. A rather negative atmosphere is produced, and your whole conversation will probably be tuned out. You are nonverbally saying, "I must get through this real fast, because I know you aren't interested in what I am saying, and aren't going to listen to me very long because what I have to talk about isn't important enough for you to take time to consider." With this type of atmosphere set, even if your mate happens to hear most of what you have said, you can most likely expect a negative response, because you have set the stage for it.

(5) Don't try to communicate with the "silent treatment," whichever special form yours happens to be, either pouting, sulking, or openly refusing to verbally respond at all over a given period of time. Obviously, silence precludes your solving *any* problems, sharing any feelings, and at times is a violently hostile weapon used to hurt one's mate. *Marriages can't be mended when you are stabbing your mate with silence!* Silence doesn't

solve problems, and it certainly isn't the example Christ set for believers. We are told in Ephesians 5:2a (AMP): "And walk in love—esteeming and delighting in one another . . ." Obviously, this precludes the "silent treatment" and says that if you are using this approach, Christ isn't in control of your life; you are, and you need to return to fellowship and follow His example, as we are admonished to do in Philippians 2:5.

(6) Don't refuse to learn how to communicate correctly. Talking on an intimate basis is very difficult—for some people, particularly men, because of our cultural preconditioning; for other people, because of the home situation in which they were raised. Some fear that they may accidentally reveal their real selves, and through the experience either be hurt or rejected. Love *requires* risk, marriage *requires* communication. Ask the Lord to give you the ability to express yourself, your desires, feelings, problems, and ask Him to change your fear of intimate communication. You can trust Him. He will never put you in a situation which, through His strength, you can't handle.

(7) Don't get highly emotional when you are conversing, either in voice tone, facially, or through tears. These are not honest ways to try to make your wants and wishes known. These tactics cut communication short, because they either totally turn your listener off, or they require a response to your emotions instead of to what you are attempting to communicate. In other words, this means that they are no longer dealing with the message you desired to share but with your emotions. There are *rare* exceptions to this rule—for example, sharing the serious illness of a loved one, a serious problem outside your marital relationship, or the death of a dear one. When Christ is in control, your emotions will be also. If you need to cry, don't do it in the presence of your mate. You may have found that you often get your way when you start crying, but don't fool yourself; you get your way because tears are confusing and frustrating to men; they don't know how to deal with them, and usually give in only to stop the flow. *The problem between you hasn't been solved;* you have just postponed it until the next time. And in time you won't have enough tears to cover the resentment you have created in your

husband, because he will realize that he is being manipulated and rebel. "There is a way that seems right to a man and appears straight before him, but at the end of it are the ways of death." (Prov. 16:25 AMP)

(8) Don't generalize when you are trying to make a statement, a point. Generalizations are a hindrance to *clear* communication—for instance, "Everyone does it," or "Women are all alike." Such comments mean nothing, because everyone *doesn't* do whatever you are talking about, nor are *all* women alike. This type of approach makes your *real* point unclear and clouds what you are trying to say. Your mate will either tune you out or miss your point when you fall into the trap of generalities. Making comparisons is spoken of in II Corinthians 10:12b (AMP): ". . . However, when they measure themselves with themselves and compare themselves with one another, they are without understanding and behave unwisely."

(9) Don't butt in—it is rude. Important points may never be completed, and it is certainly a good way to wreck communication and build walls of hostility between you and your mate. "A fool hath no delight in understanding, but that his heart may discover itself." (Prov. 18:2 KJV)

(10) There *can't* be any of "those subjects that we just can't discuss" in the intimate relationship of marriage. If you are both maturing in Jesus Christ, and He is in control of your lives, He does not war against Himself, and you *can* freely discuss anything. When a couple admits that they have those "certain subjects" that they just can't discuss, what they are actually saying is that there are certain subjects, certain areas of their relationship, which are so weak that a discussion might break the whole relationship. It is an open admission of a weak, insecure relationship, and should be turned over to the Lord to be dealt with. You won't always agree when you finally get around to discussing these "untouchable" areas, but first see what God has to say about whatever subject is the "silent" one between you and your mate. Let His Word guide you.

(11) Speak positively with your mate. Remember, you'll gather more with honest praise, love and adoration than with a negative attitude and critical spirit. If you are allowing the Holy Spirit to guide you, peace and joy will radiate from your face. *Please* remember your motivation is *most* important. You *don't* bestow praise, arrange a congenial atmosphere, etc., because you "feel" like it or to achieve a selfish end. *Every* action, plan, or outreach to or for your mate should be done "as unto the Lord." Your unceasing desire is to honor the Lord. When this dominates your life, His love will fill your home. God speaks of a positive, happy mental attitude in Proverbs 15:15 (LVB): "When a man is gloomy, everything seems to go wrong; when he is cheerful, everything seems to go right!" "Gentle words cause life and health; griping brings discouragement." (Prov. 15:4 LVB)

(12) If you blow it, admit your mistakes, your mate never expected you to be perfect anyway.

(13) Don't ride a horse to death. Once you have discussed a subject, once you both have contributed all that you currently know, and once you have checked the Scriptures to see how God would have you deal with it, then if you can't find a clear concept or principle in the Word, *wait.* Turn the subject or decision over to the Lord and seek His leading. Read II Peter 3:9. If you continue to discuss a dead-horse subject, most likely one or both of you are trying to get your own way, have the matter settled in your favor, and you will most likely fall into the sin of quarreling, from which bitterness and hostility grow. "Keep your tongue from evil and your lips from speaking deceit, turn away from evil and practice good: *seek peace* and *keep after it.*"

(14) *Don't bring in your past* or *your mate's past,* especially when you are dealing with a subject which could be controversial. Deal *only* with the two of you; leave the relatives, the dog, the neighbors, and everyone and everything else out, *period!* Clear-cut discussions are often drowned in a tank of other people, and a digging-up of old bones which should have been left buried. Proverbs has a multitude of things to say on this subject: 3:29 (AMP): "Do not contrive or *dig up* or cultivate evil

against your neighbor, who dwells trustingly and confidently beside you." 16:27 (AMP): "A worthless man devises and *digs up* mischief, and in his lips there is a scorching fire." And last but certainly not least, 17:9 (AMP): *"He who covers and forgives an offense seeks love, but he who repeats or harps on a matter separates even close friends."*

(15) Don't be underresponsive—you have *equal* responsibilities in communication. Some of you dears feel that when you talk with your mates you are carrying on a monologue because your mate isn't carrying his part of the load. Be patient. In time, when they learn the happiness and enjoyment that intimate conversations can bring, they will begin to trust and respond, but remember, *let Christ* do the changing, *let Christ* do the motivating, and please don't expect a Bob Hope overnight!

(16) Don't be a judge; be an example, a Christian example. "Why do you criticize and pass judgment on your brother? Or you, why do you look down upon or despise your brother? For we shall all stand before the judgment seat of God." (Rom. 14:10 AMP) Read for yourself Luke 6:41–49. Philippians 2:5 (AMP) admonishes us to be a Christlike example: "Let this same attitude and purpose and (humble) mind be in you which was in Jesus Christ. Let Him be your example in humility."

(17) Don't expect to move from no conversation, idle conversation, and silence to deep intimacy in a matter of days. Don't quit after the first try. Just keep on trying and keep on praying that the Lord will open your mate's heart, help break down the barriers and walls that you both have erected over the years, and teach you the beauty of true verbal communion. As you begin, keep Ephesians 3:20 in mind. It is a powerful pledge, and one which should excite your heart by the promises it holds for you personally.

Since none of us is perfect, I am sure you have seen at least part of your communication problem in one of these examples. In your heart, between you and the Lord, you know where you are not being the mate God created you to be. You know where you have built walls instead of bridges. Just confess this to the

Lord (I John 1:9) and ask Him to direct your path and make His will for you personally clear, claiming Proverbs 3:5–6. Don't wait till you "feel" differently, do as God has commanded you to do; be the right kind of marital partner, and the "feelings" will follow the correct action. Become other-centered, become a listener as Christ was, become a giver, get to truly know your mate, and leave the wall-wrecking to God. Begin today to apply God's concepts; use Christ as the supreme example of a communicator and a listener, and watch as Christ moves in and begins to make the changes in *you* that, if at all possible, will ultimately draw your mate out and unite you as God intended the day you said, "I do."

IN THE OTHER'S SHOES

The beginning of true love is caring enough to listen deeply enough that self is eliminated and you can truly "walk in your mate's shoes," so to speak. Paul talks about this type of experience in I Corinthians 9:19–27. Only openness can bring a couple to this point of communion and true understanding of the other. To commune on this level takes time, takes work, but most of all it takes love and care.

When you have developed your relationship to this point and a misunderstanding arises, you might find that you are adapted to role-reversal-playing. Role-reversal-playing is when each of you assumes the role of the other verbally, and does his best to explain how and what the other feels and desires about a given situation.

For instance, a situation in our home might arise like this: Jim has been on the road all week. He comes in tired. The phone rings and it is Bill, who wants us to go with him and Barbara to their mountain cabin for the weekend. Jim readily responds to the invitation. The idea of the quiet solitude of the mountains, the cabin overlooking the lake, no phones ringing, time to get in a little fishing and boating, excite him, and he tells Bill that we will go. When he gets off the phone, he excitedly shares the plans with me. Of course, since he has been gone all week, he has no idea that I had planned to go to a conference for marital and family counselors the next morning. What to do? We switch roles and discuss how we feel the other feels and thinks. I begin by saying what I think Jim feels and desires: "I have had so much pressure on me this week, the idea of staying in town, having to talk with customers on the phone, is just more than I can take. The mountains always seem to relax and refresh me, and I hardly ever get a chance to get away and do a little fishing and boating. Anyway, I really enjoy Bill's company, we have a lot in common, and the whole experience is like an escape into a slower, less complicated time."

Then Jim takes my position and says: "I had no idea that you would have plans for the weekend. You usually play golf on Saturday mornings and I thought that this would be an ideal time for me to take in the conference. More and more people are coming to me, questioning me, relying on my knowledge to help them with their family and marital problems. I feel very responsible to take in all the Christian counseling training that I can obtain. When I am at the cabin, you and Bill are usually out on the lake anyway, so I don't feel you'd miss me too much if I didn't go. Of course, I would really like to be with you, and I hate to disappoint Barbara and leave her with the total responsibility of taking care of both of you, but on the other hand, I feel I must attend the conference, since I have already committed myself to it. I guess you all can just make do without me."

Now each of us has a better insight into how the other really feels. We have tried on each other's shoes and walked a bit. We can now discuss what to do about the weekend. Jim finally comes up with a perfect solution. He suggests that he and Bill go ahead Friday night, and that Saturday noon, after the conference, Barbara and I drive up to the mountains in our car. He said, "You know I'd like to have our own car up there anyway, because I'd like to drive over to Highpoint on the way home. I know how much you love the waterfalls. Sunday afternoon we can pack a lunch before we leave and just spend a quiet time together, picnicking by the falls."

The weekend was perfect for both of us, because we had progressed to the point of understanding the other's needs and were able to fulfill those needs, yet find the time to be together and add another lovely memory to our love.

THE DO'S OF BODY LANGUAGE

Beyond what you say, the clarity of your statements and the time you pick to discuss your problems and desires, there are two other things which come into play in complete conversation and communication: the tone of your voice, and "body language."

(1) Speak softly, clearly, and in love. Prov. 15:1a (AMP): "A soft answer turns away wrath . . ." Studies show that in a one-to-one conversation the softer the voice, the more attention the listener pays.

(2) Your face should be as relaxed as possible, smiling if the occasion calls for it, certainly showing interest and attention to your mate.

(3) Face the person you are speaking to, if you are standing. If you are sitting, sit in a relaxed position, with your body directed toward your mate. Face-to-face arrangements indicate a couple ready to talk on a one-to-one, intimate basis; whereas a side-by-side position reveals a cool neutrality.

(4) When talking with your mate, or anyone, look into his or her eyes. If you have picked the correct time to talk about a problem, your feelings, any situation, then obviously your mate won't be watching TV, or have his nose stuck in a newspaper. The eyes are one of the most important modes of communication that we have.

(5) Sit close to your mate. Don't smother him, but perhaps pick up his or her hand and hold it gently as you share your thoughts, hopes, dreams, problems, and feelings.

(6) Be sure you have privacy when you want to communicate on a personal level. Either send the children outside to play, or be sure they are fast asleep.

(7) Often a relaxing setting is conducive to more intimate, open conversation. Soft background music might set just the right mood in which to begin.

THE DON'TS OF BODY LANGUAGE

(1) Don't yell, don't raise your voice to make what you feel is a vital point. Don't speak in monotones, which give your mate the feeling of being neutralized. They are dull and death to interesting, stimulating communication.

(2) Don't frown, fiddle with things, look at your watch, or wear a blank, disinterested look on your face. Every one of these things nonverbally says, "Hurry up and get through; I am not interested in what you have to say, and I want to get this conversation over with."

(3) Don't sit halfway across the room, or on the couch beside but not facing your mate while he is talking. These actions let him know that you are tense, and would like to escape the conversation and the situation.

(4) Don't neutralize your mate's conversation by looking at everything in the room but him. *Look at his/her face*, particularly into the eyes. *Your insecurity* is really showing when you avoid eye contact, and it doesn't make for a healthy relationship or communication. It nonverbally says, "I'm scared" or "I'm not interested," or "I don't care." All are negative signals.

(5) Sitting at a distance when involved in a serious or intimate conversation is simply telling your mate that you would prefer that there be distance in your relationship. Again you are saying that you are either afraid, don't care, or are totally negative to whatever your mate is sharing.

> GOALS: The goal of this chapter is to make you aware of how vital communication is to the marital relationship. If you are truly interested in mending your relationship and ending the communication blackout, begin to practice everything you have learned in this chapter, even when it seems silly, or awkward.

Let's face it, somewhere you are sending out the wrong signals, and they need to be replaced by the right ones. Somewhere you have built walls instead of bridges, and they need to be torn down. All of this can only be accomplished as you allow Christ to change *you,* and as you are open and willing to practice and practice and practice, continually relying on Him and His promises.

When you have mastered and applied God's concepts, have allowed Him to change *you,* when your heart has been opened to your mate and his or her needs, and your mate has responded to that love by learning to share and listen also, then the lights of communication will burn brightly, the wall will crumble, and the beauty, fulfillment, and freedom Christ promised will permeate every area of your relationship.

ASSIGNMENTS:

(1) Memorize Proverbs 3:5 and 6; Proverbs 4:2; Proverbs 7:1–3.

(2) Read and reread the whole book of Proverbs and James 3:1–18.

(3) Go to the Lord in prayer, asking that He make your heart particularly sensitive to any area where you are sending or receiving messages incorrectly.

(4) Ask the Lord to open your heart to your mate, to create in you the ability to be available to truly listen to his or her needs, wants, plans, desires, gripes, or whatever he needs and wants to share with you.

(5) Begin practicing *daily* the do's and don'ts of correct communication, realizing that you won't learn all the concepts in one sitting, but read and reread these areas. Practice and practice until they become a way of life for you. And *leave the changing of your mate's communication problems to the Lord.* Certainly don't take this book and push it under his nose, hoping or suggesting that he read this chapter. That is an obvious form of criticism, a way of saying, "I disapprove of you like you are, and here is something that you might learn from." If you do, he will most likely rebel.

(6) Review the section on body language and be sure you aren't sending out negative nonverbal signals.

(7) Begin to explore your mate's areas of interests. Study, learn, and new vistas of communication will begin to open. Begin *this week* by taking on the project of learning the basics of *one* thing your mate is interested in. I said

begin to learn. I don't mean that in certain fields you can even begin to learn the basics in a week. Continue to learn, and when you have accomplished one interest and can intelligently communicate about it, move on to others. You'll be amazed at what this will do for your relationship. You'll be silently saying, "I care enough for you to give of myself and my time to learn about your interests, and to try to make your day more enjoyable by being able to talk with and share them with you."

(8) Communication is built on trust, remember that. If trust is on shaky ground in your marriage, it has to be rebuilt. Don't expect your mate to immediately begin to tell you his innermost thoughts until you become worthy of trust.

(9) Remember, you are doing this as Colossians 3:23 (AMP) states: "Whatever may be your task, work at it heartily (from the soul), as (something done) for the Lord and not for men." As you do, the Lord will honor your service and bless you abundantly.

(10) When you have mastered the art of communication, learned the deep importance of keeping the lines open and flowing, you will have placed a strong rock under the foundation of your relationship, one that will give your marriage strength, depth and intimacy beyond words.

(11) Women: Make a list of the different ways you can begin to help your husband succeed in business.

(12) Set aside a special time each evening to be totally available to talk with your mate.

(13) Make a graph and divide it into four sections entitled: (1) Problem; (2) How did I react; (3) From God's view what should I have done; and (4) What must I do to correct the mistake. So make your lists and graphs—I don't mean to think these things out in your head; when I say list, I literally mean a written one. You'll be amazed at the insight you acquire when problems, priorities, schedules, etc., are facing you in black and white.

(14) Men: Begin today to reaffirm verbally and overtly your wives' femininity as a living, feeling, breathing woman. Plan a special dinner *out,* perhaps twice a month. Have special quiet times together, take evening walks, drives in the country, and have occasional unexpected surprises. If she collapses from disbelief the first time, don't quit. Just keep on keeping on, and your home, your love, your relationship will reap heavenly benefits.

CHAPTER 7

PROBLEM: WHO WEARS THE PANTS?

Symptoms

- Hostility and strife in the home
- Aggressive, insecure female
- Withdrawn male
- Financial problems
- Sexual problems
- Overbearing male
- Infidelity
- Rebellious children
- Open or suppressed frustration
- Reliance on tranquilizers and/or alcohol

If your marriage is listing, weighed down by one or more of the above symptoms, drifting closer to the rocks of divorce, very likely your ship is in desperate need of a strong captain, a leader.

Theodor Reik described our perverse thinking when he said: "In our civilization men are afraid they will not be man enough, and women are afraid that they might be considered only women."[1]

Now, ladies, many of you at this moment are thinking: "Oh, no, here comes that stuff on submission: The husband is the leader, and I'm the little doormat." Before you throw this book at the dog, burn it in the fireplace, or drop it in file 13, let me tell you that much has been written in the past few years on the "submissive wife." Some of it has been very good, and some of it came right out of left field; most of it failed to make the woman's position clear, and almost all of it failed to speak of the "submissive husband." Briefly stated, submission doesn't restrict, it doesn't confine, it frees! Just hold on to that thought as you read this chapter, and I believe the Holy Spirit will bring you a new and exciting vision of your marital position.

In any relationship involving two or more people moving together to accomplish a common purpose there must be a captain, a leader. When no one in the marital relationship has the final say, insecurity and confusion result and multiple problems arise. There may be constant quarreling, never-ending because each of you insists on having the last word. Since this type of family has no director, each goes his merry way, spending money, totally convinced that there is no one to account to, until the money runs out and the bill collectors start knocking at the door. In the middle of this upheaval are the children, never knowing whom to obey; Mother tells them one thing, Daddy another. In time the children tire of the internal bickering; they are confused by double rules, frustrated by having to answer to two different people, with different ideas, and rebellion sets in.

As this type of situation is allowed to continue, both mates succumb to open or suppressed frustration. If the female doesn't respect her husband's position, she may become aggressive, and domineering. Her mate may just withdraw, letting her take over, or retaliate, striving to regain his rightful position. A husband who feels that the man should be the head of the home, but doesn't understand the biblical concepts involved, often becomes a brutal bully, verbally or physically abusing his wife. As the marriage goes downhill, the problems begin spilling over into the bedroom. The sexual relationship may be destroyed because of resentment, bitterness, or because one or both of the mates begins using, or denying, sex as payment or punishment for acts occurring during the day. The concept of who wears the pants ultimately reaches through the entire relationship. It is vital that you understand God's concepts on this subject if your marriage is going to be saved.

When couples come for marital counseling, when the ties that bind are coming unraveled, almost without exception counselors find that there are problems in the couples' understanding of the husband/wife role, often taking the form of role-reversal. The biblical concepts, responsibilities, and positions outlined for the husband and wife have been broken or perverted.

THE DISTORTED DREAM

Many women reading this joined the ranks of "wedded bliss" just as Women's Lib was beginning to spread its message. We were young, aggressive, many were well educated, looking forward to exciting, rewarding careers outside the home. Our world was going to be different; we were going to do things, accomplish far beyond our mothers' wildest dreams. We were going to forge new paths, lead our "sisters" away from the dishpan and diapers, into a "fulfilling" life. Depending on whom we married, and the problems we confronted, most of us sooner or later discovered the dream was distorted, the new path we'd forged was treacherous, burdensome, and weary. Many collapsed under the responsibilities they had earlier craved, or have had to bolster themselves daily with pills or booze to stand the strain of another day. Some were deserted by a husband who wanted and needed a wife, a companion, the soft female who relied on him, not a competing, aggressive roommate. If we knew anything of the biblical teaching on the responsibilities and position of the husband/wife, we dismissed them as outdated, relics from a past time, certainly not applicable to the modern woman.

Sadly, many women learned too late that when our God-given roles are reversed, the male often becomes a responder, weak and indecisive. As the years pass, the strength of youth wanes. As the pressures compile and the wife wants to share the family burdens, she discovers through the years she created a leaner, and you can't lean on a leaner. Maybe you've done this, certainly you know women who have. These are the wives who scream about their husbands who refuse to open bills, shrink from responsibility and disappear when there is need to correct the children. These precious wives seldom perceive that they initially produced the weakling. Through their impatience, nagging, dominance and aggressiveness, they created a monster they can't live with!

The reverse is true for men, who often overextend themselves financially for any number of reasons, then ask the "little woman" to get a job, "just for a while." When she does and gets used to that extra income, money of her "own," she expects to have control and say about where it is spent. The problems resulting are obvious. Then he wonders where that sweet, gentle, feminine, dependent girl he once married is.

So now you are living with a weak, emasculated man. You've discovered your shoulders aren't broad enough to carry the load you assumed and you're mad. You hate it when the bill collectors harass you, when the children become rebellious and your mate does nothing. Bitterness and disgust fill the place where love and respect once grew.

Men, you told her once too often she was dumb, so she went back to school, learned new ideas, changed her outlook and her response to you. Now the house is a mess, she's too busy working to cook. You have that new boat, and her income has enabled you to move into that house which impresses your clients. But was it worth it? Your heart yearns for the girl you married, frustration is growing in your soul.

No matter how far your relationship has disintegrated, how twisted and confused your responsibilities and roles have become, divorce *does not* have to be your finalé. If just *one* of you is willing to turn to God, confess the mess you've made in your marriage, seek His guidance, learn and apply His concepts, rely on Him to make the necessary changes in *you,* then tomorrow can be the bright beginning of a new day, a new relationship, a new marriage.

Henry Ward Beecher put it this way: "Love is not a possession but a growth. The heart is a lamp with just oil enough to burn for an hour, and if there be no oil to put in again its light will go out. God's grace is the oil that fills the lamp of love."[2]

Before we get into God's concepts for the marital relationship, let me share the almost classic story of Lorna and Blake Nunnally, whose marriage almost reached the threshold of divorce because the "pants" in the family were being worn by the wrong person. If you have children, the Nunnallys' story should be of particular interest to you.

BLAKE AND LORNA NUNNALLY'S STORY

LORNA

While the other girls were dating, going to parties and the latest movies at the local theater, I was already changing diapers and keeping house. By the time my friends were selecting their high school graduation gowns, I was picking up my divorce papers, deserted by my husband, left with two small girls. At eighteen, I felt my life was over.

I was embarrassed, depressed, no one in our family had ever been divorced. In a town the size of Sioux Falls, South Dakota, you can't go far without running into someone you know, so for months, I stayed with Mother and Daddy, cloistered in the house, refusing to see anyone. The children, Renee and Suellen, became my life. Everything I did was for or with the girls.

The summer after my high school class graduated, some of my old girlfriends asked me to go to Panama City, Florida, to vacation with them. I declined the invitation, but Mother and Daddy found out and strongly encouraged me to go. They assured me that they would take care of the girls. I was hesitant, I wasn't sure I would fit in with the old group. But everyone kept telling me a trip was exactly what I needed, so finally I agreed to go.

Panama City was my first glimpse of the ocean. As we drove in early one morning, the whitecapped waves were washed with a soft orange glow of the rising sun. It was beautiful. We checked into our beach-front motel and spent the next few days letting our skin drink in the sun on the salt-white beach. For hours I sat on that beautiful beach, almost hypnotized by the constant roar of the ocean. Long after the sun had cast its last golden rays, I sat staring out over the unremitting surf. The moon was just beginning to find its reflection when a voice interrupted my introspection.

"Isn't it a little bit late for a young lady to be out here on the beach alone?" a voice asked.

I looked up to see a tall, sun-tanned man with sun-streaked blond hair staring down at me. "I'm sorry, I didn't hear what you said."

"I said, 'Isn't it a bit late to be out on the beach alone?' "

"I don't know, I guess I lost track of time. What time is it?"

"It's nine forty-five. By the way, my name is Blake Nunnally. What's yours?"

"Lorna Osborne," I replied.

"Well, Lorna Osborne, would you like to walk down the beach for a while?"

Without thinking, I said, "I guess so."

We must have walked for hours. Blake told me all about his childhood, his family, the fact that he'd graduated from Drake University and about the car dealership that he owned back in Minneapolis. But most of the time he talked about his "best friend"—an arrogant, cantankerous, old gray tomcat named Hector. The way he talked about Hector, you'd have thought Hector was a person.

By the time we finished talking, I felt as if I had known Blake for years. He was easygoing, comfortable to be with. For the first time in months, I was relaxed and enjoying myself.

"Now, Lorna, what about you? Did you just graduate from high school?"

Inside I wished he hadn't asked. I wanted him for a time to just think I was a nice little girl who had recently finished school and come south for a vacation, not an eighteen-year-old divorcee with two children. But there was no point in lying, so I told him everything, everything! It didn't seem to shock him or turn him off. I was surprised, but of course he wasn't planning to marry me, so why should it matter anyway? We stopped by a beach-side restaurant and had a late supper. Blake asked me to go sailing with him the following day, but I declined his invitation—I just wasn't interested. He was nice, but the children were all that filled my mind.

BLAKE

Lorna was an enigma. Most of the girls I'd met on the beach clung to guys like flies to honey; Lorna was pleasant, but cool and disinterested. The day after I met Lorna, I went sailing with another girl, but Lorna's forlorn green eyes kept haunting me. As I thought about her, my male ego couldn't accept the fact that she disliked me, so I presumed she hadn't gotten over the recent traumas in her life.

I called her on Saturday morning and asked her to meet me for breakfast. Surprisingly, she agreed. As we ate, she told me that she and her friends were going to go back to Sioux Falls the next morning. I tried again to get her to have dinner, go sailing, something, but she politely refused.

LORNA

As we finished packing the car Sunday morning, I saw Blake walking across the parking lot. We talked for a few minutes, exchanged names and addresses, and said goodbye. That was the last I expected to see of him. My girlfriends were all giddy about Blake. More than once they rebuked me for not spending more time with him, but what did they know? They seemed so young.

The drive was long, and I was glad to be back home with Mother, Daddy and the girls. They were all excited, wanting to know everything about my trip, what I saw, what we did, and who we met. I briefly told them about Blake, and then showed them some pictures we'd taken on the trip.

The following Saturday morning, I had just finished eating breakfast when I heard a car pull in the driveway. It was Blake! I couldn't believe my eyes. He had driven all the way from Minneapolis just to see me. I alerted the rest of the family to the fact that we had company and went to the door to greet him. He'd driven almost all night to get to Sioux Falls, so quickly I fixed him a cup of strong coffee and a big breakfast.

Spasmodically we dated for the next nine months, whenever Blake could take time away from the dealership and drive over. My daughters immediately fell in love with him. They clung to him like love-starved pups. Mother and Daddy liked him, but Mom felt that we hadn't met under proper circumstances. She also questioned the fact that he was somewhat older than I, and felt he was a bit of a "stranger" because he lived so far away.

In time, Blake asked me to marry him, but I still wasn't interested. I appreciated his attention, his devotion, his interest in my daughters, but I didn't feel I was ready to take another chance. I began dating other men during this time. I dated almost everyone who asked me out. I had the attitude, "It doesn't matter whether I like anyone or not, I'll just date." It was a frustrating time, a frustrating experience.

When fall came again, Blake asked me and several of my friends to be his guests for the weekend, to see the Vikings' opening game of the season. I could have cared less about the Vikings, but I did want to visit Blake at home, see how he lived, what life with him might be like, so I went.

BLAKE

The game was just a ploy to get Lorna to Minneapolis. When I finally got her there, I hoped she'd stay and marry me. After the game, I proposed to her again, and to my surprise she said yes! Immediately I took her to my parents' house in Edina to meet them. She didn't return to Sioux Falls. She stayed with us for a couple of weeks, then we were married.

LORNA

I'm not sure what possessed me, but when I got to Minneapolis, met Blake's parents, saw that he obviously was a stable man with a secure job, I guess I just decided, "Girl, you'd better get this one before he gets away." I didn't have anything good going for me at home. I'd been sort of down in the dumps, and this seemed like a way out. My ultimate goal in life was to find a real good father for the girls. I had completely disengaged myself from the situation or selection. It was a matter of somebody who would be good, somebody who could support and love the girls. I was totally wrapped up in my children, and Blake fit the bill perfectly!

I realize now that my feelings were fanatical and unhealthy. They were mostly based on the fact that when I married the first time and had the girls, everyone said, "You aren't ready to have a family, you'll never be able to raise the children properly." I was going to show them all how wrong they were. I was determined. Because others had said I couldn't, I was going to show the world I could. These weren't exactly healthy or sound reasons for marriage.

BLAKE

Lorna had had such a rough time of it in the past, I was obsessed with giving her everything. I loved her and desperately wanted her to be happy. After looking at many homes, we finally found just the home that suited her, but by the time we had looked, signed a contract, and waited for the loan to be approved, three months had passed. Three long months, with Lorna not being able to visit the girls.

Christmas week I drove my bride and my friend Hector (the cat) back to Sioux Falls to spend the holidays with her family and with my new family. Renee, the eldest, was particularly thrilled at seeing her mom again. Suellen grinned, giggled and laughed, but I'm not sure she had been totally aware of Lorna's absence. Christmas morning was a delight. The tree sparkled, the children squealed with joy as they unwrapped the presents we'd brought. Hector put on his own show, pulling on ribbons, hiding under piles of Christmas wrapping, and "helping" the children unwrap presents. As I sat there watching that scene, I envisioned many, many more happy times, our family together, hopefully children of our own, too. This is what I'd always wanted.

LORNA

Blake had bought us a beautiful lake-front home in Edina, not far from his parents' house. I was so proud. Suellen was still in diapers and Renee was not in kindergarten when we moved into our new home. Blake was wonderful. He gave me all the money I wanted to furnish our home exactly as I pleased. I couldn't believe it; the whole experience was like a dream come true. To top things off, he bought me my own car! I was so happy, so very happy for the first time in my life, that I was on top of the world. I wished Sioux Falls was closer so my friends could see me now!

BLAKE

It was so much fun doing for Lorna, she seemed to appreciate everything. She was a *perfect* housekeeper, a devoted mother, and a loving wife. I felt that life had dealt me a winning hand. Then to top off my happiness, after three months of marriage she told me that she was pregnant. We were going to have our own child!

LORNA

Blake was pleased, but I wasn't. I had a very difficult pregnancy, much of it brought on by my rotten mental attitude. I didn't want any more children. My time seemed totally consumed already. I was young and I felt I'd lived a lifetime for the two children I had; I just didn't want any more. The nine months passed slowly, each more depressing than the one before.

For four days and three nights I was in labor! I had a terrible doctor. At times I concluded I'd be better off with a vet. Sonya was born three weeks early. After her birth I mentally continued downhill.

After Sonya's birth, I seemed to go through the worst period in my life. We had been married a little over a year and I was nervous, crying, unhappy all the time. Suddenly I didn't want a home, I didn't want to take care of the children, I was miserable.

I went to several doctors, but they could find no physical cause for my mental condition. Blake finally carried me to a minister and I talked to him. He insisted that if I'd get out, plant flowers, and work in the yard while the children were young, everything would be all right. Blast it, I wasn't interested in home and gardens. This wasn't the answer, not for me. No matter how low my mental attitude got, I took excellent care of the house, perfect care of the children, but all the time I was unhappy. Like a robot, I assumed my responsibilities, my attitude was like a martyr's.

Finally, Renee started to school, and Suellen began kindergarten. But Sonya was still small and the downs continued. I was dreadfully ugly to Blake during this period. He did his very best to please, pamper, and console me, but I rejected all his attempts at comfort and happiness. After a few years of my whining, crying, complaining, and criticizing, Blake became thoroughly exhausted with me.

BLAKE

I didn't know what to do with Lorna. I'd been patient. I'd provided her with everything money could buy. I loved the children, and still she cried and moped around the house. This attitude persisted for five or six years. Finally, I just quit caring.

LORNA

Everything I did was perverse. In my first marriage I had wanted to go to church and my husband refused. When I married Blake, he wanted to attend church and I didn't. Although I had no desire, we attended church regularly, but I didn't know Jesus as my personal Savior.

When Blake finally stepped back, when he gave up and retreated into his work, I tried to do an about-face. When he quit caring, he began to stay away from home more and more. Oh, he didn't get involved in the usual extramarital activities. He didn't drink, cheat. He just worked and worked. To consume more time, he opened a second car dealership in St. Paul.

I began to surmise that perhaps I was part of the problem, but I wasn't yet willing to do anything about it. Oh, each day I would determine that when he came in, the house would be peaceful and relaxed, but each time I failed. The minute he walked through the door something inside me went off and I'd start crying.

I examined and re-examined life during this time. I thought, "Why, why me?" Other people have children. Why can't I cope? Other people are happy. Why not me? Other women enjoy cooking, enjoy gardening. What is wrong with me? Years later, Blake and I discussed this period in our lives and decided that probably during this time I had several breakdowns, but we never knew it. I was not under any medical care, and I wasn't on any pills. I just spent my days and nights crying. I was too young to know that I needed help, and Blake was at a loss as to how to help me.

BLAKE

Every evening, I met the same hysterical accusations when I came home. Lorna screaming, crying, shouting, "You work all the time, you never care for me, you never care for the children. Obviously you aren't happy at home; and buddy, I'm not either." What could I say? Words only made matters worse, so usually I just ate, picked up Hector and retreated to the TV.

LORNA

Blake didn't always retreat. Occasionally he'd burst forth with an assault on me. "All you ever do is clean the house, take care of the children. You never want to go anywhere with me. You never take any time for me. I'm just a form of security, a method of support. You don't even relate to me as a man any more." He was right, but neither of us knew how to change the relationship.

As the children began to grow up and Sonya entered school, I began to mentally stabilize. Occasionally I got out a bit. Before this, the only time I left the house was to grocery shop once a week. I had totally isolated myself, wallowing in my self-pity. I liked being alone. I could brood better that way.

When I began getting out I assumed a position of responsibility in P.T.A., then in the garden club, and then the ladies' church circle. I had had a poor self-image; actually I was totally self-centered. I'd spent all these years pitying myself, instead of counting all the blessings in my life. As I realized that I was talented in a number of areas, as my creativity surfaced, people began to praise me, and praise goes a long way. The more praise I got, the more I did, the more I poured myself into things outside the house. Still, I managed to keep things going inside the home as well. I thought to myself, "If Blake wants to work all the time, let him. I'll develop my own interests and go my own way, and he can go his."

The one thing that kept us together was the children. Blake worshiped the children, and I did too. Mine was more of the I'm-going-to-show-everybody-I-can attitude. His was a genuine love; he really loved the girls. Because the kids were the thing that held us together, we both used them as sounding boards. If Blake corrected them, I criticized him. If I corrected them, he criticized me. The children were forever in the middle of our disagreements. If we prepared an outing for them, we disagreed over where we were going to go. It was constant misery, constant fighting. Each of us was going to have the last say, the last word.

All during this time, I kept thinking, "There is something missing, there is something missing. What is it? Why can't I be happy? I have everything in the world to be happy for and I am not."

When I'd share my feelings with my mother she'd say, "Lorna, I can't understand why you aren't happy. You have a man who loves you, who has bountifully provided for you and the children. What more could you possibly want?" Her comments would only make me feel guilty. She'd constantly criticize me all during my growing up, and after my marriage. Like mother, like daughter, I reacted to my children exactly the same way—nag, nag, criticize, criticize.

BLAKE

When Lorna and I first married, our sexual relationship was wonderful; no man could have asked for more. But as time wore on, as Lorna regressed, became depressed, she began to mentally reject me. Oh, if I came to bed in a loving mood, she made herself available, but that was all. I didn't have to have her tell me she wasn't interested in sex with me. It was obvious.

LORNA

The physical desire for Blake that once burned in my heart had grown cold. I wasn't even kind enough to fake passion. I knew Blake was aware of my disinterest. I knew the rejection hurt him deeply. I suppose I just didn't care. Oh, I was a dutiful wife. I never denied him, but I was about as responsive as a limp log.

Blake wasn't part of my joy. My only happiness came in the way of compliments on my creative activities. I poured more and more of my time into flower arranging, cake decorating, canning, making jelly, all sorts of little things. I did it, not because I enjoyed it, not because the activity fulfilled me. I did it for the praise, the compliments. But the more praise I received, the more I craved. Praise wasn't a permanent type of happiness; it had to be constantly bolstered.

All these years of looking for happiness, searching for fulfillment, and nobody told me I could find it in the Lord. Nobody. Our minister at church, all the people in our families who were Christians, all my Christian friends who wondered why I was so miserable, and not one of them ever even tried to explain Christ to me, not even my parents, not even Blake!

BLAKE

Lorna's cardinal interest was our girls. They *always* came first. She was fanatical about them, then the house, and if she had time after her ego activities, sometimes she'd attempt to fit me in. That was the order of her priorities. The girls never went out that they didn't have a bow in their hair, their socks matched, their shoes polished. When they were small and she put them down for a nap, she'd polish their shoes and change their laces while they slept! She kept an extra box of shoestrings so that there would always be clean ones available.

LORNA

I stabilized a bit when the children entered school, but my rotten personality continued. When the children would come home from school, I'd scream at them about their homework, fuss at them for not eating every bite on their plates, yell if they didn't wipe their feet off before they came into the house. At night when they'd bathe, if they didn't bathe just perfect, I'd spank them. I treated them awful. If they didn't get to sleep as soon as they got to bed, I'd reprove them. When Blake would finally get in, if they'd given me a hard time, I'd tell him what they had done, which wasn't half as bad as I would describe it. Then Blake would fuss at them. When he did, I'd get on to him for the method he used in reprimanding them! Bless his heart, he was torn in the middle. He'd fuss at them because I was in tears, and he wanted so for me to be happy, but when he yelled at the children, I'd turn on him.

When Renee reached her thirteenth birthday, it was obvious to everyone that she was a natural beauty. She had natural long blond hair and doll-like brown eyes. Popularity came easily for her. At thirteen she began dating. Of course, I was right in there, helping her out in the popularity area all I could, selecting just the right clothes, and adding to her natural attractiveness with voice and drama lessons.

BLAKE

Soon we were to learn that the atmosphere which had existed in our home all Renee's life had taken its toll. Lorna's critical attitude, the strife between Lorna and me concerning discipline, had left Renee frustrated, resentful and confused. As soon as she started dating, she began sneaking around and going out with boys we disapproved of. Often she'd tell us she was going one place, and we'd find she'd gone somewhere else with someone else.

We constantly checked up on Renee. Often Lorna followed her when she left the house, sometimes I did. When we caught her lying we'd confront her, reprimand her, but never actually discipline her. Lorna was so critical that I overcompensated by being too believing and too permissive. Renee reaped the disastrous results of our unscriptural training of her.

LORNA

Until Renee was in the eighth grade, she had been a straight-A student. Then her grades and attitude began to change. I nagged and nagged, threatened and threatened, but she failed to improve.

When she turned fourteen, I entered her in the "Miss Minnesota Teen Pageant." She won third place. Renee was so beautiful; she was beginning to accomplish everything I ever wanted to do and never did. The pageant officials gave her the title of "Miss Hospitality" for the year. During the next year, every weekend she flew to a different state, where she would greet the Teen Pageant contestants, take them to their rooms, help them with any information or needs they had. The pageant officials paid all her expenses; it was an exciting time for her.

BLAKE

Also, at fourteen Renee met a nineteen-year-old boy named Jake of whom we highly disapproved. He was a high school dropout, his language crude, his appearance appalling, and on a couple of occasions when he was visiting it was obvious that he was high. She became so attached to Jake that we welcomed the idea of her traveling with the pageant on weekends because that kept her and Jake apart.

When the year was over, the pageant officials selected six girls from the Teen pageants to go to the Miss Universe Pageant, which was being held in Hawaii. Lorna and I discussed Renee's going and decided that, although this trip would be at our expense, it would be good experience for Renee. At this time we thought that she would continue to enter beauty pageants.

Renee begged and begged to go, so we made a deal with her. We told her she could go if she would promise to completely leave Jake alone, to stay totally away from him and promise never to date him again. She readily agreed! This agreement was to be a bond between the three of us. Naturally it was a bribe, a rotten form of discipline, and it totally failed. As soon as she got to Hawaii she began calling Jake, and she charged over a hundred dollars in long-distance calls to our phone. We had told the pageant officials that if she needed anything while she was gone that we would be good for the charges. She took advantage of this, charging clothes, jewelry and other personal items.

Two months after she returned from Hawaii she gave up her pageant work. All the years, the grooming, all the work we'd put into it, and she just up and quit. Renee appreciated nothing during this period of her life. We had done everything for her, provided her with everything money could buy, and when she'd gotten the fun out of the beauty business, she just quit.

LORNA

I tried to reason with Renee, explain the opportunity that she was throwing away, but she said all she wanted to do was get married. Trying to calm the situation down, we assured her that she didn't have to continue with her pageant work, but that she certainly wouldn't be allowed to get married.

My approach hadn't worked. When Renee turned fifteen, she ran away from home. The first time, she slipped out the bedroom window and left a note on her bed. It broke my heart as I read it, because it was a summary of what I would have said to my own parents if I'd ever been able to face them and put my feelings into words. In essence it said, "I know I can't please you. I know I haven't been the child you wanted me to be. I know you don't approve of my marriage. I know you don't approve of me." On and on with that thought for three pages. You see, I had been a perfectionist, and of course she could never come up to the mark, so she continued by saying, "One of these days I want you to be proud of me, so I am going away to try to make you proud." This first time she ran away, she was gone three days and nights, and for three days and nights I blamed Blake and he blamed me. I accused him because he was permissive, because I felt he let her go places I didn't approve of, because he had allowed her to begin dating too young. He blamed me because he said I was so demanding, mean, ugly, and had constantly screamed and hollered until I'd run her out of the house.

After three days, a girlfriend of Renee's from school told us where to find her. We found her just north of St. Paul, living with friends of Jake, all older, twenty through twenty-five—and Renee just fifteen!

BLAKE

When she came home, we tried our best to confine her, to watch her, but the damage had been done. She was determined to escape, to be with Jake. Lorna and I discussed it and finally decided to send her to a private girls' school in the East. We selected an open school, which provided dancing and music; it was a liberal arts school for high school students. Here she would have a multitude of advantages, things she'd never been able to study before. We'd come to our wits' end. If she'd been a boy, we'd probably have sent her off to military school, but she wasn't. But we approached the situation in the same manner. We tried to pack up our failure, our problem, our responsibility and ship it off to someone else. It didn't work. Renee didn't want to go, and she was determined not to stay. Her only way of escape was to get thrown out, so she began stealing from other girls, nothing she needed, just enough to cause the school to expel her —exactly what she wanted.

LORNA

She flew home, bringing back only what she wanted, and leaving behind almost all the expensive, beautiful clothes we'd bought for her to take to school. We had tried to transfer our responsibility, and it hadn't worked.

As soon as she returned, she ran away with Jake a second time. I couldn't stand the strain much longer. My children, not Blake, were the most important thing in my life. I felt I had failed in every other area as far as my parents were concerned, even as far as I was concerned, except with my children, and now they were falling apart, all of them. I could see Suellen coming along right behind Renee, and I had raised her the same way, and I visualized her repeating Renee's steps! When Renee left the second time, she was gone almost three weeks. We were close to the police and public officials in our area, and an all-points bulletin was sent across the U.S. for her.

The night before they found Renee, Beth, a friend who lived down the street, came over. I was alone and crying. Beth took my hand and gently explained to me how I could know Jesus Christ personally. She told me how I could have true peace and happiness in my life, even in the midst of heartbreaking situations like ours. Beth quoted portions of the Scripture which assured me of strength to face the problems of life. She explained how learning of God's concepts for our lives, our children and our family could totally change our future.

"Lorna, do you understand what I am saying? Do you understand what Christ actually did for you on the cross?" she asked.

"Yes, Beth, yes, but why hasn't someone told me before?"

"Lorna, I really don't know. I imagine you weren't ready. Would you like to pray and ask Jesus into your life right now?"

"Yes, but I'm not sure I know how to pray."

"Lorna, prayer is simply talking to God. Let's just bow our heads, and as I pray you can silently talk to the Lord, confess your sin, your need of Him, and then thank Him for loving you and dying for you. 'Lord Jesus, I desperately need You, I want to thank You for loving me and dying for me, for paying the price to make me acceptable to God. Right now I open the door of my life, my will, my all, and ask You, just as You promised, to please come in. Take this mess I've made, and change me into someone who can glorify You. Amen.'"

I prayed along silently with Beth. I was a bit embarrassed. This was the first time I'd ever heard anyone pray to the Lord personally, except a minister in church. Beth stayed with me a while longer, sharing assurances from the Word with me, and then she left.

When she left, I thought, "I don't feel any different. It is just a farce, the whole thing." But in another part of my mind I thought, "I've tried everything else, so why not?" I sat on the sofa for hours thinking, and silently I prayed by myself, "Lord, I don't understand, I don't know how to believe in You, but if You will come into my life, if You can do what other people say You can do for my life, will You please come in and try. I'm not worthy. I'm sorry, I know I've been a bad mom, a bad wife, but if You will please come in, I know You can make me whole." At that moment I knew without a shadow of a doubt that the Lord through the power of the Holy Spirit was in me. I was so excited about the peace I felt, that the next morning, just before seven, I called our minister. I wanted to talk to him, I wanted to share with somebody what had happened. I was too embarrassed to tell Blake. So I called our minister and shared the happenings of the previous evening. I said, "I know the Lord is in me, and I know the Lord will never leave me. When I prayed last night, the main thing that I asked of Jesus was that if things can't be changed with Renee, He would at least give me peace." The minister gave me no support whatsoever. I think he was a little disturbed at being awakened by a hysterically happy woman who was raving about accepting Christ, or maybe his ego was a bit hurt. I don't know. He questioned my acceptance of Christ, and I replied, "I know I have accepted Him, I know now, it is a different kind of knowing. I don't expect anything of the Lord. Before I tried to bargain with Him, but last night as I accepted Christ it was a resigning of myself to Him, and it didn't and doesn't make any difference what He does with my life. I am completely and humbly broken." The minister still seemed to have doubts, but mumbled something about praying for me, and we hung up.

That morning I went to the grocery store. Renee was somewhere in the United States, I didn't know where, but I was happy in the Lord with a peace I'd never had before. As I shopped, I discovered a new way of praying. I'd always thought one had to be alone, down on his knees, but I learned that I could pray anywhere. As I walked up and down the aisles, I talked to the Lord. I said, "Lord, if You are the Lord You say You are, and You love me as You say You do, I just want to say: Lord, You know how much I love Renee and You know she's been my whole life, and I'm sure that is why You reached me through her. But if You want her to be gone the rest of her life, if You want to take her life, or if You want to bring her home, whatever You want to do with her, she is Yours anyway. I have completely failed, and I want You to take over in both of our lives."

When I returned home, the phone was ringing, and it was the police in Virginia Beach, Virginia, saying that they had found Renee. It happened only ten minutes after I'd had my talk with the Lord. Blake flew out to Virginia Beach and brought Renee back home.

When Renee got home, I told her what had happened in my life. She listened, she seemed sensitive to what I was saying, but she didn't understand. I didn't have any time to show her the change, I just had time to tell her, "I understand why I have been the way I have all my life. Renee, I am asking your forgiveness, darling. Will you please give me an opportunity to make the right kind of home for you before you get married?" She said she would, but it was too late, too late.

BLAKE

In about four months, Renee begged us to allow her to marry Jake. "I love him. You don't know how much I love him," she'd cry. During this time, Lorna had begun to change completely. She had stopped interfering with my discipline of the children. There was a quietness and peace which surrounded her, and there were no more tears! For the first time in our lives Lorna stopped undermining my authority. But as Lorna said, for Renee it was too late. I had failed as a father just as Lorna had as a mother, and Renee was the result.

I realized that either we'd have to lock Renee up or allow her to get married. I told Lorna, "I am tired of this, our home is ruined, our marriage is ruined, our children are ruined, and I just don't care any more. I am going to sign the papers for Renee to get married. She has promised me that if I sign the papers, she will at least finish high school. She has only six weeks left."

LORNA

Blake asked me to go to the courthouse and sign the papers with him, and I obeyed, knowing or feeling that there was no hope for Renee. Blake then told me of his second condition. He said, "We'll sign the papers, she can get married, but we won't have anything to do with the wedding. Since we both disapprove of Jake, we are not going to condone the wedding, or offer her one penny of support."

At that I started crying, the first time since I had accepted Christ. Initially I refused to allow my child to get married and not be present. I didn't know what to do, so I turned to the Lord and shared the pain of my heart with Him. I said, "Lord, please help me in this situation. I don't know what to do. How can I miss her wedding, how can I miss seeing her in a wedding dress? Lord, here is this child I have slaved over for years, and now Blake says I can't even see her married. What am I to do?"

Blake interrupted my contemplation and said to me, for the first time in his life, "Lorna, if you go to her wedding, if you refuse to sign the papers, I am going to divorce you." That did it. I ranted and raved for about three days. I was in tears, out of fellowship with the Lord. "I don't care, I am not going to miss

Renee's wedding," I raved. "As far as you are concerned, what you do makes no difference to me."

When I had time to quiet down, the Lord began to speak to my heart. I began to think, "What is the most important thing in my life? The Lord," my heart said. "Well, if it is the Lord, here I am not turning to Him in my greatest need." So I prayed and prayed. In a few hours I picked up the phone and called a dear friend and Christian counselor. After explaining the situation, I said, "What should I do?" There was no question in her mind. She said, "You call your husband, tell him you are sorry that you haven't been submissive, and that whatever the situation, whatever are his wishes, that you will abide by them." This was my first exposure to submission. I didn't know the Scripture had anything to say about it. From the day I accepted Christ, for the next year, I went on a crash program. I learned everything the Scriptures had to say about marriage, the responsibilities of the wife, God's line of authority, everything. Of course I am still learning, but I learned the core of it in that first year. The Lord knew how badly I needed it.

As soon as I hung up the phone, I called Blake. Inside me a war was raging. My old sin nature was saying, "You're going to miss Renee's wedding, you'll never see her in a wedding dress. You just can't do this, Lorna." But I prayed as I dialed Blake and in my soul I knew the counselor was right, that what she had said was from God's Word. This act was completely against my nature, against the grain for me to call him, but I did, and asked him to come home, that I had something important to discuss with him.

When he came in the door, we sat down on the sofa, and I said, "Blake, I have learned that Scripture has something to say about my decision concerning Renee. I want you to know that I was wrong. It will make me very sad to miss Renee's wedding, but if that is what you want, then I will sign the papers and not attend her wedding. Whatever you want, I will do."

There weren't any words. Blake just silently started crying. When the shock wore off, he took me in his arms and said he knew how I felt, but that his wishes still stood.

Jake's parents planned Renee's wedding. They bought her

wedding dress, they did everything, and I never saw any of it. That was my first experience with submission.

BLAKE

Jake worked for a fast-food chain. Their marriage lasted two years. He was irresponsible, he didn't care, he was selfish and cruel to Renee. When she finally broke with him and returned home, she didn't even own any underwear. Here was our precious child who had had everything, everything money could buy, with nothing.

During the two years Renee was gone, I was astounded at the changes in Lorna. She often referred to the Scripture, but more noticeable was the change in her personality and attitude. She never criticized my decisions, never interfered with my discipline of the children, and was agreeable with anything I suggested for us to do, places for us to go. It was unbelievable. Of course, I didn't know what was changing her, but whatever it was, I liked it. Naturally, after having to fight for any say in our home for years, when Lorna finally backed off, I got carried away with my power. The more I demanded, the more she gave. It was a case of power going to my head. But no matter what I asked, she responded in such a loving, peaceful manner that finally I couldn't stand it any longer, and I asked her what had happened.

LORNA

"Blake, you remember the second time Renee ran away? Well, the night before the police located her, Beth came over and shared with me how I could accept and have a personal relationship with Jesus Christ. Then, when you asked me to sign the papers and not go to Renee's wedding, the Lord again stepped in, and as I sought counsel I learned about submission. In the next year I studied everything the Word has to say about marriage, my responsibilities, your responsibilities, and ours to the children. The changes in my life have come through Christ—He is the life-changer. He enabled me to accept all things and to have peace through them."

BLAKE

I could hardly believe what I was hearing from Lorna. I'll admit, I tested her more than once, but she always responded in love, no matter how difficult or trying the situation. As I saw the change Christ was making in her life, I was drawn back to totally dedicate my life to the Christ I'd accepted many years before, but had failed to follow.

Lorna's friend Beth had shared some of our problems with her husband Howard, who was an active and committed Christian. One evening while we were sitting in the backyard talking, he mentioned a seminar called Institute in Basic Youth Conflicts. He said that a year before, he and Beth had attended, and although they had studied the Bible throughout their married life, they gained new, deep, and rewarding insights from the seminar.

I told Lorna what Howard had said, and we decided to go to the seminar as a family. The first night we all felt a bit uncomfortable. It was as if Mr. Gothard had written the lessons especially with us in mind. Through the seminar I learned what my responsibilities were as a husband. I realized that Lorna and the children were all depending on me for leadership and guidance! What a responsibility. And as I searched the Word, I understood that God held me personally responsible for that position. As I understood that I had complete control of all areas of our lives, our marriage, our children, that in all the decisions I had the final say, my relationship with the Lord became closer and deeper. I had to get to know Him better, to know His Word; I had to completely depend on Christ, or the responsibility I had acquired would overwhelm me.

Lorna had taken I Peter 3 to heart, she'd never pushed, nagged or even mentioned my responsibilities as far as the Lord was concerned. Although I was a Christian, I was carnal as could be. But as I Peter 3 promises, not by conversation, but by her manner, I was led back to my rightful position and my realization of my total dependence on Christ.

LORNA

Renee was divorced and returned home. When she came home, Blake told her she wouldn't be allowed to live at home. That may sound harsh, but we both knew the kind of people she had cultivated and was still involved with, also the mature, liberal attitudes she'd acquired, and the fact that many of her friends were involved with drugs. During the two years Renee had been gone, we had done an about-face in our home, and we didn't feel that we should or could put up with what she would be doing, and how she'd influence the other children.

BLAKE

I told Renee, "This is the way our home is. We love you, we've prayed for you daily, but we can't allow you to live here because you are not willing to change and adapt yourself to our type of life. Renee, I want you to understand I'm not asking you to come home and change and show us that you've changed, or to see that we've changed; what I am saying is that unless you *know* that you can abide by our rules, in our home, then you can't live here."

"I can't accept what you ask of the other children," Renee replied. "You ask too much of them."

LORNA

Renee left that night. After she had gone, I told Blake, "This is the first time I really have to ask you to think about your decision. In the past two years I have been completely submissive to your wishes, but I want to have Renee home. I want to teach her the things we should have taught her to begin with. Blake, I want her to see in action what we have learned."

"Honey, just sit steady in the boat, abide by what I say, and I believe things will turn out okay," Blake said.

I momentarily got my eyes off the Lord and back on myself. Inside I was wanting another chance for Renee, and another chance for me to redeem myself as a mother. I spent a day crying, feeling terribly hurt and unhappy, as I doubted Blake's decision. But I didn't defy him, I didn't seek her out, I just waited, finally turning my eyes and heart back to the Lord, and begging His forgiveness for doubting His leading through Blake.

Praise the Lord, in two days Renee came back home, ran through the door, hugged her daddy's neck and said, "I want to stay home, Daddy. I'll do whatever you ask; you won't have to check up on me." That was it. She was home, and from that moment to this, four years later, she's been good to that promise.

First Renee watched us at a distance—with, but not yet a complete part of, the family. She watched as we prayed together as a family. She saw a *consistently* different mother. She saw her daddy correct the other children, and sat in amazement as I backed him up, even when he might have been wrong.

BLAKE

As fall grew nearer, I suggested to Renee that she might consider getting a job, or if she wished, we would send her to any college she wanted to go to. She said, "Daddy, I really love it here at home, but I feel like I need to get away for a while. If you don't mind, I think I'd like to try college for a time. I don't know if you'll understand, but I'd like to get as far away from my old atmosphere as possible. I've been checking into colleges, and I think if I can get in, and if it is all right with you, I'd like to go to Baylor University in Texas."

"Baylor. That's a long way off, but if that's what you want, then we'll make the arrangements," I said.

LORNA

That fall Renee went off to Baylor, and our family returned to "normal." We prayed daily for Renee. Surprisingly, she wrote often, and came home on as many holidays as possible.

As summer approached, I decided to redecorate the guest room especially for Renee, as a surprise. When she got home she was thrilled. "Oh, Mother, I love it. But the time it must have taken. The curtains, spreads and chairs all match. Did you do it all by yourself?" she asked.

"Yes, honey, I wanted to surprise you."

"Oh, Mom, I love you so much," she exclaimed.

What a difference. After two years of marriage, two years of having nothing, scraping and begging for any extra, Renee for the first time in her life appreciated everything done for her.

When it came time for her to return to college, she said she preferred to stay home. She said, "I never realized it would be so easy living under Daddy's authority. I can't believe it's so simple. I really love it. I love you both. In fact, I don't know whether I'll ever move out. You may be stuck with me forever!" I could hardly believe my ears. All this from the girl who in the past ran away every chance she got.

I have given my testimony many times, and each time I enjoy it more, knowing the promise of the Lord in Isaiah 55:11 (LVB): "So also is my Word. I send it out and it always produces fruit. It shall accomplish all I want it to, and prosper everywhere I send it." When I speak, sharing His Word, I know that someone somewhere is hearing a message that his heart has long sought. I don't need to see the fruit to know that He is planting seeds.

I am completely devoted to Blake. We have worked very hard at rebuilding our sexual relationship, and we succeeded. Through Christ we were able to salvage a marriage, rekindle dead flames, and restore the devotion that has given us a perpetual honeymoon. Before Christ, there was no hope.

BLAKE

Lorna is right. Before she found Christ our marriage for all purposes was over.

LORNA

Not only did we become survivors, but we survived to live a life which has become unbelievably happy and fulfilling. Beyond our personal relationship, our coming to know Christ and applying His concepts to our home has transformed all of our children. When people tell me you can't take a damaged teen-ager and rebuild his or her life, I have to tell them they are wrong. I saw it happen, because with Christ nothing is impossible.

Not long after we attended the Gothard seminar we began a "Family Night" at our home. This is a time when we discuss our grievances with each other. We confer about problems in our lives. We express our love, joy and care for each other, and we pray together. I think Anne suggests a "Table of Harmony" something like our "Family Night." This time together, talking straight, sharing our joys and sorrows, has brought greater understanding, nipped problems before they took root, and brought a wonderful closeness and love between our family and our Lord.

Blake and I don't mean to imply that all our problems are

solved, that we are now in a state of eternal bliss. In this life that is impossible. What we wanted to share with you is that when God's line of authority is operating correctly, when each member of the home knows his or her God-given responsibilities, when each person respects the leader, the head of the home, the father, then Christ can work and can perform miracles in that home. Each of our children now knows the Lord as their personal Savior, and it has been our joy that we've had the opportunity to share His power in action in our lives. Daily we thank Him that we were allowed the time to demonstrate how beautiful and rewarding marriage can be.

LORNA AND BLAKE IN RETROSPECT

Blake and Lorna Nunnally and the family they originally produced are a classic example of the "pants" being worn by the wrong person. The marriage itself began wrong. Lorna entered marriage on a fraudulent basis, since her main interest was a father for the girls, not her love and devotion to Blake.

Blake, who in business and other relationships was a strong, aggressive man, failed in his leadership with his wife. When he met Lorna, she had already suffered a tragic marriage, she was younger and to him represented a delicate flower which needed love and protection. These aspirations are wonderful, but Blake overdid the giving, the patience, and allowed himself to be dominated by a misguided wife.

Through tears and tantrums, Lorna controlled the house and the decisions. The underlying drive in her life was to prove herself capable as a mother. She fell into the trap described in II Corinthians 10:12. Her motivation was wrong, her priorities were out of line as she placed the children before her husband, and it almost cost her a daughter and a marriage.

She openly displayed distrust of Blake by continually interfering with his attempts at discipline. Her rebellious attitude toward Blake in front of the girls caused confusion and frustration. Their home was a chaotic place to live. By her actions Lorna was teaching the children to rebel against authority. As she rebelled against Blake, so ultimately the children rebelled against her.

What a difference when Lorna came to know Jesus Christ and

learned God's concepts and line of authority in marriage. As she studied the Scriptures and learned what marriage was intended to be, what her responsibilities were as a wife, she immediately put her knowledge into practice and their home began to change.

Lorna discovered that submission was freedom. It was trusting Christ to lead through Blake, to handle problems, to prescribe the mode of discipline through him. The burden was relieved, she was free at last—free to love, free to respond, free from the fear of failure which had haunted her every action for years. She learned that the girls' attitude toward authority was more important than any particular issue.

As Lorna quietly handed the control of the home and the girls over to Blake, the atmosphere changed from horrible to heavenly. As Blake shared, he wasn't even aware of what happened to Lorna. She didn't walk up and say, "Well, I have learned how a home is supposed to be run, so here is the outline and here are the controls." She slowly stepped back and let him take over.

After they attended the Gothard seminar, Blake for the first time clearly understood his role and responsibilities as a husband. Christ had already dealt with Lorna, so they were ready to begin a new home, to live a life of example for their children. The girls responded, not because of words, but because of the changed lives which were daily living examples. For the first time in their lives, they saw Mommy respecting Daddy's decisions, and loving every minute of it. They witnessed the birth of a new love between their parents, and bathed in its warmth. Even Renee found strength, security, and happiness in her "new" parents. The rebellion and hostility of the past melted as she lived under the authority of love.

It is exciting to know that this family of girls will go into marriage someday, not only knowing Christ personally, but knowing God's line of authority, respecting their husbands' authority, and knowing that God's concepts work because they have witnessed the miracle of their touch in their own homes.

A group of teen-agers was surveyed not long ago, and was asked which was more important to them, that their parents love them, or that their parents love and respect each other. Overwhelmingly, the reply was that their parents love and respect each other.

Is your relationship to your mate preparing your children for marriage? Are they learning God's line of authority through your example? Is your marriage, your relationship, the kind you want your children to emulate?

On the following pages you will learn what Lorna and Blake learned, what God's Word has to say to wives and husbands. Through application, your relationship can come to the place of sweet, loving closeness between you, your mate and Christ, just as it has in thousands of other marriages.

GOD'S LINE OF AUTHORITY

Just as a ship can't function without a captain, a nation without a president, a company without an executive, so God didn't design marriage to flounder, tossed with indecisiveness, leaderless. God's line of authority in the home is clearly set forth in I Corinthians 11:3 (AMP): "But I want you to know and realize that Christ is the head of every man, the head of a woman is her husband, and the head of Christ is God." This very same concept is reaffirmed in Genesis 3:16b, Ephesians 5:22–23, and elsewhere in the Bible. In I Corinthians 11:8–10 (AMP) the thought continues: "For man was not (created) from woman, but woman from man; Neither was man created on account of or for the benefit of woman, but woman on account of and for the benefit of man. Therefore she should (be subject to his authority) . . ."

I like to think of this plan that God has outlined for us to have a happy successful marriage and to enjoy the blessing He has for us personally as God's Shield of Protection. As you reread I Corinthians 11:3 you can see that God specifically outlined each role—the role for the woman, the role for the man, the role that Christ has in our relationship, and the role that the Father has in our relationship. God created this line of authority, the Shield of Protection, for the benefit of the family. Everyone has a leader to whom he is responsible and from whom he is to seek guidance. As long as everyone is in his proper place, things run smoothly.

The husband/wife relationship is an earthly picture of the relationship of Christ and His church (believers). Just as we are to be totally dependent on whom and what Christ is, wives are to relate in the same manner to their husbands, and their husbands to Christ, and to their wives.

RESPONSIBILITIES OF THE WIFE

"In like manner you married women, be submissive to your own husbands—subordinate yourselves as being secondary to and dependent on them, adapt yourselves to them. So that even if any do not obey the Word (of God), they may be won over not by discussion but by the (godly) lives of their wives." (I Pet. 3:1 AMP)

Ephesians 5 gives the clearest description of the proper role of the husband and wife. Ephesians 5:22–24 (AMP) is God's Word to wives, and *that in itself should be sufficient if you are a Christian.* "Wives, be subject—be submissive and adapt yourselves—to your own husbands as (a service) to the Lord. For the husband is head of the wife as Christ is the Head of the church, Himself the Savior of (His) body. As the church is subject to Christ, so let wives also be subject in *everything* to their husbands."

In referring to Ephesians 5:22–33, Jay Adams, in *Christian Living in the Home,* makes a statement that cuts to the very core of these verses, when he says: "The heart of these words to the husbands and to the wives can be reached quickly by asking two questions: Husbands, do you love your wives enough to die for them? Wives, do you love your husbands enough to live for them?"[3]

Just as God created the line of authority, He also provides the insight and strength to fulfill the requirements of it. (II Cor. 9:18) I realize that when Paul says, "Wives, be subject—be submissive and adapt yourselves—to your own husbands as (a service) to the Lord," those are certainly powerful words. You can read, reread, go to other translations, but there is no way to get around the thrust of those words. Paul writes it, Peter writes it, it appears in Genesis, but most important, it is *God's Word to women, period.*

WHAT IS SUBMISSION? FREEDOM

Since this is God's concept and direction for women, it would help if we understood exactly what submission means. In the Scriptures, submission is not merely suggested, there are no options which go with the verses; it is *commanded.* In other words, if you are a woman seeking God's will for your life and marriage, you are commanded to obey your husband. Certainly, your obedience will bring fulfillment, peace and joy into your life, but this *isn't* the reason for obedience. Ephesians continues by saying that we are to respond in this manner so that we might be an example of the relationship of Jesus to His church. Three times in Ephesians 5, submission is repeated. Why? Because Paul wanted to be sure the point was made, that there were no misunderstandings, no loopholes.

Submission is *not* slavery; it is not a whimpering doormat. Submission is freedom. For example, you might say I am free to sit down and write a book about music. But unless I have studied and researched the subject, interviewed those who are active in it, I may be free to sit down to the typewriter; but without discipline, without structure, without study, I am restricted by my own ignorance. Only as I take time to do the work, discipline myself to study, can I ultimately approach the typewriter, confident in my knowledge of the subject. In God's world there is no freedom apart from *discipline* or *structure.* When you come to know Jesus Christ, when you know and obey His concepts, then you have the knowledge to be free indeed. (John 8:36) The divine path of liberation for a woman is through submission.

THE IDEAL WIFE

Turn for a minute to Proverbs 31 and read about the "ideal" wife. Proverbs 31:10–29 (LVB) says: "If you can find a truly good wife, she is worth more than precious gems! Her husband can trust her, and she will richly satisfy his needs. She will not hinder him, but help him all her life. She finds wool and flax and busily spins it. She buys imported foods, brought by ship from distant ports. She gets up before dawn to prepare breakfast for her household. She goes out to inspect a field and buys it, with her hands she plants a vineyard. She is energetic, a hard worker, and watches for bargains. She works far into the night! She sews for the poor, and generously gives to the needy. She has no fear of winter for her household, for she has made warm clothes for all of them. She also upholsters with finest tapestry; her own clothing is beautifully made—a purple of pure linen. Her husband is well known, for he sits in the council chamber with the other civic leaders. She makes belted linen garments to sell to the merchants. She is a woman of strength and dignity, and has no fear of old age. When she speaks her words are wise, and kindness is the rule for everything she says. She watches carefully all that goes on throughout her household, and is never lazy. Her children stand and bless her; so does her husband. He praises her with these words: 'There are many fine women in the world, but you are the best of them all.' " Is that the type of wife you are? Maybe not. But it is the kind of wife you can become. Remember the rewards that this verse says come in following God's concepts.

Did you really read this verse? If you did, you noticed that this is certainly not the picture of a suppressed woman. This woman has many activities, many interests, and important responsibilities. She is obviously talented, and her husband has wisely allowed her to develop her skills. This is a true picture of a liberated woman, but it is also God's picture of a submissive woman. Active as she is, you will notice all her ingenuity and activities are directed toward improving and glorifying her husband and her home.

Now, for a moment, let's break down these verses and take a deeper look at this "ideal" woman. In verse 13, "She finds wool and flax and busily spins it." We see the attitude in this verse—it is one of happiness, eagerness. Another translation says, "and works with her hands in delight." Is this the way you approach your daily household duties, or do you, as many women do, spend half the morning griping and complaining about the day's work? There you sit facing a pile of plates covered with dried egg, and think, "If I were a man, I'd be out meeting all sorts of exciting people, eating lunch in nice restaurants, traveling, but here I sit. Oh, poor me."

Ladies, if you only knew. As I have told you, Jim travels about five days out of every week. Just like you, I used to imagine all the fun, the exciting places he saw, the opportunity to meet new people, and sample unusual foods. Finally I had the opportunity to go on the road with him, off and on for a couple of months. It took about two weeks of living out of a suitcase, sleeping in a different bed every night, good food, bad food, cranky customers, demanding clients, and noisy motels to cure me for the rest of my life. I'm amazed at how he does it, day after day, year in and year out. I don't envy him any longer. I respect his fortitude for being able to live and cope with the life God's given him.

The main picture we derive of this "ideal" wife is of one who responds to all her duties, her activities, with enthusiastic delight. She provides for her family, buys and sells property for her husband, is active in helping the poor, and still she has time for herself. Her gowns are beautiful, she is pleasing to the eye, a woman who adorns herself well, and is an honor to her husband. Lastly, note that her husband has a place of prominence. Because he wisely chose a good woman, she has praised him, emotionally supported and obeyed him, making him able to assume more responsibility, and to gain a place of honor among the elders of the city. Proverbs 31:28–31 concludes by saying that her children shall rise up and call her blessed, and her husband constantly boasts and praises her. That's what I call happiness. How about you?

QUESTIONS AND PRACTICAL APPLICATION FOR WIVES

Women, if you have just discovered that the wrong person is wearing the pants in your home, and things are in a mess, begin right now to make practical changes. First, go to your husband and tell him that you have just learned that you have been wrong in assuming the role and responsibilities that God delegated to him. Don't generalize, tell him specifically the areas you have infringed upon. Ask his forgiveness for not trusting his ability in these areas, and assure him that you are confident in his God-given capability to handle every decision. Share with him that from this point forward, with Christ's help, you are going to be the companion, wife, housekeeper, mother, and lover that he needs.

Don't be surprised if he tests you for a time. For some men this is going to be such a change they may not actually believe it. As you are faithful to apply God's concepts, rely on His strength to do His will in and through you. The honesty of your change will be apparent.

As your husband begins to step out, making decisions where you had control before, be encouraging, trusting, and the confidence that you have crushed in the past will begin to reappear. Be a happy follower; the more relaxed you are, the stronger, more able he will become.

As you maintain the right relationship with Christ, He can directly deal with your husband. Remember what you are actually doing is trusting Christ, so don't panic, thinking, "What if he makes a wrong decision? What if he disciplines the children wrong?" Christ promised to lead through your husband, so when you fail to trust your husband, you are actually failing to trust Christ!

If you have always held the reins of discipline in the home, you can begin turning them over to your husband by responding to your child's next request with, "Go ask your father. He is the leader in our home," or whatever variation of that is natural for you. Then, no matter what Father decides, you support him, period. In this, you not only increase his confidence in himself and his leadership, but you are being a living example of God's lines of authority for your child.

If you are handling the bookkeeping for the home because your husband asked you to, then continue. If you are handling it in order to control the flow of funds, or because you feel your husband isn't capable, then you are out of line and need to return the responsibility to him. Often budget problems arise because the wife has been the bookkeeper out of choice, and the husband has no idea of the cost of living, of the income and outflow of funds. If you have spent half of your life trying to make ends meet, you have been carrying a burden that God didn't intend for you in the first place. The responsibility of supporting the family is the husband's. (I Tim. 5:8) Naturally, you are to be logical about money, not spending or charging beyond your husband's means.

While we are talking about money, let me share this with you. *Never, never* make comments like, "We can't afford that," or, "Aren't you proud how I have made ends meet this month." They are the biggest put-downs to a man's ego, and can thoroughly discourage him with relation to his job and advancement.

If your husband makes a wrong decision, financial or otherwise, which you were mentally opposed to, don't delight in saying, "I told you so." You will undermine his desire and capability in leadership.

"Is there any positive way I can know God's will for my life?" Yes, there is. When something arises, first check God's concepts concerning the subject. *Always go to the Word,* then pray about the matter. If there is still any question in your mind, ask your husband. Remember, God *promised* to lead through the husband. Whether he is a Christian or not doesn't matter. Whatever he says goes. Now, if his answer and what you feel is God's will aren't the same, you may pray about it again. God can step in and change your mate's mind. Proverbs 21:1 (AMP) says: "The king's heart is in the hand of the Lord as are the watercourses; He turns it whichever way He will." Since God is capable of changing the mind, the heart of a king, I'll assure you, if He has a plan for you, He can also cause your husband to go along with it, perhaps through a change in circumstances, if it's truly His will.

Along this same line often comes the question, "Well, if I am to obey my husband, what if he suggests that I go to a questionable movie, or nightclub, or the like?" Usually these situations are merely the fearful "ifs" in your mind, and never actually occur. On the other hand, they occur once in a while when a husband is really testing to see if you are actually going to obey, no matter what. If you find yourself in a situation where, for example, your husband suggests going to a questionable place, you are to lovingly agree. I have read testimonies from women who followed this, and before they left the house their husbands changed their minds. God intervened. Other women have shared how this situation was turned into a time of blessing. As they were obedient, their husbands saw the truth of their words, and the Lord protected them in whatever situation they encountered.

God's line of authority and Shield of Protection is for your personal benefit. If you are responding correctly to your husband, then you will be protected from unnecessary pressures, burdens and worries. When questioned about an unpaid bill, or harassed by your neighbors who are complaining about your dog getting into their garbage, you only have to reply, "I'm sorry, that is not my responsibility; you will have to take that up with my husband." Since I've learned to enjoy my husband's protection under God's Shield, that is one of my favorite phrases. It doesn't bother me a bit that the person on the phone may think, "Oh, poor unemancipated little woman, she can't make any decisions," because I know from experience what a mess I made and what pressures I suffered before I came under Jim's authority and protection.

When you are trying to decide if an activity or involvement is within God's will for you, determine first if it interferes with your first duties as a wife and/or mother. Next, is it an activity or involvement that your husband may feel he has to compete with? Does it make you financially independent? If your answer is yes to any of the above, then don't do it.

RESPONSIBILITIES OF THE HUSBAND

Ladies, if you are feeling that the Lord really laid one on you when He commanded you to submit to your husband, spend some time reading the responsibilities the Lord has given your husband. I think you'll realize your load is much lighter.

In Ephesians 5:25–33 (AMP) we read God's directives to husbands. "Husbands, love your wives, as Christ loved the church and gave Himself up for her, So that He might sanctify her, having cleansed her by the washing of water with the Word, That He might present the church to Himself in glorious splendor, without spot or wrinkle or any such things—that she might be holy and faultless. Even so, husbands should love their wives as (being in a sense) their own bodies. He who loves his own wife loves himself. For no man ever hated his own flesh, but nourishes and carefully protects and cherishes it, as Christ does the church, because we are members (parts) of His body. For this reason a man shall leave his father and his mother and shall be joined to his wife, and the two shall become one flesh. This mystery is very great, but I speak concerning (the relation of) Christ and the church. However, let each man of you (without exception) love his wife as (being in a sense) his very own self."

Men, in these verses you are told that you are to personify Christ's leadership over the church. Christ's leadership is always right, always wise, always kind, loving, considerate, forgiving, always in right relationship with God's concepts and commands. This is *your* responsibility!

"Impossible," you say. Certainly it is, for sinful man. But as you are open and willing for the Holy Spirit to work in and through you, as you learn to walk with Him moment by moment, daily studying the Word, you will begin to approximate Christ's example. (Phil. 2:5) Just as there are no loopholes to submission, you as a husband are responsible to be the head of your home, your wife, your children, just as Christ is the head of the church. The Scripture says that the husband is to reflect Christ in the marriage. You are responsible to exemplify Jesus Christ by your leadership.

Men, before you take this book and run to your wife, to show her that God said you are the head of the family, the boss, you'd better wait and learn what He expects of you. These verses in Ephesians are not your heavenly edict to become "bully of the year." They put you men in the position of being the aggressor, or the initiator in the relationship. If you are fulfilling verse 25 (AMP)—"Husbands, love your wives as Christ loved the church and gave Himself up for her"—you are not going to have much of a problem about your wives' fulfilling verse 22, which relates to submission. God has clearly *commanded* you to love your wife. He only requires that she respond as a service to Him. The problem with many marriages is that you gentlemen want the response before you are willing to give, and that is the reverse of what God ordered here. If you aren't getting the right kind of response from your wife, maybe you ought to check out how you are fulfilling God's commands for you!

God didn't just give you a title. He expects action. He requires responsibility. You are directly responsible for everything that happens in your home. Nothing should be going on in your home of which you are unaware. You are directly responsible for the discipline of the children. Although you can delegate part of this responsibility to your wife, God still holds you accountable for their actions. The spiritual leadership is also on your shoulders. Nothing should be taught or done in your home without your approval, because God is holding you accountable.

"Anne, you have got to be kidding. God can't hold me responsible for all these areas, can He?" He can and He does. Look back in the Word for a moment. Remember in Genesis when Adam and Eve first sinned, it was Eve who began the process. But when God came to the garden, who did He call for? He called for Adam, He spoke to Adam. He rebuked Adam and held him responsible for the actions of his wife. In I Samuel, the second and third chapters, we read about Eli and his two sons. I am sure you recall that Eli was a priest of the Lord. Poor old Eli. Obviously, he was so busy with his duties at the tabernacle that he failed to take time to properly train and discipline his own children. The Scripture described his sons as "vile and immoral." Finally, God became very angry with Eli because of his indifference concerning his children, and in I Samuel 3:13 (AMP) it says: "And I now announce to him (Eli) that I will judge and punish his house for the iniquity of which he knew, for his sons were being a curse upon themselves and he did not restrain them." Did you notice God didn't make one mention of their mother? He held Eli, the father, completely liable.

Certainly, taking the spiritual leadership of the home will be easy for some, and very difficult for others. To begin with, you can't be the spiritual leader if you don't know Jesus Christ. After you have come to know Him, you need a knowledge of the Word, and that will only come through study, prayer and perhaps listening to good Bible-study tapes. Of course, you need to be in a good Bible-teaching church, under a real man of God. If you are new in the Lord, you might begin by having short devotions after dinner. If there are children in your family, Kenneth Taylor's excellent *Devotions for the Children's Hour* will provide you with illustrations, a short story, Scripture verses, a few questions for the family to discuss, and a closing prayer. There couldn't be a simpler way for a beginning father in the Lord to start devotions in his home. Perhaps as a family, you might take an hour a couple of nights a week to listen and discuss a good

Bible tape. In time, as you study the Word, your knowledge will increase and you will feel more comfortable in this position. (Women, let me warn you, if your husband is new in Christ, and you are a mature Christian, this is going to be a difficult position for him to assume. Please don't correct him, don't criticize him, learn to keep quiet and let him lead. Pray for him, ask the Lord to give him the strength to adapt and carry the spiritual leadership.)

Men, keep in touch with God daily. Set aside some time for private prayer. Remember, God isn't concerned with your manner of speech, but He looks and judges the heart. More time on your knees will bring you closer to Him, and make a better, stronger leader of you. (Luke 11:10)

Being the head of the house means being a good leader. A good leader doesn't have to beat his followers over the head to get their attention, or to have them conform. Christ is your supreme example of leadership—leadership based on love, kindness, and consideration. It does not mean making all the decisions and plans without consulting your wife or the children. A good leader gives serious consideration to the ideas and desires of each member of the family, just as in business, the best corporation head knows how to delegate responsibility, knows how to motivate others to respond to him, work for and with him to reach a common goal. With all that God holds you directly accountable for, if you don't learn the secret of being a good manager, all your time will be taken up with home responsibilities and you'll hardly have time for work. Therefore, be a smart manager, learn the talents and interests of each member of your family, and direct these energies into productive areas of accomplishment. Encourage your wife and your children to develop and use their unique God-given skills. That is the secret of being a good leader, not to thwart and suppress but to encourage and inspire.

God gave you a wife as a helpmate; let her be one. If she doesn't know how to properly manage a house, teach her. If she is interested and capable of helping you in business, let her. As the leader, you aren't to be standing over everything that happens in the house, only be aware of what is going on, and step in when things get out of line, or changes need to be made.

In our modern society, where most husbands have very little time at home, where more and more men travel much of their lives, leaving the raising of the children and the running of the home completely with the wife, men need to make a *special* effort to keep in touch with the happenings of home. Husbands, be aware of needs, changes, discipline problems and frustrations your wife may be facing.

In I Peter 3:7a (AMP) Peter, a married man himself, tells how to treat a lady, a wife, how to bring this happiness into full bloom in your home. "In the same way you married men should live considerately with (your wives), with an intelligent recognition (of the marriage relationship), honoring the woman as (physically) the weaker, but (realizing that you) are joint heirs of the grace (God's unmerited favor) of life." Here Peter is telling you men that God created your wife with a more delicate nature, that because she is a woman, she must be treated tenderly and gently. In other words, you shouldn't expect her to act like a man, work like a man, nor should you treat her like one. When God created woman, it was to be a completer for you as a man, and in this position do you realize that *you* are the center of her life, and that that is a delicate position? It is as if you were holding a fragile flower, and, believe me, you can crush and destroy it so easily. Like a precious flower, she must be kept in the center of your love, protected from too much pressure. She is God's gift to you, and He is daily watching how you respond to, care for, love and cherish that which He made just for you!

"But Anne, I just don't love her any more, I don't feel anything." When a marital relationship has reached this stage, it is a sad situation, but God still commands you to love her. Now you are wondering, How can I love her when I don't "feel" anything? To begin with, remember that you are to emulate Christ, and how did Christ relate to us when we were still sinners, when we cared nothing for Him, denied Him? He gave His life on the cross, the supreme expression of love for us. If you sit around waiting for a "feeling" of love to reappear, you'll be sitting forever. God said to love your wife. Love is an *action* word, a *giving* word. God didn't say, When you "feel" like it, love her; He said, *love* her and the "feeling" will follow. You are still the head of your home, and if there is no love in that home it is your fault.

God holds you responsible to rekindle the flame. How? By giving. Giving of your time, your care, your interest, your money, but most of all giving of *yourself*. Don't wait until tomorrow. Begin right now, today, and every day from now on. Plan something special, do something thoughtful, begin relighting those fires, and as you are obedient, the "feelings" you long for will return.

The heart of the message in Ephesians 5:22–25 is that not only is the wife to be submissive, but that you are to love your wife so that she will want to be the submissive woman God created her to be. You won't have to worry about how to control her if you are loving her in this manner. The Scripture says that you are to love her enough that you would even be willing to give up your life for her. *Submissiveness goes two ways:* The woman is to be submissive to the man, and the man is to love and cherish the woman as *his submissive* response to Christ—as Christ does the church.

QUESTIONS AND PRACTICAL APPLICATIONS FOR HUSBANDS

If you have just discovered there is role-reversal in your home, that you've failed to assume the position of leadership God designated for you, begin by seeking God's strength and help. (Ps. 28:7) Then go to your wife in private, tell her you've learned that God commissioned you to be the head of your home; ask her forgiveness for your lack of protection from worries, burdens, and jobs which should have been your responsibility. Be specific in describing the areas which are reversed. Then share with her your plan to adopt your proper role and responsibilities.

Show her in the Scriptures how God ordained the husband's position. Many women may feel you're just trying to be domineering and bossy. Your mate may not be familiar with God's line of authority. Gently share with her that henceforth you anticipate respect, a companion, not a competitor, and obedience. Be patient, loving; lead and guide her as you bring the changes. On the other hand, be firm, and above all be consistent. The respect you desire is a quality which is built on firm, stable leadership.

After you have spoken to your wife, speak to your children. If they are young, you're fortunate. You'll have few changes and you can begin now to teach them in word and example the proper relationship in marriage. If the children are older, make a list of rules and principles. Apologize to the children if you have failed to set the proper example, or failed to discipline them correctly in the past. Tell the children that many of the frustrations, quarreling and problems in the family have arisen because you failed to actively accept your position of leadership and authority in the home. After you have apologized for areas of past failure, explain how from this point on you will expect them to be under your authority, and to respond with the right attitude. So there will be no misunderstandings, give them each a copy of the home rules and principles which you expect to be performed and/or followed. Depending on the children, their age and their background in the Word, you should seriously consider following your talk with a brief discussion of what the Scriptures say in relation to children, their obedience, respect, relationship, and responsibilities to parents. A list of Scriptures relating to this area are provided for you in the back of this book.

How do you create a good follower? Well, God created women to be responders, but they do not become devoted followers through pressure, criticism or browbeating. Let your mate know how much you need her support, ideas and advice. Often great insight can be gleaned from talking through a problem or situation, and in the process you are making her a part of the solution, a closer part of you. As you integrate her more and more into different areas of your life and business, you'll soon find an excited wife who is sincerely interested in your life and readily supportive of your decisions.

Most important in your remodeling process is *consistency*. Once you have thought through a plan or problem and reached a decision, be staunch. When a father begins to doubt himself, fear of failure takes root in his heart; the stability of the whole family is weakened. When you make plans, decisions, follow through. Naturally, there will be times when unforeseen situations and emergencies will arise, which will require a change in plans. Be assured when situations like this occur, wives and children are very flexible and understanding under these conditions.

Just be certain that you have *real* justification for the alteration of prior arrangements. If you've established their faith in your consistent stability, then they'll happily follow you and harmony will exist even in the midst of disappointments.

As a true leader, you must lead with firmness, but with gentle consideration for the members of your family. God dictated your position in the family; therefore, you are not to allow others to undermine your position, manipulate you through tears, pouting or other forms of pressure, into wrong judgments. Remember, God is holding you responsible.

As a leader, you must display confidence, speak with assurance. If you are daily in the Word, learning God's concepts, then you'll be secure in your judgments. Your confidence will be contagious to the rest of your family.

Don't panic if you blow it once in a while. Failures are human. Don't fear leadership because of your fear of mistakes. God created you for this position and has amply equipped you to function in and through it as you rely on Him. As you apply His concepts, His commandments to your family and to your decisions, failures and mistakes should be confined to a minimum.

As I have suggested in the chapter on communication, you should seriously consider a "Table of Harmony" for your home. Although the final decisions are yours, as a good leader you'll want to hear the ideas, views and desires of every member of your family.

So your finances are in a mess, or there are constant fights about money, what to do? First remember I Timothy 5:8 (AMP): "If any one fails to provide . . . especially for those of his own family, he has disowned the faith (by failing to accompany it with fruits), and is worse than an unbeliever." Remember, God placed you in the position of being the family provider. Sadly, there are many women who have to struggle and do without basic necessities because their husbands refuse to discuss even a simple budget. When God placed you in the position of the provider, He meant an open, happy giver, not the stingy miser who requires his wife to beg for every extra penny, or to ask his permission about every personal item purchased. If you have a normally intelligent wife, she should be allowed private funds of her own, to spend as she pleases. A basic household budget should be set up apart from her "private funds." Most of you like to come home to an attractive, well-groomed wife, or you're very concerned about your wife's appearance in front of clients, customers and friends. Well, guys, there are a *few* women who seem to be natural beauties, who would look good in gunny sacks, but they are the exceptions. Most of us aren't that fortunate. It takes work, a decent wardrobe, an occasional visit to the hairdresser to make us the "doll" you expect. This is one area where you usually get what you are willing to pay for.

Be sure that when your children reach the age where they are old enough to understand a little math, that you begin them on a small allowance, explaining that they are free to use it as they please. The older they become, the more funds they will require. When they get old enough to get a summer job, let them. Nothing teaches the value of a dollar like working for it.

Guys, if you are sincerely interested in a revived, exciting relationship, let me share a secret with you. As a man you probably don't need to be reassured of your wife's love, verbally. Women are different. They need action and words to be reminded and reassured of your love. They need romance, not once in a while but *every day.* Unfortunately, after the honeymoon, most men neglect those romantic words, needed kisses and moments of spontaneous passion. *Don't!*

If you have denied or deprived your wife of affection, overt romance and love, she will literally wither and die. There is no pain so deep as that experienced by an unloved, ignored wife. In Genesis God's Word dictated: "Your desire and craving shall be for your husband . . ." Genesis 3:16 (AMP) says this desire is deeply embedded and needs *you* to fulfill it. Perhaps you fail to identify with such a need; maybe in lieu of love and attention you've escaped into work, as Blake Nunnally did. This escape doesn't fill the void for a woman. If you are seeking to be God's man, begin to *openly* express your affection *daily*. Apply the steps in the chapter "Rekindling the Flame." Don't—repeat, don't —wait until you "feel" attracted to her, "feel" romantic. Act now and trust God to revive the "feelings."

What about those tears? Men, I realize that tears, pain or an upset wife cause frustration for you. Because you're undecided or insecure in how to console her, or solve the problem that's disturbing her, you react in anger, disinterest, or open hostility. I'd wager that every man reading this who has, at one time or another, found his wife in tears, has said, "Honey, what's wrong?" Sometimes she explained, sometimes she said, "Nothing." Buddy, when she says "nothing," she doesn't mean it. But you accepted the answer and walked out leaving her wailing, right? Perhaps there is something seriously wrong and she is too upset to talk about it. Maybe it is just the time of the month that she is extra sensitive. Whatever, most women react with the "nothing" answer because they aren't willing to beg for the comfort they need. Don't let the situation threaten your masculinity because it momentarily appears baffling. Nine times out of ten, the solution is only an arm's length away. Your arms are the protection she needs, the shield that shelters her from the pain or disappointments of the world. Her innermost soul craves your consoling love and sympathy. If you are supportive of her in times such as these, you'll win her undying love, respect and devotion.

As you now think through all the areas that God has directed you to lead in, remember that if you allow your home to be ruled by your wife, a multitude of problems can arise, many of which we have already discussed. Beyond these, the charm, the femininity which drew you to your mate can be destroyed as she assumes masculine roles. Sociological studies have shown that rebellious children and homosexuality are most often produced in broken homes, or in the home where the female is dominant! Are these the problems you want for your home?

As you begin your leadership, as you assume the role God created for you, I'd suggest that you read three excellent books written by men, for men, which will go into depth in every area of your responsibilities: how to develop leadership qualities, family finances, self-confidence, paths to a peaceful home, how to deal with and discipline children, and how to satisfy the needs and inner desires of a woman. For a deeper study, check your local bookstore for copies of *Do Yourself a Favor, Love Your Wife* by H. Page Williams, *Man of Steel and Velvet* by Aubrey P. Andelin, and *Total Man* by Dan Benson.

As you step out, remember the promise in Philippians 4:13 (AMP): "I have strength for all things in Christ Who empowers me—I am ready for anything and equal to anything through Him

Who infuses inner strength into me (that is, I am self-sufficient in Christ's sufficiency)."

NO FIFTY-FIFTY DEAL

You've heard all your life that marriage is a fifty-fifty deal; well it's not. God requires 100 per cent from each of you in your God-given responsibilities. Your roles are of *equal* importance in God's eyes. They just manifest themselves in different areas. In other words, *different doesn't mean inferior.*

Our individual worth is not judged on God's line of authority. God sees each of us, male and female, as unique individuals of equal importance and worth. Galatians 3:28 (Berkley) says: "There is neither Jew nor Greek, there is neither slave nor freeman, there is neither male nor female, because you are all one in Christ Jesus."

We need to study God's Word so that we can come to a fuller understanding of His plan for us as individuals and as marriage partners. As you adjust more and more to His plan, you will begin to see wonderful things happening in your marital relationship.

GOALS: The purpose of this chapter is to share God's divine line of authority for the home. It is my prayer that the Holy Spirit will open your hearts, giving you true understanding of your roles and responsibilities as set forth in the Word. Who wears the pants, who is the leader in your home, is of ultimate importance as you strive to rebuild your marriage. The goal accomplished when you learn and apply God's concepts as shared in this chapter will be a properly run home, where peace and happiness abide, and true love again radiates between husband and wife.

ASSIGNMENTS:

(1) Begin by asking the Holy Spirit to show you personally any and all areas where you have departed from your God-given role. Ask God's forgiveness and guidance as you begin to correct your errors.

(2) Memorize Psalms 127:1.

(3) Read Proverbs 3:1–7; review I Peter 3:1–7, I Corinthians 7:3 5, Ephesians 5:22–33 and Proverbs 31:10–29.

(4) Pray, claiming the promise of John 16:23–24, asking God to give you a desire to fulfill the position He has designed for you.

(5) Begin daily to respond to your mate as Christ would. When in doubt, think, "How would Christ act? How would Christ respond in this situation?" (Eph. 5:1–2)

(6) If you have not already attended, I would *highly* recommend that you both attend Bill Gothard's Institute in Basic Youth Conflicts. I promise you that you will come away with a deeper understanding of God's line of authority, self-image, conflicts in the home, successful living, the marital roles, and much more. The seminars are life-changing experiences, and if you have teen-agers, take them along. The schedule of seminars may be obtained by writing:

Bill Gothard
Institute in Basic Youth Conflicts
Box One
Oak Brook, Illinois 60521

(7) Make a list of all the little jobs your mate has been asking you to do since year one and try to accomplish at least one every other day till your list is completed.

(8) Men, make a list of the house rules, regulations, and responsibilities for each of your children. Be sure the children understand for each rule, regulation, or responsibility there is an appointed punishment if they fail to obey. Be sure the punishment is consistent with the "crime."

(9) As the spiritual head of your home, men, establish a set time for Bible study in your home, beginning this week.

(10) As a couple, sit down and make a budget allowing for household expenses, savings, entertainment, payments, etc., and a personal fund for your wife.

CHAPTER 8

PROBLEM: SEX WAS GOD'S IDEA

Symptoms

Total disinterest	Distorted sexual education
Overemphasis on the physical	Fatigue
Worry	Adultery
Fear	Impotence, frigidity
Feminine or masculine manipulation	Unsettled differences
Unconfessed guilt	Jealousy
	Suspicion

Neither Hollywood nor *Playboy* created sex. For some of you, this may be a shock. But sex was God's idea, His creation and, used in its proper bounds, receives His hearty blessing!

God realized that married love needed more than verbal communication to express itself. Therefore, in the beginning, He provided a beautiful and effectual way for a couple to completely and vividly convey the love, devotion and oneness of their souls. Elton Trueblood states it this way: "One of the most significant things to say about sexual intercourse is that it provides husband and wife with a language which cannot be matched by words or by any other act whatsoever. Love needs language for its adequate expression and sex has its own syntax."[1]

It is *very* important that you realize and understand sex from God's point of view, recognizing God as the creator of the marriage act. In Genesis 1:27 (AMP) we read: "So God created man in His own image, in the image and likeness of God He created him; male and female He created them." The soul of man was created in the image of God. That means, just as God has essence, man has essence. God's essence in part is His perfect character. Man's essence consists of his soul, his self-consciousness, his emotions and his volition. The part of us which was created in God's image is invisible and intangible. But God gave us a tangible, visible way of manifesting what is a reality in the soul, and this is done through the body. The body is the second part of the verse; it was also created by God, *male* and *female*.

In Genesis 1:31 (AMP) it says: "And God saw *everything* that He had made, and behold, it was very good—suitable, pleasant—and *He approved it completely.*" The approval included the creation of the maleness and femaleness. God was pleased with the creation and called it *very good.* This verse clearly shows us that sex was God's idea.

In Genesis 2:24 God performed the first marriage ceremony. This ceremony is the divine pattern which all mankind is to follow. God designed man to be monogamous, not to inhibit man, restrict his pleasure or fun, but to liberate him, to give him maximum joy under God's protection and provisions.

Genesis 2:24 (AMP) says: "Therefore a man shall leave his father and his mother and shall become united and cleave to his wife, and they shall become one flesh." The second part of this verse describes the sexual copulation that the husband and wife are to have in marriage. In fact, in this verse, the *union is actually commanded.*

In the last verse of this chapter of Genesis we see how comfortable and relaxed a husband and wife should be in marriage. Verse 25 (AMP) says: "And the man and his wife were both naked, and were not embarrassed or ashamed in each other's presence." Adam and Eve are the only couple who ever had the freedom and pleasure of entering marriage and making love with no preconceived ideas, no hang-ups and no inhibitions. They were designed by a Holy God, commanded to make love, and they blissfully enjoyed the ultimate gift of God between a man and woman. It is God's desire that you also come to understand the ecstasy and delight He provided in the physical congress of marriage.

In the Song of Solomon, we have the opportunity to read the very vivid, detailed language of the sexual relationship. The Song of Solomon shares how exciting and enchanting God means for this portion of your life to be. If you are an unbeliever, or a new believer, and have always regarded the Bible as dull reading, I suggest you read the Song of Solomon—if possible in the Living Bible Translation, particularly the sixth chapter, verses 1–10, and all of the seventh chapter. The whole book describes the courting and physical affection between King Solomon and the Shulammite maiden. The language isn't in the slightest offensive, and it is an example of how gratifying and rapturous God means this part of your life to be.

Hebrews 13:4 clearly tells us that the marriage bed is honorable in *all* ways. The second part of the verse reminds us that it falls from honor only when adultery enters the relationship. Of course, God is ready to forgive an adulterer when the offending party is truly repentant. The main thrust of this verse is that the marriage bed (whatever a married couple jointly finds satisfying and enjoyable in that bed—of course, I don't mean sado-masochism) is glorifying to God, because He meant it to be a real, functioning, delightsome part of marital unity. Proverbs 5:21 (AMP) says: "For the ways of man are directly before the Lord, and He carefully weighs *all* man's doings." God watches all our action and interaction and this includes the physical relations in marriage, and He greatly approves. As with the verse in Hebrews, His wrath is reserved for those who violate His plan and pervert or distort sex beyond the bounds of marriage.

As we have seen, even in our physical makeup, God created man's love to be predominantly aggressive and protective. The wife's love should be responsive and receptive. Sex is based on the concept that man initiates the love and woman responds to it. As the husband and wife come together in sexual union they become one physically and one in the self-consciousness of their souls. In this act they are helping each other to like and appreciate who they really are. They are both giving out of their own free volition—in a way, submitting to each other. Your thoughts are to be centered on how you can please your mate. In the consciousness of your souls you are adapting to each other's way of life. The physical unity brings the consciousness, the soul, the emotions into an elegant oneness, which makes the act so deeply meaningful.

As you analyze your own marriage *please* keep in mind that most of the time sexual problems are merely the rash that alerts you of deeper discord in your relationship and in actuality is *not* the major conflict.

SEXUAL COMMUNICATION AND EDUCATION

The LaHayes state it very well in their book *The Act of Marriage:* "God has never put a premium on ignorance, and that includes sex education. His statement 'My people are destroyed for lack of knowledge' is as true in this area of life as in the spiritual. Millions of married couples accept a second-rate experience because they don't know much about the reproductive organs and sexual functions and are unwilling to learn."[2]

I am not suggesting that sex education belongs in the school system, far from it; sex education belongs in the *home*. The problem in the school system is that God's viewpoint is not taught. On the other hand, the home obviously has failed with many of our generation, so I have suggested two books on sex, dealing with every aspect, in the assignment chapter of this book. Obviously, I can't cover the total subject in one chapter. But if you are having problems in the bedroom, don't continue to wander frustrated in your ignorance. If you really desire to be God's man or God's woman, you owe it to your mate, if not to yourself, to learn all you can about the human body, the erotic zones, the needs and desires of the male and female.

Even for those of you who feel you are fairly well versed on the subject, I'd still suggest you do a bit of reading, a rethinking on the subject. Often, after a few years of marriage, if we are satisfied with our physical relationship, we tend to get on dangerous ground because we fall into ruts. The ruts may not be bothering you yet, but your mate may be bored to death. Varied approaches, innovations, are what keep the bedroom an exciting place. Few mates have ever wandered from the partner who is constantly exciting, always thinking of new ways to please. The death blow in the bedroom comes through *selfishness.*

Everything that God created about the body is beautiful; there are no parts sectioned out as "dirty." If God has given His approval to you as His creation, then you should never be ashamed to discuss with your mate your likes and dislikes. Before you do this, please learn the basic names for the various parts of the body. When you begin to talk to your mate, the atmosphere will either be free and liberating if you are relaxed and knowledgeable about what you are referring to, or stifled and inhibited if you can't seem to say the words vagina or penis, and try to talk around them with a lot of "You know what I mean." It is important that you are familiar with the basic anatomy of both the female and the male, and the purpose and function of those parts. It doesn't take years of study to become knowledgeable. It does take care—care for your mate, care for yourself, and concern that you are not *defrauding* your mate by your ignorance.

There is no way that there can be improvements in the bedroom unless you are willing to admit to yourself and your mate that there are unfulfilled needs in your physical life. If you have totally understood God's viewpoint on sex, you should have moved to the place that you feel liberated enough to share with your mate that either you are not being satisfied, or you'd like more variety in your relationship, or to inject inventive new ideas yourself. While you are sharing your needs, be sure to ask your mate if he or she is totally satisfied sexually. If he/she says no, ask him/her to *specifically* share with you how you can better gratify his/her desires. Learning to communicate your feelings and desires is the key to sexual contentment.

As we discussed in the chapter on communication, your mate is not a mind-reader; *you* must assume responsibility for communicating your own sexual needs, desires, and feelings. The same is true for your mate. You can't read their minds either, and they are responsible for relating to you their pleasures. This isn't a matter of selfishness, of "I'll tell you what I want, then I expect immediate ecstasy." What we are talking about is being open, learning to communicate your wants and desires. Once you are aware of what makes your mate happy, then *you* are responsible for fulfilling them to the best of your ability. *BUT*, if you don't talk, if you refuse to tell your mate of a need or frustration, then you have no one to blame but yourself.

You can both save yourselves years of hit-and-miss guessing games by taking a few minutes to talk. Certainly, things may not go perfectly the first time you try new positions, as you attempt stimulating areas that you've never tried before. Realize you are human beings, *allow for mistakes*. We humans are so totally unrealistic. If a man had to perform as perfectly on his job every day, or a woman had to cook as idealistically, as each of you seem to expect to perform in the bedroom during every encounter, people would think you were nuts. Give yourself room to grow. Room to grow means allowing for mistakes, some frustration, but the experience will ultimately be a beautiful, fulfilling one. *Don't make a perfect sexual climax your abiding purpose.* Learn to relax and enjoy the excitement and thrill of the moment. In other words, let go, don't let half your mind wander off evaluating your performance. If you approach sex in this manner, you'll miss half of the fun, the closeness, because you aren't totally participating, completely involved with your mate. So quit judging and start enjoying.

Next, do your real communicating apart from actual love-making. Since sex seems to be the most sensitive area of any relationship, be *very* careful about not sending negative signals, especially during the actual act. When you are engaging in your pre-love-making conversation, decide on some sort of signal, a word, a pat on the head, something that will tell your mate that whatever is happening during the marital act is either disturbing, uncomfortable, or that you simply desire a change for greater pleasure.

When you want to send positive signals to your mate (these are of course always welcome, ego-building and enhancing to the relationship), it can be done in various ways. You can either verbalize your pleasure, or transmit your delight through movement, sighs, or the like.

If you are very bashful, or just learning real sex knowledge, and feel you simply can't talk to your mate, try writing down your feelings and desires sometime during the day. If both of you are inhibited in this area, you can both begin by sharing in this manner, exchanging notes maybe after dinner, sometime during the evening, but don't wait until you are getting ready to crawl into bed, because there may be times when your messages need clarification, and if you are relying on writing, bedtime isn't the time. As you become more comfortable about expressing yourself, as your knowledge of anatomy becomes clearer, you will want to put this limited manner of communication away, and begin to share with each other face to face.

Last but not least: in communication, don't fake it. Women,

we are particularly bad in this area. Certainly don't demean, or cut down, your mate during intercourse. But when you are communicating later, you need to be honest if you are not gaining satisfaction in your current approach. Be honest but kind. Honesty can always be put in a kind fashion. For instance, a wife who is not being given enough time during foreplay might later say: "Honey, I know it is probably me—you know how slow I am about everything—but the next time we are making love, it would be helpful if you gave me more time." Or: "Honey, I must have a slow motor; I feel I need more foreplay stimulation." In this approach, there is no blame involved, but the need and message have been communicated.

SEX BEGINS AT SUNRISE!

Sex doesn't start the moment you enter the bedroom or the bed. It starts at the breakfast table, it begins in the relationship that you have with your mate as a way of life. Sex begins in the mind. Your mental attitude has everything to do with your physical relationship. If you think sex is dirty, your brain will never let you relax and enjoy the gift of oneness. Hopefully, as you've read this chapter, you've come to understand God's viewpoint, and with a changed mental attitude wonderful joys now await you.

A smile in the morning, kind words, a goodbye kiss before the day's work, are all mentally turning you on or off for sex in the evening. As Dr. David Reuben has pointed out, what is or isn't expressed, those unverbalized reassurances and moments of affection will affect your feelings about each other throughout the day. A couple who has learned to relate their most intimate thoughts, feelings, fears, joys, and triumphs never feels the need to seek companionship beyond their own bedroom. Those fleeting minutes of love at night are completely interwoven with all the shared love, memories, friends, and fulfillment of every day, month, and year of your marriage. When a couple truly learns this, they discover a powerful deterrent to infidelity. The mate who denies his or her partner satisfaction is breaking a command of the Scriptures (I Cor. 7:5) and is truly asking his or her mate to seek fulfillment elsewhere!

BUT YOU DON'T KNOW MY WIFE

I Corinthians 7:3 (KJV) says: "Let the husband render unto the wife due benevolence . . ." The word "render" actually means to give totally of one's self. You guys must realize that a female is a person to be loved and cherished, every day, not a sex machine that you turn on when the desire hits.

Since God created the woman as a responder, she needs to have your love and affection to respond to. If she has nothing to respond to, you will discover that she will react in one of two ways. She may become extremely nervous, pouting, bitter, resentful, and spend her days nagging you to death. Or she may turn to some form of escapism. Women used to escape by spending long hours gossiping across the kitchen table with the next-door neighbor, or pouring their frustrations out by overactivity in the ladies' circle, or some cause-oriented group. Unfortunately, in the past decade, more and more women are escaping into the tranquilizer bottle, or the carefully hidden bottle of booze! Who's responsible? Well, God says you men are!

With leadership comes responsibility. Too many of you have turned your leadership into whip-cracking sessions, acting like a drill instructor instead of a loving husband. You want sex without the accompanying responsibility.

In I Corinthians 7:3 (KJV) it says: "Let the husband render unto the wife due benevolence: and likewise also the wife unto the husband." Did you notice the wife comes second? Why? Because she is to respond to your benevolence. Most of you are businessmen and realize that in order to get a return you have to invest something. In marriage, the principle is the same. When a man invests nothing in his marriage, he not only receives nothing, but a negative atmosphere takes root in his home. God made woman a simple creature to relate to and understand. In Genesis, we read that she is simply to complement and complete the man. She becomes complex when she has nothing to complement and complete but negativism. So, men, if you are having problems in the bedroom, you'd better take serious account of how you are fulfilling your God-given responsibilities toward your wife. Are you providing an atmosphere of love and devotion? Do you show her daily little signs of care, concern, a hug in the morning, a kiss before you leave (and I mean a kiss, not a peck in the direction of her face)? If you aren't setting an atmosphere of love, then not only are you the loser in the bedroom, but you are responsible before God for failing your wife in these areas.

SATAN'S DISTORTIONS

Anything that God has created is good. Satan seeks to distort, to abuse, to destroy in some way. In the area of sex, he will cause some people to either put all the emphasis on the body, to the exclusion of the soul, or all the emphasis on the soul, to the exclusion of the body. There are some groups (they are rare, and I should hope that they continue to be so) that say the body is evil, and therefore even in marriage you are not to have sex. To continue to be truly spiritual, you are to live with your mate in a brother/sister relationship. The total emphasis is on the spiritual, or the soul. Then there are other groups, which are far more predominant. You see their thought patterns displayed on the movie screen, the TV, in almost every magazine that you can pick up, and their approach says the body is all-important. In essence, if you aren't built with a certain curve here, and bend there, then you have had it. The whole emphasis is on the body. You know, when I listen to many of the modern commercials, I'm amazed that you and I were ever conceived. How did our parents ever do it without the right deodorants, the sex-appealing toothpaste, mouthwash, and foot deodorizers?

Both extremes are wrong. God wants you to come to His divine balance. You see the imbalance began with Adam and Eve when they sinned. (Genesis 3:7) If you recall, the first thing they did when they sinned was to sew together fig leaves to try to cover up their genitals. They presumed the problem was in their body and what was showing. It wasn't in their body at all; it was in their soul. The soul problem is the one which needed to be corrected. Just as they did, we have a tendency to put the emphasis on the wrong thing. We either think of sex in a promiscuous manner or that sex is dirty, filthy, even in the marital relationship. Some approach the physical union as a duty one has to perform, and if they feel any pleasure they feel guilty.

What we need to do is learn God's divine balance, see that what He has provided is something beautiful. But in order to enjoy this celestial, fulfilling relationship, there must be boundaries. God has set boundaries, limits for our protection, to keep the happiness there, rather than destroy it. Let's talk about some of the ways that Satan has distorted sex, so we can be aware of them.

I suppose his ace in the hole is, first and foremost, adultery. We are told that the sin of adultery destroys the body as well as the soul. In I Corinthians 6:15–20 (LVB) we vividly see how this is accomplished. "Don't you realize that your bodies are actually parts and members of Christ? So should I take part of Christ and join him to a prostitute? Never! And don't you know that if a man joins himself to a prostitute, she becomes a part of him and he becomes a part of her? For God tells us in the Scripture that in His sight the two become one person. But if you give yourself to the Lord, you and Christ are joined together as one person. That is why I say to run from sex is sin. No other sin affects the body as this one does. When you sin this sin it is against your own body. Haven't you yet learned that your body is the home of the Holy Spirit God gave you, and that He lives within you? Your own body does not belong to you. For God has bought you with a great price. So use every part of your body to give glory back to God, because He owns it." God is clearly warning you here not to get involved in adultery, that it will destroy your body.

Let's look at some of the ways illicit sex does destroy the body. First there is the high risk of contracting a venereal disease. I don't know about your part of the country, but around here V.D. is about as prevalent as the common cold. Next, it can cause the sexual extremes which lead to nymphomania, excessive sexual desire in the female, or the corresponding problem in the male known as satyriasis, which means that the male is driven by a desire that never finds fulfillment. To the opposite extreme it is often the basis for frigidity in the woman, and psychological impotence in the male, usually brought on by guilt.

The next distortion that Satan seems to be having a heyday with currently is best explained in Romans 1:21–28 (AMP). "Because when they knew and recognized Him as the God, they did not honor and glorify Him as God, or give Him thanks. But instead they became futile and godless in their thinking—with vain imaginings, foolish reasoning and stupid speculations—and their senseless minds were darkened. Claiming to be wise, they became fools—professing to be smart, they made simpletons of themselves. And by them the glory and majesty and excellence of the immortal God were exchanged for and represented by images, resembling mortal man and birds and beasts and reptiles. Therefore God gave them up in the lusts of their (own) hearts to sexual impurity, to the dishonoring of their bodies among themselves, abandoning them to the degrading power of sin. Because they exchanged the truth of God for a lie and worshiped and served the creature rather than the Creator, Who is blessed forever! Amen—so be it. For this reason God gave them over and abandoned them to vile affections and degrading passions. For their women exchanged their natural function for an unnatural and abnormal one; and the men also turned from natural relations with women and were set ablaze (burned out, consumed) with lust for one another, men committing shameful acts with men and suffering in their own bodies and personalities the inevitable consequences and penalty of their wrongdoing and going astray, which was fitting retribution. And so, since they did not see fit to acknowledge God or approve of Him or consider Him worth the knowing, God gave them over to a base and condemned mind to do things not proper or decent but loathsome." I think that pretty well states God's position on the distortion of homosexuality.

Before you write me and tell me all about the people you know who have shacked up and played around for years, and still seem to be functioning normally, let me share these thoughts with you. The body has a delicate wiring for our sexual makeup. Illicit sex, whether homosexual or heterosexual, causes the wiring in time to short-circuit. When this occurs then the above results in some form usually take place. These malfunctions in the sexual wiring don't usually occur overnight. Sometimes it is years before the wiring blows a fuse. Beyond the biblical view, the world itself is aware of this problem. They produced a pathetic but good example in the film *Carnal Knowledge*. It vividly portrayed a man, proud of his sexual prowess, shacking up with one woman after another, year after year, but in the end you see a tired, depressed human being, totally impotent, languishing in anxiety because he was finally reaping what he had sown. Remember Galatians 6:7 (AMP): "Do not be deceived and deluded and misled: God will not allow Himself to be sneered at —scorned, disdained or mocked (by mere pretensions or professions, or His precepts being set aside). He inevitably deludes himself who attempts to delude God. For whatever a man sows, that and that only is what he will reap. For he who sows to his own flesh (lower nature, sensuality) will from the flesh reap decay and ruin and destruction; but he who sows to the Spirit will from the Spirit reap life eternal."

God isn't a kill-joy. His warnings are for our benefit, not to take the fun out of life. Proverbs 6:32 (AMP) reminds us how sexual sin destroys the soul: "But whoever commits adultery with a woman lacks heart and understanding—moral principle and prudence; he who does it is destroying his own life." The King James Version says, ". . . his own soul." How is his soul destroyed? God has designed the soul to respond to Him in the right way, to keep our sins confessed to Him moment by moment, to respond rightly to fellow man. When we do not do this, guilt is produced. The guilt will cause mental as well as physical problems. It may cause you to distrust your mate and distrust yourself. Jealousy can be a by-product, I'm not saying that everyone who has a problem with jealousy has committed sexual sins, but Romans 2:1 (AMP) does remind us that whatever we judge another of is what we are guilty of ourselves, so that is something to take into consideration. Once you have gotten involved in illicit sex, it is easy to lose respect for yourself and be constantly confronted with self-condemnation. All of these things can bring on extreme mental strain. In fact, just trying to keep an affair secret can bring on a good deal of worry, anguish, fear of being caught and the like. All these areas are difficult to live with, and the only way that they can be resolved is to go to God and claim I John 1:9, realizing that Jesus Christ paid on the cross for that sin, just as He paid for your bitterness, revenge, or any other sin. Claim His forgiveness for the sin and move forward to establish new and right patterns.

Another area where Satan has distorted sex is in the area of autoeroticism. Perhaps you are more familiar with the term "masturbation." In I Corinthians 7:4, we are reminded that we do not have the right to be involved in this activity. I Corinthians 7:3–4 reminds us that our bodies belong to our mates and we are to arouse each other's bodies, not our own. In I Corinthians 6:12, in the second part of the verse, we are reminded that we are not to become a slave of anything or be brought under its power. We are to be under the power of only the Holy Spirit, not in bondage to our own self-gratification, which often happens when masturbation becomes a form of sexual outlet. Now, I am strictly speaking of autoeroticism as actively practiced by you, individually. I am not discussing it or discrediting it as a part of stimulation during marital relations.

Although the Scripture is silent on this and even Christian writers in this field vary in their opinions, I feel that since your body does belong to your mate, it is best that they do the stimulating. If you get involved in a practice of stimulating yourself, even during love-making, it could get to be *self-oriented* instead of *other-oriented,* and the desire for *self-gratification* could take precedence over care for loving and satisfying your mate.

The next distortion is probably as near as the magazine counter or book rack at the local drugstore. Sometimes you find it near a check-out stand in the grocery, and certainly the newsstands and "adult bookstores" are full of it. Its name is *pornography.* Most of those who are regular readers of pornography are people seeking vicarious sexual experiences. These people either can't or won't have a normal sex life, so they seek fulfillment in an artificial world of books, pictures, and descriptions of characters who are usually sexually more aggressive than they. In the majority of cases, pornography is combined with or followed by masturbation. For years men have been the leading consumers, but recently more and more women have become involved. Obviously, this is another of Satan's distortions. Since pornography is generally a substitution for normal sex, it is defrauding your mate. *Anything* that replaces the husband-wife physical relationship is a creation of Satan. As with other fetishes, pornography may begin with a book or magazine now and then. But for those who don't adhere to God's viewpoint on sex, pornography may replace their mates as sexual outlets.

"But how can I know what to read and what not to read?" you ask. You know whether your motivation for purchasing certain books and magazines is based on literary content, or whether you are seeking sexually explicit books. The next time you settle down with a book to get "turned on," just remember God is omnipresent; He knows exactly what you are *thinking*, *feeling*, and, yes, He knows what you are *reading* and He knows why!

Other areas of distortion are in the form of "blue movies," better known as "adult films." Much of the current "sensitivity" training also falls into this category.

GOD'S VIEW OF SEX

If you want the proper viewpoint of anything dealing with sex, it is as close as God's Word. He will tell you everything about it. You don't have to feel that you are missing out on anything. As you read through the Old Testament, you'll read the most descriptive things having to do with sex that you have ever read. What is the difference between it and pornography? It is not pornography, because it is not glorified or glamorized; it is kept in the proper perspective. God shows you the different distortions and perversions, but He also shows you the effect they have on people and why they are not to be allowed to become part of your life. So go to God's Word. Find there the proper viewpoint.

In the Bible we discover that sex was God's idea from the beginning, and He designed it to be pleasurable for you and your mate. Genesis 18:12 (AMP) shows you that God has designed sex to be a "pleasure" relationship between the husband and wife. As you read there, Sarah and Abraham were both past the reproductive age. There was no more sex as far as they were concerned. Then they were told that they were going to have a child! Genesis 18:12 (AMP) reads: "Therefore, Sarah laughed to herself, saying, 'After I have become aged shall I have *pleasure* and *delight*, my lord being old also?'" She knew God was giving them something back that had passed, but with it she was expecting *pleasure* and *delight*, not only for herself, but for Abraham also. Proverbs 5, I believe, is one of the major Scriptures that emphasizes how sex was designed by God to be a wonderful, pleasant experience for both husband and wife. Proverbs

5:15 (AMP): "Drink waters out of your own cistern (of pure marriage relationship), and fresh running waters out of your own well."

Here God is paralleling the sex desire in the husband/wife relationship to the way you feel when you are very thirsty, how you are satisfied by drinking cool water out of a well. I am sure you can readily identify with that. How good it feels to drink that cool, refreshing water. God is saying that the same analogy is between the marital relationship—that you are to go to each other and both of you are to be completely satisfied, as the thirst was satisfied when you drank from the well. He compares the wife to a cistern. Those of you who live in the country know that a cistern is a deep well that has a lid over it. The lid protects it from all impurities, but then the one that owns the cistern comes to it, removes the lid, and the deep cool water fills him, satisfies him. The same is true with the marital partner. You are to be covered from other people, except your mate. Your mate is the only one who has the right to uncover you, and you *both* have the right to be totally satisfied.

"Let your fountain be blessed (with the rewards of fidelity), and rejoice with the wife of your youth." (Prov. 5:18 AMP) God is reminding you again that you are to *rejoice,* that this is to be a pleasant experience for both of you. Then in the nineteenth verse: "Let her be as the loving hind and pleasant doe (tender, gentle, attractive): let her bosom satisfy you at all times; and always be transported with delight in her love." More specifically, the latter portion of this verse, when translated from the original Hebrew, would read: "You will always wander up and down her body in the area of her love." Taking these verses in conjunction with other Scriptures—I Corinthians 7:3–5, which reminds us that our bodies belong to our mates; Hebrews 13:5, which states that the marriage bed is undefiled, honorable *in all*—God is showing us that His viewpoint of sex is free, liberated, that wives and husbands are free to satisfy their mate's sexual desires in any way they *both* enjoy. In other words, *there is no perversion is the marital relationship,* period. Wives, remember that we are to be submissive. If your husband suggests something new, don't miss out on the fun. God's viewpoint is total freedom. You are liberated to satisfy your mate's desires, completely and totally. *The perversion comes when it is done outside the husband/wife relationship.*

Before you write and ask, Do I mean this, that, or if the other is all right? I'll state the major areas which usually come up for questions. I am saying that you are free to engage in oral sex, the use of vibrators, if that turns you on—although I would caution you that the constant use of a vibrator may form a desire for a level of stimulation which your mate cannot meet through normal means. You may engage in mutual masturbation during foreplay for stimulation. You may choose any position that you enjoy, although I think in time you'll discover that many that are written about take a contortionist to perform. You can leave the light on, turn it off, make love in the bed, the bathtub, wherever you desire, as long as you have total privacy. All the above-mentioned variations, and some I probably forgot or haven't as yet run across, are *never* to totally replace the basic form of intercourse that God created for His creatures.

As you adjust to God's view on sex in marriage and begin to make it a part of your life, you will not only be rightly influencing the marital relationship and gaining the pleasure that God created for you, but you will be influencing your children. Freely express affection to your mate in front of the children, giving your mate a hug, a kiss, telling them you love them, because the relationship they see between the two of you may be the only marital course your children will take. Daily show them the joys and devotion. Make your interaction a living daily example for them. Judge Phillip Gilliam stated that of the 28,000 juvenile court cases that he judged, the lack of affection between father and mother was the greatest cause of juvenile delinquency that he knew.

SIDE BENEFITS

Did you realize that the Lord has provided some wonderful physiological benefits for women that occur during physical union? Physically fulfilling copulation is a tremendous emotional release. This is one area where the overworked, pressured, up-tight woman of today can totally let go and experience the ultimate joy and fulfillment that the Lord created for her. The feeling of completeness and tremendous release of tension have no parallel.

Secondly, as a woman is enjoying God's gift of sex, her body is renewing itself! Research has shown that during sexual union, large amounts of the sex hormone estrogen are produced. This hormone not only sustains healthy female organs but contributes to firmer skin, a flexible spine, healthy hair, and better distribution of the body's subcutaneous fat! So, ladies, a wife who is fulfilling her role as God intended her to has many wonderful experiences and benefits to enjoy through her physical expression of love toward her husband. Isn't God great!

WHAT ABOUT BIRTH CONTROL?

Birth control is the responsibility of both mates. For too long the burden has been on the woman, in the use of various foams, diaphragms, creams, IUDs, the faulty rhythm method, and probably most used, the pill. Every one of these methods fails to be foolproof; some, for particular women, are even dangerous. I would suggest that you read and study various methods, then consult your personal Ob-Gyn before deciding which is preferable for you personally.

I would like to suggest that you consider Natural Family Planning, which is particularly helpful for fertility awareness. This method of family planning can be used effectively to achieve or avoid pregnancy, *depending upon the motivations of the couple*. It is usable for women with or without regular menstrual cycles. This particular method brings both husband and wife into the beautiful intimacy of family planning. For information on this concept write:

> The Couple to Couple League, International, Inc.
> Post Office Box 11084
> Cincinnati, Ohio 45211

Use any form of family planning you desire, except abortion. Abortion does not prevent conception, but kills a life already begun. This action should be considered *only* when the mother's *physical* life is actually endangered.

PROBLEMS, QUESTIONS, AND HANG-UPS IN RELATIONSHIP TO SEX

Let's get down to some specific areas which might be a problem in adjusting sexually. It is important that we realize, before we go into specific problems, that because the physical union in marriage is an expression of the soul's oneness, it is already a reality. If there are sex problems, most of the time they are manifestations of a deeper soul problem. You will want to go back and evaluate. "Have I violated any of God's concepts, God's commandments? Am I helping my mate to like who he or she is? Am I giving him or her the freedom to go and be the person he or she wants to be? Am I accepting him or her exactly the way he or she is?" Women, are you submitting *willingly* to your husband's leadership, since this position in the home is one that God ordained? You must respect and admire him, not necessarily because of what he does, how he acts, but because God has given him that position. Are you centering your thoughts around how you can please your mate throughout the day? Are you appreciating your mate, and are you adapting to his way of life? Men, are you remembering the little things, the romantic actions and words, the opening of your soul through communication, talk which will bring your wife closer to you? As you do these things, soul problems will begin to be worked out and in the majority of cases the sex problems will take care of themselves.

Darien Cooper told me of a woman who came to her course who had, by normal standards, been called "frigid." She neither desired sex, nor had she ever had an orgasm. As she realized that she wasn't responsible for her husband, but for how she reacted to him; as she learned to confess her sins, to unburden herself of bitterness, disgust, jealousy; as she, through the power of the Holy Spirit, began to admire and praise him, *just as he was,* and as she applied the concepts from God's Word, she told Darien that their sex life had become fantastic. That is exactly the way it ought to be. Usually when we are rightly relating to our mate, fulfilling the role God gave us, then the bedroom blossoms. You have to realize that you can't carry the baggage of the day into the bedroom at night; if you do, that baggage will come between you and your mate.

MEN AND SIGHT STIMULATION VS. WOMEN AND THE CAVEMAN APPROACH

It is important to realize that a man is usually more stimulated by sight than a woman. Your husband watches you getting ready for bed and is ready for physical union. What a mess! There you are ready for a "long winter's nap," and he's crawling into bed, motor running! If you understand the male makeup better, you will understand why this has happened, and can keep from responding with a collection of female excuses, knowing that he truly needs you. Men also seem to respond to smell, perfumes and powders. Capitalize on this and use it.

On the other hand, there are some of you gentlemen who completely fail to understand the female responses. You either approach the bed stark naked, thinking that that is going to arouse wild passion, when in the majority of cases it turns your lady flat off. Or you drag into the bedroom, crawl out of your work clothes, forget that baths can be taken even if it isn't Saturday night, and flop into bed in droopy underwear. That isn't sexy or stimulating; it's stupidity, and nine out of ten times turns your lady off. Think through your desires. You enjoy coming to bed with a wife in a pretty nightgown, clean, sweet-smelling, all tucked in between soft sheets, right? Well, sirs, so does the little woman. Lack of personal hygiene is one cause of mental and sexual frigidity in females. It is very difficult for us to get turned on to unshaven faces, the perspiration of a day's work, dirty nails, and bad breath. In essence, the game works both ways; you should be willing to give as much as you enjoy getting. It takes only a few minutes to shower, put on some deodorant, slap on a little after-shave, and put on a *clean* pair of shorts, or pajamas; and don't forget to brush your teeth, and use a good mouthwash or mouth deodorant. You'll find that in the little time you take to make these changes, a more excited, responsive wife will await your arms.

WHAT IF YOUR HUSBAND APPEARS TO BE IMPOTENT?

If your husband doesn't appear to have any desire toward you sexually, what should you do? First, don't jump to the conclusion that there is another woman involved. The most important thing is, again, to go back to the soul relationship and see if there are any concepts you are violating. Have you been belittling him? Have you been putting him down? If so, then it is very hard for him to relate to you in a warm, responsive way in the sex relationship.

There is the slight possibility, and you should *not* assume any kind of guilt, that your husband is physically impotent. If God has shown you that you are completely following His concepts, responding and interacting rightly with your mate, then the problems may be totally your husband's. For some reason, counselors are facing this particular problem more than ever. The basic problems *in almost all* cases are mental and emotional, *not* physical. Impotency is known to occur between a husband and wife when an affair is in progress. This type is usually brought on by guilt. In other cases women have allowed themselves to be placed on a pedestal so high, so perfect, that their men can no longer relate to them. This is often referred to as the Madonna Complex.

Then, there is impotency which occurs during the heavy use of alcohol or drugs. What has recently been recognized is that very often, after the use of the alcohol or drugs is stopped, there comes a period, from a few weeks up to a year, when the male continues to be impotent. His mind still feels the need of alcohol or drugs to release some distorted inhibitions so that he can function. He may simply fear failure, because his old crutch isn't available to him. As I interviewed a number of women, I was amazed to discover that this is a very prevalent problem. Some of these poor couples had been to doctor after doctor seeking help with no success. Few of the physicians contacted were even aware of this after-alcoholic-drug impotency problem. It is very important that the man who is planning to go off the bottle or drugs is made aware of this problem when he "dries out." If he is not aware of it, then attempts intercourse and discovers a state of apparent impotence, he may be so emotionally frightened by the experience that he either returns to the bottle, or his fear of failure keeps him from attempting sexual intercourse again. If you need more detailed information, Dr. Ed Wheat has a Christian, medically oriented section on impotency in his book *It's Intended for Pleasure,* published by Zondervan.

What does the mind have to do with potency? Almost 90 per cent of impotency is emotional. Your biggest problem once you experience apparent impotency is "fear." Don't allow the fear of failure to dominate your thought. God wants you to have a wonderful, fulfilling sex life, so turn your fear, your problems over to Him, rely on Him. In other chapters we have discussed how to deal with depression, and the answer to fatigue, overwork, obesity are obvious, so no solutions need be discussed here. If you have a relaxed mental attitude and want to give it a try, then go ahead. Tim LaHaye states: "No amount of hormones will cure a man who *thinks* he is impotent."[3]

WHAT ABOUT FRIGIDITY IN THE FEMALE?

Frigidity is basically a meaningless word. It has been used to cover the gamut of subnormal sexual responses of women, from occasionally missing an orgasm to total abstinence from sexual intercourse. Women were created to have regular and frequent orgasms if they so desire. Only in the past few years have physicians and the male populace come to realize what many women knew all along, but were afraid to discuss, and that is that *every female orgasm that occurs is basically clitoral.*

If any one person is responsible for generations of frustrated females, it is dear Dr. Sigmund Freud, who decided after a bit of research that clitoral orgasms were childish, and that when a woman matured, she would put away childish things and only respond to vaginal orgasms. Thank heavens, the subject has finally been taken out of the closet. Reputable studies have been done, and they've all proven the old "master" wrong. The frustration many women have suffered because of this distorted approach is pathetic.

Therefore, men, since so many women still have a problem either never having had an orgasm or only experiencing it on occasion, obviously some of you have approached sex with your thinking in Freudian gear! Most women want to be hugged, kissed, and loved beyond the bedroom door. Far too many ladies complain that the only time their husbands touch them is as a prelude to sex. Women need to feel they are lovable and desirable without those overtures always leading to sex. Touching, long, gentle passionate encounters as foreplay give a female the assurance and feeling of being totally loved. The very closeness of you, the sweet intimacy which develops is very stimulating to her. If you take time to learn your wife's most sensitive body area, then spend time giving her pleasure, what a tremendous experience you will both have. Remember, *every* female orgasm is created by stimulation of the clitoris, either directly or indirectly. Some women experience clitoral stimulation merely through the thrusting movement of the penis in the vagina. But if this were enough to stimulate all women, the problem of so-called frigidity would never have existed. Therefore, for many other women the husband will need to stimulate the clitoris directly with his hand during intercourse. Women who've never experienced orgasm before because they didn't experience it through vaginal penetration have discovered that they weren't alone; many others were "suffering silently" too. It is time husbands realized that they are probably operating under a distorted view of female orgasm. Seek to discover exactly how to bring your wife to the peak of orgasmic pleasure. If that sounds "sinful," it isn't; it is exactly what God meant for it to be—*heavenly!*

WHAT ABOUT SEXUAL FREQUENCY?

There is no standard, no matter what you have read in sex manuals. Certain couples seem to want to, and do, copulate almost every night; other couples, as little as once or twice a week. "What is normal?" God set no norm on this. Make love, enjoy it as often as you like, and don't allow yourself to be influenced into thinking that there is some basic number of times one should copulate because a book or magazine says so. In other words, make love often enough to satisfy your and your mate's desires, because God's Word has warned about defrauding your mate, and how temptation enters a relationship where little physical love is expressed. (I Cor. 7:2–5) If you want to see femininity nipped in the bud, just show me a woman who is ignored, unloved, seldom sees any expression of affection—you might as well shoot her, because emotionally you've already killed her.

Start checking yourself out. If your wife looks like warmed-over death, has severe nervous problems, seems to have lost that youthful spring in her walk, the glow from her face, and somewhere along the way, most of her self-respect, in 99 per cent of the cases you have a love-starved female.

WHAT ABOUT A VASECTOMY?

Just as most sex begins in the mind, the lack of potency because of a vasectomy takes its false roots there also. The operation has nothing at all to do with the way a man feels or performs in sexual union, unless he thinks it will. A vasectomy stops *sperm* flow, not semen. When a couple has completed their family, some choose this as a positive method of permanent birth control; but might I again suggest that you investigate the Natural Family Planning concept, where each mate shares an active, intimate part in the couple's birth-control planning. This method offers a sweet togetherness, which most seem to lack. But if you prefer, there is certainly nothing wrong with having a vasectomy, and it certainly won't affect your sex life at all. For some couples it may be the simplest, safest answer available.

DOES A HYSTERECTOMY AFFECT THE FEMALE CAPACITY FOR SEX?

A hysterectomy no more renders a female less of a woman than would the loss of a finger. Ninety-nine per cent of the problems arising sexually after a hysterectomy are emotional, brought on either by the woman's own fear or by some thoughtless comment by the male.

As we discussed before, the clitoris is the main point of sexual stimulation and this operation has no effect at all on this area. Many women have actually reported higher sexual desires since hysterectomies than at any other time in their lives. I feel much of this desire is based on their being relieved of the fear of pregnancy. As with all areas of sex, sex begins in the mind. When that organ, the brain, is intact, you have no excuse except emotional self-pity, which comes between you and a healthy, fulfilling sex life.

If you have recently faced what women used to feel was the "dread" operation, and you feel incomplete, or if you are facing the prospect of one soon, then you are probably thinking, "Well, Anne, that's fine for you to write all this logic, but you don't really know." Well, I do know. I went through the same thing in my early thirties, and gals, I am functioning as well as ever, if not better. It is all a matter of mental attitude.

IS IT NECESSARY FOR A WOMAN TO HAVE AN ORGASM TO REALLY ENJOY SEX?

Most women aren't going to experience an orgasm every time they have marital relations, throughout their lives. But anyone who says that it isn't really necessary for a woman to experience orgasm to thoroughly enjoy sex as God designed it is usually a selfish male who hasn't the slightest idea what he is talking about. Once you learn how to have an orgasm, you'll probably never go back to thinking: "It is enough to make your mate happy." Making your mate happy, fulfilling him, and gratifying him are important, but it should be a two-way street. If you aren't having orgasms, or are running off to the bathroom to relieve your frustration, now is the time to share with your mate the problems you are experiencing. The two of you should begin to experiment until you come to a point, position, whatever, which is mutually stimulating and capable of bringing you to a climax too.

SEX AND THE TV

Good relationships have been turned into mediocre ones, and bad ones have completely been destroyed because one partner desires to watch the late-night movie, or Johnny Carson (America's answer to contraception). In my estimation, TVs ought to be barred from the bedroom. The longer the boob tube is on, the more physically tired you become, and if nothing else, that is a detriment to a good physical relationship.

Secondly, it is very difficult to be engaging in the most personal, intimate relationship between two creatures of God when in the distance you hear a comedian saying, "It isn't that I have a big nose, it's just that I have a small face." Or what a put-down when one of you peeks over the other's shoulder to see if the butler really did it! In other words, concentration becomes difficult. I'd suggest the TV be placed in the den where it belongs, and replaced with a nice radio or stereo with quiet mood music.

THE SEXUAL WEAPON

Sex is *never, never* ever to be used as a weapon, or for punishment, or manipulation. Recall I Corinthians 7:4–5, that our bodies belong to our mates. If you deny your mate sex for any reason—anger, bitterness, jealousy, guilt—you are acting like a *prostitute.* You are selling your affections for the right reactions, the right privileges or gifts, a changed way of thinking. It is all the same. You are still holding out for a price. If this is the case, your mate may go looking for a better bargain, so don't be guilty of that. You are actually defrauding your mate, and that is a sin in God's eyes.

CAN A WOMAN TAKE THE INITIATIVE SEXUALLY?

Can a woman ever take the initiative sexually? Certainly, she can. It is important to realize that with some men, it is important for her to do so, particularly with the man who is questioning his masculinity, or has a fear of rejection. It would be very encouraging for him to know how much his wife desires him sexually, and he would be assured of not being rejected because she has taken the initiative.

But it is also important again that we keep the balance. Realize that it is fine to take the initiative, but don't go overboard. For example, consider Page, who married a football player, the "catch of the century." Since she entered marriage with an inferiority complex, a feeling of inadequacy, she tried to offset this by being overly aggressive in trying to satisfy Steve. Her approach totally turned him off. Be aware to keep the balance in this area.

REST AND SEX

Keep in mind that having a satisfying sexual relationship takes planning ahead. Think ahead on how you are going to meet your mate's needs. Don't wear yourself out during the day. Women, take a nap. Men, skip that last nine holes on the golf course. Be ready to go to bed when your mate goes. Then when you are together, give your mate your undivided attention. Don't destroy your intimate moments. In the middle of union is no time to ask questions: "Did you remember to feed the cat?" or, "Did you see those grades Jack made on his report card today?" Give your mate your *total* attention. As you take all these things into account, applying all the concepts in this book—especially acceptance, trusting Christ, the Big "I" and communication—you will be able to tip the scales so that you will never have to face adultery in your marriage. Or, if it currently exists, you will become the winner, the survivor, as you come to know how to rightly respond, as you learn what your mate's real needs are. As you are satisfying these areas, your mate will be drawn to you.

In all the areas of sex, particularly the areas where you may currently be having problems, keep in mind Proverbs 11:25 (AMP), which states a concept that I believe you can apply in these situations: "The liberal person shall be enriched, and he who waters shall himself be watered." As you plan how you can fulfill your mate, stimulate his or her desires, how you can make positive plans throughout the day, how you can be most pleasing to your mate, then you will succeed in giving your mate a satisfying experience and enjoy one yourself. There is nothing that brings a person to a fulfilling sexual experience like knowing how exciting, stimulating and satisfying he/she has made the relationship for you.

SUGGESTIONS FOR MAKING YOUR PERSONAL LIFE MORE STIMULATING

(1) Be sure you always have privacy; parents' bedroom door should have a good lock, and use it.

(2) Be sure you start your romance in the morning; set the mood for the day, especially the evening.

(3) Once a week, call and tell your man, or your wife, how exciting and desirable he or she is to you.

(4) Always be prepared for sex, mentally and emotionally.

(5) Never forget that praise goes both ways, and is certainly a strong cornerstone as you build a healthy sexual relationship.

(6) Ladies, buy some new nighties, and before you do, see what your mate prefers. I just discovered while writing this book, that for years I've been wearing the wrong kind. Being tall, I thought I looked glamorous in the long, flowing type. Out of curiosity, I asked Jim which he preferred, and he said, "Baby dolls!"

(7) Guys, surprise her with a get-away weekend for the two of you. Pick a romantic setting—the mountains, a lake, or maybe the seashore. Make this a very special time just for the two of you, and I mean in a pretty motel, with hot and cold water, not in the back of a fishy-smelling camper!

(8) Ladies, begin to consider him, and think about the meals he really prefers, and begin to prepare a very special one; farm the children out for the evening, and have a candlelight dinner alone, or perhaps in front of the fireplace.

(9) Don't let your sexual life get in a rut. Why not try some different rooms, the pool (if it is private), or (at night) a secluded beach.

(10) Set the mood. Some evening, in lieu of the radio, I'd like to suggest two albums or tapes which have soft mood music and the sound of rain falling in the background. They are recorded by the Mystic Moods and are entitled "One Stormy Night" and "One Stormy Weekend." Let me state very clearly, I neither like nor approve of the Mystic Moods' record jackets; on the other hand, why throw the baby out with the bath water?

(11) Depending on your personalities, and your size, and the size of your bathtub, try a double-bubble bath before retiring.

(12) Guys, when you are ready to go out for the evening, try noticing your wife for a change; really give her one of those long stares, the kind you used to. Tell her she's attractive, or her attire is stunning.

(13) Flirt with her in public. I promise you that the reaction when you get home will be beautifully rewarding.

(14) Remember, God created sex for our pleasure and enjoyment. *Don't* make it a time of trying to be absolutely perfect; allow for mistakes. Don't make it a workout in calisthenics; relax and enjoy. In other words, don't keep a sex manual under the bed and pull the thing out every few minutes to be sure you are proceeding on schedule!

(15) Men, please remember special days—Valentine's Day, birthdays, Mother's Day, anniversaries. If you really want to get a loving and devoted response, bring a small present home in remembrance of the day you met, or the day you proposed!

(16) I realize that God created flowers first, but I think maybe He fashioned Eve right beside a flowerbed. It doesn't have to make sense to you, but one of the quickest ways to a woman's heart is through a surprise bouquet of flowers! Try it, and let me know the results.

(17) Ladies, remember the song that was popular a few years ago, "Wives and Lovers"? Get a copy. Those words hold a mountain of truth. Wives should always be lovers too. In fact, a good wife is, as the old saying goes, a lady in the parlor, and a tiger in the bedroom.

(18) Ladies, if your husband travels, as my Jim does, every so often slip little love notes in his suitcase or briefcase before he goes off to work.

(19) Both of you take a minute every month or two and drop a romantic card to your mate.

(20) Women, as we have discussed, men are usually more stimulated by sight and smell than we are. Check with your man before investing in some erotic perfume guaranteed to have him chasing you around the house. Let him smell it first. And you might tell him what kind of after-shave turns you on. Some women are as sensitive to after-shave and cologne as men are. Jim and I have learned the hard way that some fragrances not

only didn't have us chasing each other but almost made us sick to our stomachs.

(21) How about buying some new sheets, perhaps satin or nylon? They are a change for most people and an invitation to more than television watching.

(22) Ladies, in particular (but gentlemen, too), there is nothing that relaxes a tired guy, revitalizes him like a good rubdown.

(23) Some couples have found that soft lights, candles, black lights or smoky mirrors on the ceiling are their forte. The black lights and smoky mirrors are usually preferred by the younger set. Please let me warn you, if mirrors are your thing, have them professionally installed. Improper installation can cause serious injuries.

(24) I have a friend who has made a fake fur throw for her bed. Her husband thought it was delicious—particularly with her in it.

(25) Ladies, leave the curlers and facial cream for when he is out of town or after he leaves for work.

(26) As we have discussed before, for both of you, give your mate a new body to respond to, a new you. Take off any extra weight. You'll look better, feel better and certainly be more confident. A new body will be a magnet to your mate because it is a new and unknown entity.

(27) If your city is large enough, you probably have a club of some sort that for a small fee supplies you with discounts at many of the best restaurants, theaters, and dinner theaters. This is a good way to stay within the budget, and still have a special evening out—one a week if possible.

I could write a complete chapter on ideas and suggestions I've either read or heard of, but I think the above are about standard, without getting into some of the ridiculous ideas I've had passed on to me while writing this book.

Most important is really coming to understand God's viewpoint on the marital relationship. I think Tim and Beverly LaHaye sum this point up well when they say: "*Everything* a Christ-controlled Christian does is spiritual. That includes eating, elimination, spanking children, or emptying the trash. Why isolate sex in marriage as if it were in a category all by itself? Many spiritual Christians pray before going to bed, then in a matter of minutes engage each other in foreplay, stimulation, coitus, and finally orgasm. Why isn't that just as spiritual as anything else couples do? In fact, we believe the more truly spiritual they are, the more loving and affectionate they will be with each other and consequently the more frequently they will make love. Actually, coitus should be the ultimate expression of a rich spiritual experience that continues to enrich the couple's relationship."[4]

GOALS: The goal of this chapter is to help you understand God's viewpoint on the marital act better, to bring you to the divine balance that He would have for you in this, one of His most beautiful gifts to His children. Hopefully, it has helped you learn how to better give and receive pleasure, and express your love and oneness of soul in a physical way, which you might not have truly understood before. Most of all, I pray that after reading and understanding this chapter, your physical union will become a relaxed and enjoyable one.

ASSIGNMENTS:

(1) Read Genesis 1:27 and 31, Song of Solomon 6:1–10 and 7:1–4, Hebrews 13:4, I Corinthians 6:16–20, Proverbs 6:32, I Corinthians 7:2–5, Ephesians 5:21–33.

(2) Memorize I Corinthians 7:3–5.

(3) Begin today to add newness to your marital life by saying or doing the unexpected. Use one of the suggestions to add spice to your sex life.

(4) Learn Satan's distortions, and flee from them.

(5) If you have had a wrong view of sex, misused it, denied your mate, or been involved in distorted sex, go to your Heavenly Father, confess your mistake, claim I John 1:9 and open your eyes to the exciting relationship He has created for you.

(6) If you continue to have problems in the bedroom, review the preceding chapters to be sure that you are applying God's concepts correctly, and that no jealousy, bitterness, manipulation, or the like have crept through the bedroom door.

(7) Men, please throw out your Freudian ideas and be man enough to realize that you may not have learned all there is to know about sex in the locker room. Ask the Lord to give

you an open mind in this area, and begin to read Christian books on the subject, and learn, for your sake and your wife's.

(8) No matter how much both of you think you know, a review of any subject usually adds knowledge. I would *highly* recommend that you secure a copy of Tim and Beverly LaHayes' *The Act of Marriage,* published by Zondervan, 1976, and *It's Intended for Pleasure,* Dr. Ed Wheat and Gale Wheat, Revell, 1977. I think these are the most thorough and *complete* Christian books on sex currently on the market. Read them together! (In recommending any book, in writing any word, I feel that the Lord holds me directly responsible. Therefore I must add this footnote concerning the LaHaye book. I find only one area that we disagree in, and if it were not such a vital area I would overlook it. I *do not* agree with the LaHayes' position on abortion. I feel the Word has more to say on the subject than they allude to.)

CHAPTER 9

PROBLEM: THE BIG "I"

Symptoms

A stubborn spirit	Critical or cynical attitudes
An unforgiving nature	Loneliness
Rebellion to God's authority	Withdrawal and daydreaming
Restlessness and frustration	

In the preceding chapters we have discussed many concepts from God's Word which, when applied, can transform your marital relationship from frantic to fulfilling. As you begin to learn and apply these concepts to your daily life and relationship, you may find yourself wondering, "What concept applies in this situation?" or "I don't recall God's command in this instance." Certainly learning and applying a different way of acting and reacting doesn't become habit overnight. But once you have become acquainted with the Big "I," you will discover that deciding what to do, how to react, how to relate, and most of all, how to love, is much simpler.

Most of us stood at the altar, riding high on the emotion called "love." Few of us saw marriage beyond the vine-covered cottage of Hollywood dreams. There was hardly a thing we wouldn't do for our lover, and he or she for us. But when honeymoon time was over and the enchantment began to dull, the Big "I" began to surface. All of a sudden, we wished someone had told us about the routine of housework, the responsibility of supporting a family, the 2 A.M. feedings, mortgages, and the rest.

Women discovered that Mr. Wonderful has a habit of leaving the dresser drawers pulled out, closet doors open, newspapers all over the den floor. Perhaps he doesn't have the social or financial aspirations you desire, he's often late to dinner, he leaves most of the responsibility of the children on your back, and in general expects much more than you ever anticipated giving. You guys sadly discover that Baby Doll isn't always "in the mood," is dedicated to the constant use of credit cards, never learned how to cook, greets you each evening with an endless list of complaints, and basically asks more of you than you want to give. You have decided that marriage isn't what it was cracked up to be. You want more out of life than this, and to be frank, you want out. Congratulations, you have just met the Big "I."

There are no marital problems that do not involve the Big "I." Most divorces happen because of the Big "I." "*I* can't stand this situation any longer. *I* want my freedom again. *I* don't love my mate any more. *I* didn't know what my mate was really like. *I* don't have anything in common with my mate. *I* don't find our sexual life exciting any longer. *I* can't stand the responsibilities of marriage. *I* love someone else." Who are all these comments concerned with? The Big "I."

Self-centeredness, the Big "I," is not only disastrous to the marital relationship, but its side effects can be emotionally crippling. The Big "I" can be born of a stubborn spirit that wants only its own way; when its wants aren't fulfilled, unforgiveness begins to breed. A life-stifling loneliness grows and ofttimes drowns itself in self-pity. As loneliness and/or self-pity are allowed to fester, often we withdraw into ourselves to avoid more pain and disappointment. Depression occurs, we consult a physician, take tranquilizers, but continue to sink because we haven't taken care of the root of the problem. We give way to daydreaming about how things should be, could be, or might have been. Perhaps in a lonely moment we reach out for God's Word, looking for an answer, only to find that He commands us to *give,* and we turn deeper inward, refusing God's solutions, rebelling against His authority. The cycle becomes endless. Restlessness and frustration surface.

We feel like the Psalmist when he cried: "My tears have been my food day and night, while they keep on saying to me, 'Where is your God?' These things I would remember and pour out my inner soul, for I used to walk on with the throng in their van to the house of God, with the voice of joy and praise, a multitude that kept festival. Why are you bowed down, O my soul; why so restless within me . . . ?" (Ps. 42:3 AMP) At this point many decide the only answer to their pathetic lives is divorce.

But there are other solutions which are more fulfilling to you as a person, and you as a Christian. Christ says in Matthew 11:28–30 (Berkley): "Come to Me all you who labor and are heavily burdened, and I will give you rest . . . For My yoke is easy and My burden is light." You see, any time we are ready to let go, He is ready to take over.

Now you are faced with some choices. Have your solutions solved your problems? Have rebellion and withdrawal been fulfilling? Did the pills bring lasting answers? Do you want to continue in this maddening cycle? Are you really enjoying your misery? Or, do you want to be God's child and rest in His love, assured that His answers always work, that He loves you more than you love yourself, and that whatever He asks will be for your good? God is a gentleman. He won't force His concepts, His answers on you, but if you so choose, *all you have to do is ask.*

Now that you understand that the root problem is the Big "I," we can go right to the Scriptures and find its cause. Proverbs 11:24–25 (Berkley) says: "There is one who gives liberally, yet he grows richer, and one who withholds what he should give, and suffers want. The charitable soul will be enriched, and he who waters, will himself be watered." If you are as dry as a bone, then obviously you have been more concerned with getting watered than in watering. "But wait a minute. Why should I give? Why should I care? I mean, my mate doesn't do anything for me." You see who you are still concerned with? You are still focusing on *getting*. Luke 6:32–33 (AMP) tells us: "If you (merely) love those who love you, what quality of credit and thanks is that to you? For even the (very) sinners love their lovers—those who love them. And if you are kind and good and do favors to and benefit those who are kind and good and do favors to and benefit you, what quality of credit and thanks is that to you? For even the pre-eminently sinful do the same."

To begin to rebuild your marriage, to rekindle your love, you must first die to self, and that is often a painful experience, but the rewards are tremendous. (Eph. 4:22–24) Luke 6:35–36 (AMP) says: "But love your enemies, and be kind and do good—*doing favors so that someone derives benefit from them; and lend expecting and hoping for nothing in return,* but *considering nothing as lost and despairing of no one;* and *then your recom-*

pense (your reward) will be great–rich, strong, intense and abundant–and you will be sons of the Most High; for He is kind and charitable and good to the ungrateful and the selfish and wicked. So be merciful–sympathetic, tender, responsive and compassionate–even as your Father is (all these)."

When I say you must die to self, I mean that God's directives, His commandments, His desires must become more important than your own–as He daily leads you, as you allow Him to mold and conform you to His image.

You must also give Him your expectations and desires. Almost every little girl has dreamed of her knight in shining armor, and every boy his fairy princess. If you continue to carry unrealistic expectations into your relationship, trying to force your mate into a mold no human can fill, then you are dealing a death blow to your relationship. The best marriages are still made up of two human beings, and as much as they may love each other, at some time, at some place, they will disappoint one another. Your stability *must* be dependent on who and what Christ is, not who and what your mate is. "For (as far as this world is concerned) you have died, and your (new, real) life is hid in Christ." (Col. 3:3 AMP) When you can incorporate this into your life, *then everything in your relationship will become a bonus and a reward,* because you will be relating to your mate as Christ does to us—*giving everything, expecting nothing.* This is one of the most *vital concepts;* it can change your marital relationship from hell to heavenly. *Please* reread this paragraph and ask Christ to open your heart and soul to teach you these deep truths. Then pray and fully read John 14:6; 16:21, 23; 15:4–12.

Most people enter marriage thinking about those things in the relationship that will make them happy and fulfill *them.* If your thought patterns don't change, you'll soon become disappointed. You will become frustrated because all your dreams, your desires, aren't being satisfied. From your standpoint, you probably will feel that if your mate would change, everything would be wonderful. For your relationship to be saved, *you* have to move from these unrealistic desires and expectations to the opposite end of the pole . . . in essence, stop being consumed with self.

Happiness and contentment come when you turn your desires over to Christ. Psalms 37:4 (Berkley): "Have your delight in the

Lord and He will give you the desires of your heart." Now that Christ is in control of your desires, you are free to satisfy the wants and needs of your mate.

You may think that you don't fall in this category, that perhaps selfishness isn't a problem in your relationship. But whose desires and wishes do you consider when you accept or reject a social engagement? When you are thinking about buying a new car, do you consider the family, or trot out and buy that sporty model you have been wanting since you were a kid? When you ladies select clothes, do you consider what your husband would like to see you in, or what you want to be seen in? Men, when you plan the family vacation to include only camping and fishing, whose desires are at the top of the list? When you plan a dinner party, do you invite those you wish to visit with, or those your mate would prefer to spend an evening with? Have you disciplined yourself well enough that you have a relaxed time for each other in the evenings?

Because of our sin nature, all of us tend to look out for "old number one." Yet, we have the perfect example of love shared many times throughout the Scriptures, and the heart of every verse is "give."

If you often fall into this trap, congratulations, you can join the rest of us humans. As you are first learning and applying God's concepts, keep the Big "I" in the front of your checklist. When your memory fails you about what to do, how to react, always remember: "Who am I really thinking about, caring about, or considering in this situation? Is it my mate and our relationship, or the Big 'I'?" Before you open your mouth, before you make a decision, go through this quick checklist: (1) Who is in control of my life—me or Christ? (2) If I am in control, use I John 1:9 and get back into fellowship before you move on. (3) Who are you thinking of? Is this decision best for me or my mate? In essence, is the basis of my decision the Big "I" or my mate's feelings, thoughts, wants, interests, or comfort? As you are obedient to Christ's directions for interrelating, He will abundantly fulfill you. (Eph. 3:20)

I like the way Mary Cholmondeley expresses it: "Letting out the reins—Every year I live I am more convinced that the waste of life lies in *the love we have not given, the powers we have not used,* the *selfish prudence* that will risk nothing, and which, shirking pain, misses happiness as well. No one ever yet was the poorer in the long run for having once in a lifetime 'let out all the length of all the reins.' "[1]

Selfishness is the root destroyer of marriage. Honestly begin to analyze your true basis for decisions. If you are completely honest with yourself, you will quickly realize that much of the time your marital problems are rooted in selfishness. *Don't* concern yourself with your mate's selfish actions; turn his/her actions and responses over to God. Proverbs 21:1 (LVB): "Just as water is turned into irrigation ditches, so the Lord directs the king's thoughts. He turns them wherever he wants to." Leave the directing of your mate to the Father. God is concerned with what you do and why. Proverbs 21:2 (LVB): "We can justify our every deed but God looks at our motives." Know that God is concerned with the motives of your heart, and as you become more and more sensitive to the Holy Spirit, He will make you more aware of areas where you are putting the Big "I" first. As far as your mate is concerned, God can work more quickly when you are allowing Him to work to mold *you* daily into the likeness of Christ. Your mate is God's responsibility, and you can leave him/her in God's hands, knowing that He is faithful and capable in and through all situations.

GOALS: To daily stay in God's Word. (Ps. 119:11) Learn more of Him so that you can become the wife or husband that He created you to be. Daily give your hopes and expectations for your mate to God and then step back trusting in Psalms 37:4–5.

ASSIGNMENTS:

(1) Memorize Luke 6:31, Colossians 2:7, Colossians 3:17.

(2) Using I John 1:9, confess your areas of selfish, unrealistic expectations to the Lord. Ask Him to change your direction, your desires, and to give you His peace right in the situation that you are in. (Phil. 4:6–7)

(3) Read John 15:1–12.

(4) Moment by moment, consider each thought and action and analyze, "Who am I thinking about—me or my mate?"

(5) Remember daily that the most we can give to another is ourselves. Keep your priorities in order so that you will

begin to have more time to spend on things your mate would enjoy.

(6) Each day try to discover some unique need or desire of your mate's and do your best to fulfill it.

CHAPTER 10

REKINDLING THE FLAMES

"But we just don't love each other any more," you say. "There are no feelings left. You can't rekindle the dead embers of a dead love." How often I've heard this cry. But, would you believe, after a couple really understands what love is, they can learn to love again? The "feeling" they are frantically searching for returns. Remember what God said about real love in the Song of Solomon 8:7 (AMP): "Many waters cannot quench love, neither can floods drown it . . ." I Corinthians 13:8 (AMP) says: "Love never fails—never fades out or becomes obsolete or comes to an end . . ." And Song of Solomon 8:6 (AMP): ". . . for love is strong as death . . ."

I know you are thinking: "If God is right, then I guess we never loved each other, because obviously our love has come to an end." Maybe what you called "love" has temporarily faded, but I imagine what you are calling "love" is really "feeling." This is not the type of love the Scripture speaks about. In our modern society we have developed a distorted picture of love. We seem to feel that love is something that uncontrollably happens to us—rather like getting high. But, like getting high, this Hollywood type of love always ends in a downer. Love isn't a "feeling" you conjure up while sitting under the stars, or that swoops down on you on a moonlight cruise. It isn't remembering "your song," or making out in the back seat of a car.

True love isn't panting and drooling after one of the opposite sex. Nor is love actually any form of touching or embracing, although it can be expressed that way.

Remember Todd Winters discussing this point in his story. If you will recall, he said that they had to "learn" to love all over again. Their prior relationship had been based on "feeling" and it had failed, but when they were reunited, they were so excited about the Lord, they got right into the Scriptures and God showed them what *real* love was. I'm sure those of you who have been terribly hurt, particularly through marital unfaithfulness, probably feel dead inside right now. The experience of pain, fear, rejection has pushed whatever "love" feelings you once had to the farthest part of your mind and heart. You've probably come to the point that you are afraid to feel, afraid to care. Now you think that what used to be can never be revived. Maybe what used to be shouldn't be revived; perhaps it should be replaced with the *real* thing this time. As far as your feelings are concerned (Todd and Melony Winters can tell you; so can Pamela and Howard; and yes, Anne and Jim also), however dead you feel inside, no matter how large the stockpile of fear, bitterness, and resentment is, love, *real* love, can be revived. We are just a few of the living examples of how, when God's concepts are applied, miracles can happen in marriage, and in our case, even after divorce. Believe us, with God *nothing* is impossible. Jesus said in Luke 18:27 (AMP): "But He said, 'What is impossible with men is possible with God.'" (Gen. 18:14 and Jer. 32:17)

You may think that love has died, but still the desire to save your marriage burns on. In marriage, love builds on love, and it doesn't go away just because of one evening of infidelity, one fight that got out of hand, or any other overt happening.

The "feeling" that you called love may have disappeared, but that is *no excuse to split and run.* God says that we must *learn* to love. Sound strange? It certainly did to me when I first encountered it in the Word. "Learn to love? Why, that is the silliest thing I ever heard of," you are thinking. If love were automatic, if it were the type of instantaneous feeling that movies depict and songs are written about, how could God command it? He couldn't. God isn't in the business of commanding "feelings"; He is in the business of commanding *actions.* He makes this command clear in John 13:34 (AMP): "I give you a new commandment, that you should love one another; just as I have loved you, so you too should love one another." Ephesians 5:2 speaks of walking in love, and Matthew 19:19 commands love. If love were feeling first, God certainly would not have commanded it.

In the intimate relationship of marriage, God again commands love in Ephesians 5:25 (AMP): "Husbands, *love* your wives, as Christ loved the church and gave Himself up for her." He says to the wives in Ephesians 5:33 (AMP): ". . . and let the wife see that she respects and reverences her husband—that she notices him, regards him, honors him, prefers him, venerates and esteems him: and that she defers to him, praises him, and *loves* and admires him exceedingly." Some of you are thinking, "That certainly does it. I could never love my mate that way. God is asking the impossible this time." Before you start looking for that scriptural loophole, remember that the Lord also commanded us to love our enemies! There is no way out, friend or foe. We are admonished to *love*.

Now, before you panic, remember that God would never command us to do something that He didn't provide a way to fulfill. (Phil. 1:6) He has clearly taught us, through His own example, exactly what "real" love is. Now, if you still want to split and run, if you persist in failing in your marital obligations, remember that you are rebelling against God. Hebrews 12:6 (AMP) tells us: "For the Lord corrects and disciplines everyone whom He loves . . ." Scripture goes on to say in Proverbs 11:29 (AMP): "He who troubles his own house shall inherit the wind."

Now that you feel I have placed you between a rock and the proverbial hard place, let me continue for one more thought. Perhaps you feel that God is directing you to "seek" happiness, "seek" love, "seek" pleasure and fulfillment. In a sense He is, but He doesn't intend for you to pursue these things directly. Love, happiness, fulfillment, etc., are all by-products of a life in right relationship to Christ. He reminds us: "Seek ye first the kingdom of God, and all these *things* will be added unto you." He states in Psalms 37:4 (AMP): "Delight yourself also in the Lord, and He will give you the desires and secret petitions of your heart." That is, delight yourself in Him, not in your desires, and then He can fulfill Ephesians 3:20 (AMP): ". . . Now to Him Who by the (action of His) power that is at work within us, is able to (carry out His purpose and) do *superabundantly, far over* and above all that we (dare) ask or think—infinitely beyond our highest prayers, desires, thoughts, hopes or dreams." Isn't that fantastic?

Now that you understand that you aren't to make a mad dash to pursue the "elusive butterfly of love," let's learn what God actually had in mind when He commanded us to love. He said in John 15:12 (AMP): "This is My commandment, that you love one another (just) as I have loved you."

Let's take a moment and analyze exactly how did, and does, God love us. Certainly, He doesn't just love us with some whooped-up mushy feeling. When we turn to the Scriptures, they describe His love. John 3:16 (NIV): "For God so loved the world that He *gave* His one and only Son . . ." John 1:12 (AMP): ". . . He *gave* the authority to become the children of God . . ." Galatians 2:20 (AMP): ". . . Who loved me and *gave* Himself up for me." Matthew 7:7 (AMP): "Keep on asking and it will be *given* you . . ." I could go on, but I think you get the point. Love, throughout the Scriptures, is umbilically bound with *giving*.

Remember, what you thought was "love" was feeling, and *feeling is always self-centered,* looking out for what *I* want, what *I* can get; whereas *love is always other-centered.* When you read the Scriptures about Christ's love, Christ's giving, keep in mind that none of these are preceded by "if you feel like it." Old actions and reactions will have to be changed, but you know that it is possible, because Christ said so in I Corinthians 10:13. Certainly, thinking of your mates first, of their needs, their wants, their desires, won't come easily. To begin with, you will certainly have to make it a conscious part of your thinking and your actions. But, remember that Christ never said, "Feel, then do"; He said, "Do, give," and in time, the "feeling" will be the by-product of the action.

Think about some of the people you have read about in this book and recall how they went from a state of mental estrangement, through Christ, to a state of real love—which was followed by the "feelings" we human beings call love.

I can personally testify to a time in my life when I never thought I would have any type of "feeling" for Jim again. But, as I learned how to be the right kind of a wife, when I became more interested in giving than getting, things changed. There are days now when I'd almost like to "attack" him when he walks in the door. He has again become to me the most interesting, stimulating, desirable man on earth. You can experience this in your relationship too.

In our relationship with our mates, we give, we do, we interact in a spirit of love, not because we expect to get, but because *God said to. Don't get your priorities mixed up.* We are not to be obedient in order to obtain a desired end. We are to obey because God has commanded it, because we know that He knows what is ultimately best for us. If your giving is with an attitude of expecting to get, it will be fake, and it will neither be honoring to the Lord, nor help the growth of true love in your relationship.

"Well, Anne, the whole thing makes sense, but I don't think I can pull it off," you say. You are exactly right. God never expects you to take His commandments, His concepts, and try to make them work on your own strength. When we are in Christ, we have the very Spirit of Him living within us, always ready to be our source, our strength, our power, to love when we don't "feel" like it, to give, to share, to risk; He is only waiting for *you* to let Him.

Now that you understand what true love is, now that you know that even though you can't, Christ can, you are ready to begin. If you haven't been accepting your mate just as he/she is, with God's help begin. If you have avoided conversations with your mate which made you uncomfortable, begin. Learn to be a giver by listening, really listening to what your mate says, the desires and fears he/she has. Particularly study the fifth chapter of Ephesians, which discusses a husband's and wife's responsibilities.

WIVES, REMEMBER

Wives, if your home hasn't been the clean, relaxed place your husband would want to come home to, give of yourself and change it. Set your priorities in order, and the housework and the extras will fall into their correct place. Become inventive in the kitchen, in your interests, in your conversations and in the bedroom. Think of all those things that he has been asking you to do for so long; make a list and get them done. Don't just dress up for an evening out with friends; remember to keep yourself attractive at home. *Your husband is the most important person in the world.* He is the one you want to impress. Remember, when you were dating, those special things that made your man happy? Put them back into practice. If you want a never-ending honeymoon, get yourself ready for one, and act as if you were on onc.

If over the years the pounds have caught up with you, there is a four-letter word that you should seriously consider: *diet.*

If I hit a touchy subject there, let me share a secret about dieting that I found most useful. Number one: to please your husband, you are responsible for keeping yourself looking as nice as possible. Extra pounds never look good in the latest fashions. I know the old joke, "There is just more girl to love," but most men don't seek out this type, and you know that. Since I hit my thirties, I have had a constant battle with the bulges. For many reasons, most of which were merely excuses to indulge myself, I became a confirmed eataholic! Just knowing that those extra pounds weren't good for my health didn't motivate me. Being tall, I was able to hide a good bit of weight, until finally Jim said, "I am ashamed to be seen with you." That should have done it, but mentally it didn't. I rationalized, "Well, who is he to talk? A little dieting wouldn't hurt him either." At first, I had feelings of resentment and rebellion. Then the Lord reminded me that I could always know His leading through Jim. I thought, "Maybe the Lord is trying to tell me something. Certainly if Jim wants me to lose weight, and the Lord says I am to obey Jim, then if I refuse, I am really refusing to obey the Lord!" That sank in.

As my thoughts continued, I recalled my past impressions of Christian women (long-faced little old ladies with their hair in buns and dowdy dark dresses). I realized then that not only did I have a responsibility to please Jim, but I was a representative of Jesus Christ, and as His representative I had the responsibility of looking the very best I could. I didn't want others to see me and think, as I had once, that Christianity couldn't be much fun, since most of the Christian women I encountered as a child looked as if they spent most of their time eating—probably because that was the most exciting thing they could do. If you need to diet, get with it, don't cop out with excuses. Remember, even in dieting, with Christ all things are possible. I was sharing with a friend the other day my attitude about dieting. I told her, "It can be summed up in a few words, Jackie. I diet as unto the Lord, and it works."

Men, "diet" isn't reserved for "women only." Stop for a minute, go look in the mirror; turn sideways. Do you look as though you just ingested a ripe watermelon? Does your stomach hang so far over your pants that you've quit wearing a belt because no one would see it? Are you carrying so many extra pounds that your chin looks like a turkey wattle and your legs chafe when you walk? Be honest, would you like your wife to take care of her figure like you do yours? Believe it or not, guys, we women care just as much about the excess inches around your waist as you do about ours. Do us both a favor, get back in shape—for us, for yourself, for your health.

Ask your man what type of hairstyle he likes, and if it is at all possible with your hair, get it, do it, and keep it. I used to have waist-length hair, but because Jim never said he liked it, I presumed he didn't care and I cut it all off. After a couple of years of a little boy haircut, which I enjoyed very much because it was so easy to keep, Jim finally said, "I wish you would let your hair grow out." I could have screamed. All those years he had liked the long hair, and because of a lack of communication, I never knew it. You can see from my picture on the back of the book that I am letting my hair grow out again. Of course, we have agreed that waist-length hair at my age is a bit much, but now he is happy. Of course, the long hair used to take much of my time, but like everything in our lives, I knew the Lord wanted me to please Jim. But I also knew that He wouldn't have me spend the time it used to take me to keep such a mass of hair, so I prayed about it. I told Him, "Lord, now You know what Jim wants me to do with my hair, and You know that it used to take up much of my time just fixing it. If You want me to let it grow out, I'm trusting that You will let me find a style and a cut that won't consume much of my time." He did!

When I wrote the first draft of this book, I didn't write about gifts because I didn't want anyone to presume I was suggesting that one of your aims in being the right kind of wife is to get material things. But so many ladies have asked me to speak on this point that I will take a moment to do so. First of all, men are not the creatures of detail and remembrance that we are. Often they would be, but their minds are full of other duties and they simply forget. Making them feel that your heart has been broken for life doesn't make the situation better; it only makes them feel guilty, and you miserable. In a million other ways they say they love you, by providing for you, by loving you, by protecting you. If you happen to be married to a "forgetter," can't you at least allow him one human error? Secondly, you never get by asking, hinting, or nagging. Remember, a gift represents the fact that he thought about you, whether it is a toaster or a mink coat. I have reminded the men that often we women would prefer more personal items, but whatever he gives you—from the most beautiful diamond ring, the latest in fry pans, to a dress or pants suit that you'd rather not be caught dead in—be thankful, be gracious, *use it, wear it,* and let him know how much you appreciate his remembering you. His remembering you is the point, not the present; whether it is just a card or something expensive isn't the issue; *the thought is what counts and nothing else.*

If you are the type who takes every present back and exchanges it for something else, don't expect him to continue to give. You are, in essence, putting him and his taste down, and lady, you are in trouble. *Never* say, "Oh dear, this is really nice, but I was down at the store the other day, and I saw a dress I just really loved. Would you mind terribly if I took this one back and exchanged it for the one I saw?" Obviously, he liked the dress he bought you, so who are you thinking about—his likes, desires, feelings, or the Big "I"? Make it a basic policy that you only make exchanges when you are given items which actually don't fit. Then try to get a dress or whatever like the one he picked out if at all possible.

Now for those ladies who say, "But he never remembers, he never buys me anything. What do I do?" Again, remember that men and women are different, and it will take him time to become the thoughtful husband that God created him to be. Meantime, you become the kind of wife he cares so much for, thinks about so often, that he will begin to remember. And when he does, no matter *what it is,* you react as if he has just given you the crown jewels. As you become the wife he needs, the helpmate he wants, those little remembrances will come your way, but you must be that right woman first.

Just consider this: who in the world wants to give to a wife who is a dowdy mess in a filthy house with a nagging mouth? Or, do you think the desire to give grows in a heart that is being pushed to be something different?

I experienced the difference in Jim, from our last marriage to this, in the giving department. In the ten years of our first marriage, I can't recall anything he gave me that ever cost more than twenty-five dollars, and I think his mother dragged him out and had him buy that. Of course, the cost isn't the issue, but most birthdays were forgotten, anniversaries were never remembered, and I think if I'd gotten a card from him I'd have dropped dead. Since we've been remarried and I've learned to be the kind of wife he needs, the kind of wife God created all of us to be, you can't imagine the difference.

We had sold our old home and had been living in an apartment for three years while we looked for a new one. I looked in a medium-price range which I felt would be comfortable for us, and Jim kept saying no. I couldn't understand and began to feel he just didn't want the responsibility of a home, and that we'd be stuck in that "cotton picking" apartment the rest of our lives. But guess what? Instead of the nice little houses I kept picking out, he went out and chose the kind of house I had always wanted but never dreamed we would have (see Eph. 3:20).

Often we put our man down with comments like, "Oh dear, we can't afford that." What you can and can't afford is *his* responsibility, not yours. I kept looking at extremely practical things, not wanting to put pressure on Jim. But what Jim was hearing me say was, "You can't afford to provide for me in the manner most of our friends live." I don't mean to imply that you are to suggest the most expensive things. But let your man do that if it is his desire. And if he does, don't put a damper on things with the "We can't afford it" bit. There is no point in continuing the list of things Jim has graciously given me. Naturally, the value of the gift isn't the issue. The point is, he remembers. Sometimes he gets busy and forgets until the last minute, and then runs to the drugstore and just picks up a card, but you had better believe I cherish that card as much as everything else he has done, or ever will do for me.

Patience, ladies. These miracles didn't happen overnight, and on occasion he'll forget, just like you do. Don't put so much emphasis on material things; they never made anyone really happy. The nice house, fine car, and lovely clothes would be nothing without him. He is the issue; not what he can, will, or wants to give you. The fact that he has given you him is enough. It should be enough for all of us.

Whatever your man's interest is, whether it's politics, golf, fishing, football, the stock market, begin to learn about it. Some of you will discover those "Sunday games" that you used to hate can become a real time of togetherness for you. I didn't say that you would ever come to love his interest as he does; that isn't the point. You do it because you love him, and these interests are part of him. Don't complain about communication if all you ever discuss with him are problems with the children, what the neighbors are doing, or what went on at the local garden club. If you are honest in wanting to become a part of his interests, believe me, in time he will bubble over sharing with you all the things about them you don't understand. You will discover, as he will, that if you care enough to study his interests, to communicate better with him, to make his life more enjoyable, he will respond with such love that you'll feel like praying, "Lord, stop for a minute. You are about to bless the socks off me."

There are many other areas. As you are available to the Holy Spirit, He will continue to bring new ideas to your mind.

Wives, as you read the next section, which deals with God's directives to the husband, don't be misled into thinking that since God placed the direct responsibility of the family on the husband's shoulders, that this is your loophole to cop out on your job. God holds *you* responsible for becoming the right kind of loving, caring, respectful, obedient wife in His eyes. He never said, "You are only responsible to do this if your husband contributes to the relationship, or if your husband is a Christian, or if you feel like it." He directed us to learn His concepts for us as women, to put them into practice in our marriage relationship, as a service to Him. As we are doing this daily, striving daily to become the wives God intended us to be, then in the process He will have the opportunity to do everything possible to heal the wounds in our marital relationships.

HUSBANDS, REMEMBER

Husbands, in Ephesians Christ places the major responsibility of a loving home atmosphere on you! If there is strife in your home, if your children are disobedient, whatever is the problem, remember Christ placed *you* in the position of leadership, and as the president of the corporation, you are also responsible for the condition of it. This doesn't mean that you are to force changes through anger, brutality, or bullishness. It is your responsibility, in love, to gently, lovingly lead your family back to harmony. Reread I John 4:19 (AMP): "We love Him, because He first loved us." *You* are to take the initial action. Don't sit around waiting for the right reactions, just keep on keeping on, and the love will begin to flow.

Men, if you aren't the head of the house as the Scriptures describe, then you are putting untold burdens on your wife. "But she likes to run things," you complain. She may think that she likes to run things because she has had no other choice for so long, or because you have been so irresponsible that she has felt that she had to take over. Either way, she is carrying a burden which God never intended her to assume, and it is *your* place to take over.

If you have a complaining wife, listen the next time she starts in on you and see what she is *really* saying. Is she reminding you about that hole in the screen door that she told you about last winter, and now flies are getting in the house? Who is at fault? It was your responsibility in the first place to keep the house in good repair. Perhaps in your neglect of your male duties around the house, you have created the "complainer" that you now think you can't live with.

If every evening about the time you sit down to read the newspaper, your wife comes up wanting to talk, and you respond with a couple of bored "yeahs" and she starts screaming that you never listen to her, goes into a lecture about the children, the house and her needs, then stomps out—guess what? You have one frustrated wife. Next week she'll probably run out and start marching for Women's Lib, and then you will really have a rebellion on your hands.

Men, whether you know it or not, some things about housework and child care are less than exciting. Sometimes, after spending the day talking to a two-year-old, it would be refreshing to have an adult respond to you once in a while. I'm not complaining; I wouldn't exchange places with my man for all the tea in China. I know I am just exactly where the Lord wants me to be, and probably your wife does too. But once in a while we do like to talk, to share with someone who understands more than "See Dick run, watch Puff play."

Men, when you come in, greet your wife as you used to when you were dating. I don't care if she looks like warmed-over death. Maybe that was the kind of day she had, or maybe there is no excuse for it at all. But you take care of your responsibility, which is to love her, and see the response you will get. Some men give their *dogs* more attention, petting, and love than they do their wives, and that is the truth. A woman is like a flower; if you'd like to see that lovely young flower you first met, begin to water the garden with a kiss, a hug, loving words, and just watch how the flower will blossom. When a woman is appreciated, she is inspired to do more and more, to look better and *better*. Let her know that you are glad to be home with her, that you are looking forward to spending the evening with her, and then give her a hug, a kiss, a swat on the bottom, whatever is your own private message of love. Set aside a time in your evening when she *knows* that you are going to be *totally* available to listen to her. Believe me, men, the dinner will be better, you can throw out the Pepto/Tums, she won't be interrupting you any more, and the walls will begin to come tumbling down.

Don't wait until your wife gets as frustrated as one woman I read about. The story said, "A housewife called the Sanitation Department to pick up a dead mule in front of her house. The Department sent several men and a truck, but suddenly she changed her mind. She asked the men to take the mule upstairs and put it in the bathtub. 'I'll give you ten dollars each for doing it,' she said. They didn't understand it, but after all, ten dollars is ten dollars, and so up to the bathroom it went. Afterward, they asked, 'Why, ma'am, did you want the mule in the bathtub?' 'Well,' she said, 'my husband has come home every night for thirty-five years and pulled off his coat and shoes, grabbed the newspaper, sat down in his easy chair, and said, "What's new?" So tonight I'm going to tell him.'"

If your home usually looks like a tornado has hit it, perhaps your wife's mother never taught her how to manage a home, or perhaps she has no incentive to make your home respectable.

Just as you need encouragement and compliments when you finally land that big account, so does your wife. She has struggled all day, thoroughly cleaning a room, just to have everyone come in, say nothing, and begin messing it up all over again. Perhaps if she were complimented once in a while, perhaps if everyone would assume their *own responsibilities* and pick up after themselves, she might be encouraged to move on to another room. I doubt that you men are aware of it, but picking up those things left around the house by husbands and children is one of the most time-consuming and discouraging jobs there is.

Most men take their wives' housework for granted, yet expect praise for the job they do. Do you realize that she may be needing just that praise to get her started? Begin by encouraging her to put the den in order, and when she does, praise her, and the room. Maybe the next day you might do a few little things in the living room or dining room, and as she sees that you really care what the house looks like, as you encourage and praise her, your castle will sparkle like a diamond.

When things finally get in order, be sure that you keep *your* part straight—newspapers picked up, ashtrays emptied, office work where it belongs—and make sure that the children do the same. This transformation shouldn't take much time. Then encourage her by saying something like, "Gee, honey, things look so nice, why don't we have some friends over for a get-together?"

Remember, God said: "Husbands, love your wives, even as Christ also loved the church." I know some of you are thinking, if I really reacted to my wife as the Scriptures say, she would turn into a lazy, spoiled, self-centered female. Wrong! God would never have commanded you to do something that would create a monster like that. What will happen is, you will see a God-created miracle right before your eyes. You won't believe how your woman will respond in joy, abound in love, and revere and honor you.

Men, for years we women have been told how to keep the "romance" in our marriages. But how about you? You know by this time that God created *you* as the aggressor, and she as the responder. But it is awfully hard to respond day in, day out, year in, year out to a man who is walking around but who, as far as romance and the emotional feelings that he shows his wife are concerned, might as well be dead. I know a lot of these "dead" men, and they are usually the loudest complainers about wifely lack of interest either in herself, in him, in his work or in sex. Have you ever wondered why? Possibly for years she tried and tried to please you, and received no response. She dressed for you, tried new hairstyles for you, and no response. She did everything in every book she could find, and still no response. Finally the hopes, dreams and desires crumpled into ashes, perhaps along with her health and looks. With some of you she was trying to reach the unreachable star. You are so consumed with yourself, your interests, your desires, your needs, that you never noticed. Finally she quit, and you started complaining. There is hope. You can still change this situation, but the way back is going to demand of *you personally, not of things,* but of *your time, your attention,* of *your interest* and *your love.* You might even have to give up that Saturday golf game for a while, and spend time taking quiet walks with her, listening to the deep inner needs of her soul. But as in any relationship, if you want the most, the very best, you, being the God-created aggressor, are going to have to get off the tee.

If things aren't going too well in the bedroom, remember that God created men and women differently. A wife who has been ignored, overburdened by responsibilities which you should be assuming, starved for communication, probably isn't going to turn into a red-hot momma the minute she walks through the bedroom door. A woman's love is basically a soul type of love first, and if you are cutting her out of your life, clamming up in the communication department, she will find it very difficult to commune with you in the total, giving, intimate way the Lord would have for both of you.

Remember the way you treated your wife when you were dating. Now, when you go out socially, do you show her the same attention? Do you open the car door, the restaurant door, or pull her chair out for her? Have you allowed your wife to be put into strained situations at parties because you wandered off to be with the boys, and some loose male tried to take over for you? I often see husbands who use their lovely wives as their passport to the right parties, their ladder to "success." Women aren't bracelets that God gave you to dangle on your arm; they are delicate creatures, created by God, and put in your care and under your protection. In social situations, remember your *first* responsibility is to *your wife,* not the boss's wife, not your best friend's wife, but *your* wife. She is the one who is deserving of your time and attention. If you begin interacting with her in this way, you will reap the most marvelous benefits on earth.

If being proud of your wife, if praising her in front of others is about the most embarrassing thing you can think of, let me tell you something, men. The few men we know who show their wives love, attention, comment on their accomplishments, etc., are the most popular men in our group. Men really look up to a man who is the type of man God created him to be, and women adore him. This kind of man just can't lose. Just think, people swooned for years about the Duke and Duchess of Windsor because here was a man who wasn't afraid to declare to the whole world how much he loved this woman. We have some close friends, and they are one of the most adorable couples I know. And do you know why? Because both of them are so proud of each other, and they aren't afraid to say so.

The road to a woman's heart is paved with the "little things." The birthdays, anniversaries, valentines, and other special days remembered. You don't have to go out and buy an expensive present. A loving card, an expression of your love and remembering is often enough. Occasionally pick up some flowers for *no* reason at all. What a response you will receive. Plan a trip back to your honeymoon spot, a weekend in the mountains or at the beach. Remember, God created you to be the aggressor, but you have to pave the way with love, care, and *most of all, a giving of yourself.*

"Judson is so thoughtful, so romantic, he never forgets our anniversary," Freda told her neighbor.

"Well, you are certainly lucky," Merle commented. "What did good ole Jud give you this year?"

"Oh, Merle, he gave me the most beautiful harvest-colored, metal-lined trash compactor. It is the deluxe model, you know. It even has an automatic air-freshener! I was so thrilled I haven't taken my eyes off it since he presented it to me!"

Sound ridiculous? Certainly. The point is, men, when you are considering gifts for us, remember that where presents are concerned most women aren't really very practical creatures. If you give us a new vacuum, or superdooper fry pan, we may appreciate it, but don't expect us to glow from ear to ear. We'd much rather have those precious things like a beautiful piece of jewelry we can treasure forever and often say, "John gave that to me." Oh, how loved and proud that makes us feel. Perhaps you might consider our favorite perfume, a lovely nightgown, or something else which spells romance. I guarantee you'll love the response.

I could write a book on "workaholics," men who—either for their own ego or because they'd rather give of material things than of themselves—have neglected their wives, hardly know their children, and then wonder why things are going to pot at home. You rationalize, "Look how hard I am working for you." Get off it. You are working for yourself, either for things you want materially, or because it is cheaper to give the family a new car, a new home, a new swimming pool, than to give them you. *You* are what they want, *you* are what they need, and if you don't wake up to that fact, all the work you have done will amount to nothing, and be split up in the courts between child support and alimony! Men, believe me, *we'd rather have you more* (and things less) than any other thing in the world. Most wives are dying inside for companionship, for time with their mates. God is holding *you* responsible for the stability in your home. You may be a success in the world's eyes, but if home is hell on earth, you aren't being the man God expects, and in time you will sadly reap what you have sown, either in divorce, estrangement, rebellious children, or worse.

Certainly, you can't start making all these changes tomorrow. Begin by confessing your failures, your lack of leadership to the Lord (I John 1:9) and ask Him to show you the areas of your life which need changing. Secondly, get in the Scriptures and learn what God has to say about being a man. Muscles and brawn do not a man make; only God can make a man, and only God can remake you into the kind of man whose wife will respond and love him, and whose child will honor and respect him.

THE "WHENS"

Before you can progress, you may have to overcome a disease called "the whens." Many of us have found that this disease has been one of the major factors in our failure. Have you ever thought or said, "When I get married, then I'll be happy"? Or, "when we have children"? or "when we can take that vacation"? or "when we have more money"? or "when the children leave home"? or "when I can get out more"? or "when that big promotion comes along"? These are just some of the "whens" that hold people back. They are usually material things. And when we acquire them, they never fill the void that we thought they would.

One of the most deceptive things about the "whens" is that if they become a reality in our lives, we sadly find that we still aren't happy. Our marriage is still the same, the kids are still disobedient, and we are no better able to cope than we were before. The base of your life operations is all *wrong* if the "whens" are its foundation. The "whens" never fulfill, they are never stable, they are always changing. Only when Christ is the foundation can life be happy, fulfilling and stable. If you aren't happy now, if you can't follow Christ's concepts now, then your basic motivations are all wrong. Christ wants you to find your marital success *right where you are. He* must become the *basis* for your happiness, then the "whens" will disappear. You have to come to the point that Paul does in Philippians 4:11b (AMP): ". . . for I have learned how to be content in whatever state I am." This is what Christ wants for you, to become content, happy, exactly where you are, *today, this moment.* He wants you to rely on Him for your every need, your every desire, and as you concentrate on Him, He will supply more than you ever dreamed of.

Learn to enjoy the now. So many people are so busy living in their tomorrows, or dredging up yesterday's disappointments, that they let the precious moments of today slip by. Learn to appreciate the day the Lord has given you. (Ps. 118:24) Learn how to relax and enjoy a quiet evening in front of the fire, caring conversation, those special times alone. Don't let tomorrow interfere. I noticed the other night that I was about to make that mistake; it certainly is one of my weak areas. Jim wanted to play a game.

We are great game players at our house. But I realized that it was already late, I was tired, and besides, the next day both boys had basketball games and I would have to get up early. My immediate reaction was "No." Then I remembered, when Jim and I were divorced I had longed for these simple times, these moments together. Now I was letting them slip by in my rush to reach tomorrow.

Learn to make the most of every moment together, whether it is watching TV, playing a game, or having a quiet talk. Every evening doesn't have to be spent discussing the children's problems, future needs, or the cares and strains of the day. Beam in on your mate, and the love that shines from your renewed relationship will radiate throughout your household. *Now* can be beautiful; just learn to let it.

NO INSTANT CURES

Some of you picked up this book looking for that pill, the instant cure for all your problems. In our modern society we have become accustomed to instant everything—instant rice, instant coffee, and microwave ovens. We've been led to believe if we use the right toothpaste, drive the right car, and use the right deodorant, that everything will fall into place, and love will rush to our doorstep. In such a frantic society, we expect instant problem-solving too. In one sitting, one reading, you hoped your whole world would be changed. That may well be true, but lasting, constructive changes can *only* come through *learning God's concepts,* and *daily, moment by moment,* applying those concepts to our lives, actions, and reactions. If there is a magic word in effecting marital changes, it is *discipline.*

You know how many times in the past you have determined to change an action or an attitude, only to find, after the initial desire had waned, that you returned to your old ways. For a time you were encouraged, for a time there was some change, but in the end you were almost back where you started. Each year, many people determine on New Year's Eve to do this or that in the new year, only to find a few weeks later that all those glorious resolutions have failed, just like those in years gone by. Possibly you feel like Paul when he wrote in Romans 7:15–22

(LVB): "I don't understand myself at all, for I really want to do what is right, but I can't. I do what I don't want to—what I hate."

The way out is through Christ, the method is through *discipline,* allowing the Holy Spirit to break old habit patterns and create new ones. I Timothy 4:7–8 (NASV): "On the other hand, discipline yourself for the purpose of godliness; for bodily discipline is only of little profit, but godliness is profitable for all things, since it holds promise for the present life and also for the life to come." Then, exactly what are we talking about? Certainly if we read Webster's definition of the word *discipline*—"to train or develop by instruction and exercise esp. in self-control; to bring under control; to impose order upon"—we can readily see that it isn't a sudden change that God is talking about. God expects continual, daily, moment-by-moment effort and change.

Christ refers to this daily exercise in Luke 9:23 (NASV): "And He was saying to them all, 'If anyone wishes to come after Me, let him deny himself, and take up his cross *daily,* and follow Me.'" Christ wasn't speaking of denying yourself special treats, certain enjoyments, which you might conceive would bring you closer to Him. He was speaking of denying your "old" self, the "old nature," and daily taking on the new one, which is constantly available to you through the power of the Holy Spirit making you able to live God's way, not man's. It is a matter of saying, "no" to your old self, and "yes" to the new one.

To break the old habits and to instill God's concepts won't come automatically. First of all, you must become aware of all your wrong directives, wrong actions, wrong responses; then these must be evaluated in the light of God's Word. What does God have to say about bitterness, jealousy, anger, adultery, resentment, etc.? Then, moment by moment, as the Holy Spirit makes you aware of a wrong habit pattern, you must confess it, put it behind you and move on. In time, as you are *constantly* in God's Word, learning the mind of Christ, the Holy Spirit will be more and more able to trigger your mind to avoid a wrong action or reaction.

Still skeptical? Do you feel that you have been in your old ways too long to change? Well, probably you have! But through God's grace, and the power of the Holy Spirit, you too can change. God doesn't ask you to make these changes alone. This is beautifully explained in Philippians 2:13 (AMP): "(Not in your own strength) for it is God Who is all the while effectually at work in you—energizing and creating in you the power and desire—both to will and to work for His good pleasure and satisfaction and delight."

"But it sounds like work, and what if I fail?" you ask. The first time you reach out and fail, the first time you determine through the power of the Holy Spirit you won't lose your temper, you will have those meals on time, you will remember your wife's birthday, and then you "blow it"—remember, Rome wasn't built in a day. Everything takes time. And in the meantime, God's grace can supersede your mistakes. Romans 8:28 (AMP) tells us: "We are assured and know that (God being a partner in our labor) all things work together and are (fitting into a plan) for good to those who love God and are called according to (His) design and purpose." The verse doesn't say that all things are good, but that God can make all things (those booboos, those wrong responses) work together for good as long as you are relying on Him.

This isn't a sink-or-swim situation; God has made provision for your situation. As you *daily* take in His Word, *daily* walk with Him, He is always there to support you, to uphold you through difficult situations, until, through discipline, His reactions become your reactions, His concepts become habit.

"I don't think that I have the patience to endure any more," you say. "I mean, how long does the Lord expect me to be patient?" James 5:7 (AMP) tells us: "Be patient, brethren, until the coming of the Lord." That covers a good bit of time, doesn't it? At the moment, you may be convinced that you probably can't hold out until the weekend, much less the coming of the Lord. Right? I know you are in a hurry and you wish, in all sincerity, that the Lord would get "with it." Often we feel this way, wishing that God would get with the program. But, you see, He often allows us to endure difficult situations, disappointments, even heartbreaks, because some of us are only teachable when we are flat on our backs.

Accept whatever situation you are in; seek to know what the Lord is trying to teach you through it. Perhaps the Lord wants to develop patience in your life, not only for the present situation, but to conform you more to His image and develop in you a stronger character. Whatever He is trying to teach you, seek to learn it now. Don't do as I have often done and squeak by one problem just to have Christ put a like situation right back into my life because I still haven't learned the lesson He was trying to teach me the first time. Believe me, if you patiently wait on Him, He will come through.

HOW AND WHY TO STUDY

If you are to take God's concepts and have them make permanent changes in your marriage, in your life, you can only do this God's way, through study and discipline, Psalms 119:11. You must set a time *each day,* if at all possible, for the study of the Word and prayer. "Have the roots (of your being) firmly and deeply planted (in Him) fixed and founded in Him—being continually built up in Him, becoming increasingly more confirmed and established in the faith, just as you were taught, and abounding and overflowing in it with thanksgiving." (Col. 2:7 AMP)

If you are not constantly taking in God's Word, if you don't have a thorough working knowledge of His concepts, precepts, commands, how can you fulfill the following desires and commands of the Lord: Deuteronomy 6:6–7 (LVB): "And you must think *constantly* about these commandments I am giving you . . . You must teach them to your children and talk about them when you are at home, or out for a walk; at bedtime and first thing in the morning."

In Matthew there is a discussion of a man who was doing wrong, and it says he did so because he did not know the Scriptures. Matthew 22:29 (AMP): "Ye do err, not knowing the Scriptures, nor the power of God." In Romans 15:4 (AMP): "For whatsoever things were written (in the Scriptures) were written for our learning, that we through patience and comfort of the Scriptures might have hope."

"Well, Anne, I tried to read the Bible once, but I just couldn't understand it." Possibly you picked up the Word before you knew the author, and to truly understand and love this book, it is *essential* to know the writer personally. I Corinthians 2:14 (AMP) says: "But the man who isn't a Christian can't understand and can't accept these thoughts from God, which the Holy Spirit teaches us. They sound foolish to him, because only those who have the Holy Spirit within them can understand what the Holy Spirit means. Others just can't take it in." This simply means that nonbelievers are unable to grasp a real and deep understanding of God's Word because the Holy Spirit, which indwells every true believer (Col. 2:9–10) also gives a believer insight and understanding and interest. The nonbeliever doesn't have these things. One must first come to a personal knowledge and belief in the substitutional work of Jesus Christ on the cross for you personally, then interest in study will follow.

It is rather like trying to read a book on the detailed workings of computers. If you are a computer expert, you can understand them, but if you know nothing of computers, the book will look silly, be confusing and you won't understand it, and could care less about reading it. So are the things of the Spirit; to those who don't have a personal relationship with Jesus, they don't make sense; they are often silly, and certainly they are of no interest. But for the Christian they are the very breath of life, see Psalms 119:114. For how can we live as Christ asks us to unless we are constantly applying His concepts?

If you are totally unfamiliar with the Word, you might grow faster in your Christian experience through good, sound Bible study tapes. Many busy men have found that they really began to grow in their relationship to Christ and their family by listening to Bible study tapes in the car, to and from work. Women often find that their spiritual maturity has blossomed when they listened to God's Word on tape while they cleaned the house, sewed, or did the ironing. If you don't have good Bible study tapes available to you, *please* write me and I will send you literature on how to get started, and where to obtain tapes which will help you grow spiritually, and through them help you master God's concepts and your marital relationship. The more you read and study, the more the Holy Spirit can make you aware of needed changes in your life, Psalms 119:160. As Christ chips away the bitterness, fear, rejection, anger, and despair, a new person will emerge, one who can act and react to his/her mate as God intended. Your presence, which used to turn your mate off, will become a magnet to draw him/her to you, and perhaps in time to Him. (I Cor. 7:14)

GOALS: Your goals for this chapter are to begin to understand and practice *true* love. You can spend the rest of your life reading, but nothing will change in your life until you put into action what God says is true. G. K. Chesterton put it this way: "I do not believe in a fate that falls on men however they act; but I do believe in a fate that falls on them *unless they act.*"[1]

ASSIGNMENTS

(1) Memorize John 15:12.

(2) Seriously consider John 14:21.

(3) Begin a daily prayer life, make a list of those things you wish to thank the Father for, those things you wish to share with Him, and those things which need changing in your life. Share all your heart's desires, claiming John 16:23. Pray for patience as God begins to work in *your* life and your marriage.

(4) Wives, make up a schedule for your household duties and stick to it. You'll be amazed at the order which will develop in your home.

(5) Husbands, "wife" isn't another word for servant, so remember you will save her much valuable time if you'll quit littering the house with newspapers, office reports, clothes, etc., and begin to pick up after yourself and create a new responsive mate, one who is less burdened and more relaxed and loving.

(6) Both of you must dismiss the "whens" of your lives and begin to live in the *now.*

(7) If you are both Christians, set aside a specific time for Bible study together, either by listening to a tape for daily studying, or a planned mode of Scripture study. The eternal triangle of man, woman, and God will bring your lives and love closer together.

(8) Both of you, begin to show your love in word and deed.

(9) Begin to turn each other on and self off.

(10) Learn that God's word for love is *give,* and *give,* and *give* again. Love is an action word, and after the action comes the "feeling" we call love. Every time you begin to think

about the "feeling," think about Christ's example of love, which was the ultimate in giving.

(11) Ladies, when you realize the financial responsibilities your husband faces, remember to tell him how much you appreciate his ability to provide for you and the children.

(12) In rekindling the flame, list the problem areas in your relationship. Beside each problem write God's concept or solution. Now begin to apply God's answers.

(13) When the diet is over, ladies, and the new you needs a new wardrobe, instead of the masculine pants suits you've worn for so long, why not pick out some soft, lovely feminine dresses, step back, and watch him notice!

(14) Fix a nice dinner every evening this week whether you're in the "mood" or not. Add some creativity to your nightly table setting, perhaps flowers, candles, or the like.

CHAPTER 11

EMOTIONAL BARRIERS TO HAPPINESS AND HOW TO OVERCOME THEM

After you have learned God's concepts, even when you reach the point that their application to your marital relationship is almost as natural as breathing, don't get too comfortable, thinking, "Well, we finally made it." Certainly, when any major marital wound has been healed, it is a day to celebrate and praise the Lord. But when the major tears are mended, you need to realize, like everyone else on the face of this earth, that there will always be day-to-day trials and problems which can become emotional barriers to your happiness if they aren't dealt with correctly. *How you face and handle these can be the most important vitamins you can give your marriage.*

I am sure as you have progressed in the study of God's Word, you are beginning to discover areas of your life that you were previously unaware of—problems, defects, and difficulties that you now recognize need to be changed. Vividly, you understand the truth of Isaiah 55:8–9. As you have studied God's concepts you have come to realize, "I don't think the way God would have me think; I don't act or react in the manner He would desire." *Congratulations,* that is one large step toward a changed you, a you Christ can conform and fashion more in His image.

As you face day-to-day annoyances, *don't panic.* Remember that in eternity past, Jesus Christ knew that you would encounter that very problem, that very strain. He knew what temptations you would be facing at this very moment! And He supplied for every one of them. *Victory has been provided.* Christ is just waiting for you to go to His Word and discover the solution, how to respond, how to relate, how to become a survivor, a victor over this particular problem. In Proverbs 24:3–4 (Berkley): "By wisdom is a house built and by understanding it is established; for by knowledge the rooms are filled with all precious and pleasant riches."

Pretend for a moment that your mind and soul have rooms

which God wants to fill with His Word, His promises, so that the house may be firm and sturdy. When we have properly furnished the rooms of our minds with His furniture (His Word), then the moment a storm threatens our homes we can go to the correct room, knowing His Word, claim the knowledge we have stored there, and triumph over the upheaval swirling around outside. This is exactly what Proverbs 24:3–4 is talking about—that through wisdom and understanding, a house, a marriage are established, and that when the storms rage outside, you have the right provisions stored to carry you through, to fill you and minister to you until the turbulence passes. Then you can step out into the sun, a triumphant survivor.

As the wind howls around you, you can relax and have inner peace. It is truly exciting that many times it is only through pressures, problems and trials that we really grow. While you are residing on planet earth, this is the only time you will have the opportunity to flourish and grow in this way. When you go to heaven to be with God, there will be no more problems. But while you are here, you have the fantastic opportunity of seeing God's power at work in your life, to give you peace and inner happiness when all about you is chaos and despair.

In the next few pages we are going to go through the most common problems, trials, and strains that confront most marital relationships. How you react at tense periods is most important to the growth and stability of your relationship. I know that since you have progressed this far in the book, you are vitally interested in God's will and direction for your life, and your marriage. It is therefore important to know how He would have you deal with everyday annoyances and problems.

(1) How should you respond when you have made a mistake? You are to handle your mistakes, failures, sins as exactly that and nothing more. We are all going to blow it once in a while. The key is: *don't* become discouraged; *don't* put yourself down, thinking, "There is no hope for me, I'm just a lost cause." First of all, you must realize that you are human and you are going to make mistakes. The important thing is not that you make a mistake, but how *you respond* to it. If you respond in the correct manner, then God can use that to make you more like Jesus, help

you to grow and develop the character traits that He would desire to create in you.

Beware, the tendency of your old sin nature is to blame someone else for your sin. Remember in Genesis 3, when the Lord confronted Adam, he responded with, "Well, it was that woman Eve that You gave me," and Eve, when reproached, passed the buck to the serpent. Neither wanted to take responsibility for his or her own actions. Seriously, recognize the tendency in each of us to blame someone else and not take the responsibility for our own actions. This blaming is a fruit of the old sin nature, and it is the wrong way to respond; it is the road to failure, not the path to victory and maturity in Jesus Christ.

"He who conceals his transgressions will not prosper, but he who *confesses* and *forsakes* them will receive mercy." (Prov. 28:13 Berkley) The key response when you have failed is: admit it, confess it to God, claiming His forgiveness through Jesus Christ's payment on the cross for you. You didn't earn or deserve it, and you never will. It is God's gift at Christ's expense, and He wants you to receive it and move on, allowing Him to make the changes in you. If you have wronged someone else, you *must* also ask their forgiveness; or if the case requires, you are to make restitution. Understand that in Christ there is no condemnation (Rom. 8:1); you are no longer condemned if you have accepted Jesus Christ's payment for you personally.

(2) How am I to react when my mate fails, sins, or disappoints me? "Beloved, never avenge yourselves, but leave the way open for (God's) wrath; for it is written, 'Vengeance is Mine, I will repay (requite),' says the Lord." (Rom. 12:19 AMP) Open your heart to Proverbs 17:9 (LVB): "Love forgets mistakes, nagging about them parts the best of friends." The message of the Scriptures is that you are to respond to your mate's failures and mistakes exactly as Jesus Christ does to yours! How does Christ relate to your mistakes and how does He treat you? "Be gentle and ready to forgive; never hold grudges. Remember the Lord forgave you, so you must forgive others." (Col. 3:13 LVB) So when your mate really blows it, remember that you do too and that God forgives you even though you don't deserve that forgiveness. On the same basis, you are to forgive your mate. What

they have done, whether they deserve forgiveness, isn't the issue; the issue is that this is the way Christ would have you respond. Remember the words of the Lord's Prayer, and Isaiah 43:25 (KJV): "I, even I, am He that blotteth out the transgressions for Mine own sake, and will not remember thy sins." God forgives and forgets, and that is the same thing that you are to do when your mate fails. You are to *forgive and you are not to remember it any more!*

You begin by first of all *not reminding your mate of the mistakes he/she has made, ever again.* You forgive your mate. How many times? In Matthew, Christ says seventy times seven and more. Next, you *never* mention the incident to another person, not your mother, not your prayer group, no one but God, *period.* Lastly, you don't allow yourself to think on it. When it comes to your mind, immediately apply Philippians 4:6 (AMP). If there is any sin on your part, any bitterness, resentment, jealousy, you confess that and give it to God. Then you turn your mate's mistake, sin, wrong over to God: "God, I am committing this act that my mate committed against me into Your hands. I thank You that You are capable of handling it. Now it is Your problem, not mine." Now apply Philippians 4:8, fixing your mind and thoughts on good things about your mate—perhaps his or her sense of humor, creativity, honesty, whatever. Think on these and leave the wrongs to God. Then in verse 7 claim God's peace.

In the beginning your mind may flash right back to the sin. What do you do then? You just turn it back over to God, thanking Him for His control over it. Again return to thinking positive things about your mate. Every time your mind wanders back to the situation, apply God's formula. As you do this over and over, in time you will discover that it will seldom occur to you. As you are faithful to follow God's formula, you will find that, with an act of your will, it will pass from your mind.

You see, the problem with most unpleasant things that we can't forget is that we keep them constantly before us. In many instances, you have been actively remembering them, rehashing them in your mind. Perhaps in some cases you are making yourself feel very "righteous" by comparison, thinking how spiritual a person you must be to have put up with such an act . . . you are on an ego kick and out of God's will.

I was counseling a young woman the other day who had just been reunited with her husband. She told me that she was having a difficult time forgetting the affair in which he'd been involved. As I questioned her, she admitted that she had kept a number of letters written to her mate from the "other woman." I advised her God couldn't open a door to heal their relationship as long as she held onto the sins of the past, sins which she said she had forgiven. Many of you probably have skeletons, just as she did, buried in the back yard, rotting, corroding, smelly, and yet every so often you go out there, dig them up, and relive all the disgusting memories. You'd better throw those bones away, because God can't clean house and heal your marriage as long as you want to fill your life with filth from the past.

As you are obedient to God, as you apply His formula to forgive and forget, that "feeling" of forgiveness will soon take root in your heart. Proverbs 12:20 (LVB) tells us that ". . . joy fills hearts that are planning for good!" When God's thoughts, God's actions are filling your thoughts and mind, then joy will begin to fill your life and marriage.

(3) How do I rightly respond to criticism? Good question. Proverbs 23:12 (LVB) reminds us: "Don't refuse to accept criticism; get all the help you can." When you truly understand that God is often using your mate in your life as one of the primary tools as He molds you more and more into the image of Jesus Christ, then you can view your mate's remarks from a different vantage point. View it as God speaking to you; you can take that judgment, evaluate it and in your heart say: "God, what is it that You want me to learn from this? What, Lord, are You trying to change in my life?" Take a moment and listen to your mate's comments with your heart. Perhaps you can discover areas that you aren't fulfilling. Perhaps you can learn about new desires of your mate. Just turn off your emotion long enough to listen. When you react to criticism in this manner, you won't respond in hostility or with excuses; you will respond graciously, thanking your mate for bringing particular faults or unfulfilled duties to your attention.

"But, Anne, what if the criticism isn't valid?" If your mate is demanding more of you than is humanly possible, you might in love say, "Honey, I really want to please you. I want to be the mate you need, but I am having a very difficult time trying to accomplish all that you have requested of me. Would you please sit down with me and evaluate the things I have to do and help me formulate a time schedule as to how I can accomplish them." Then when you sit down together, your mate may be able to point out some things that you are doing which aren't necessary, or good for you. If he is actually demanding too much of you, he will be able to recognize this as he tries to budget your time. Perhaps this is something you need to do around your "Table of Harmony." As you are open before your mate and the Lord, God will honor that and work out a happier existence for both of you.

How should criticism be given? I would hasten to remind you that criticism should be handled by both the giver and the receiver in love. Proverbs 17:24 (LBV) says: "Kind words are like honey—enjoyable and healthful." Try to make your statements of disapproval in a loving and kind manner. Harshness never hastens learning, and if you want to make a point, do it in love, gently, and you will find that your mate will be more responsive than in the past to your loud comments, flagrant blaming, or the rehashing of everything he or she has done wrong since getting out of diapers! Stay on the subject. If you have a point to make, something that you are unhappy about, make it. Don't *ever* allow your comments to drag in *other situations,* or other people, etc.

Women, I particularly want to make a point here with you. We women seem to be born with the desire to give advice to our mates. We see logic and sense in what we are saying and think that our mate should take our comments in the same way. If he doesn't respond the first time, we repeat it until he does. We call it advice; he calls it nagging! Do you know what the Scriptures say about this? Proverbs 21:9 (AMP) says: "It is better to dwell in a corner of the housetop (on the flat oriental roof, exposed to all kinds of weather) than in a house shared with a nagging, quarrelsome and faultfinding woman." I know how you feel. Often what we are "nagging" about are things which truly seem to need correction, or the "advice" we are giving is actually the better way, but, women, our men don't take our comments that way. A wise lady once told me, "Anne, you know, unasked-for advice is actually veiled criticism!" She was right, but the truth surely hurts. I had never thought about it that way. I bet you haven't either.

"But, Anne, if I don't tell him ten times, then the grass will never get mowed." Well, if your nagging usually centers on his area of responsibility, then you are overstepping your bounds. You might remind him once, *politely*, but then turn the situation over to the Lord. Your husband isn't blind; he can see that the grass needs cutting, or the leaves need raking, just as well as you can, so after you have mentioned it once, *shut up*. If it grows knee deep, it still isn't your responsibility to remind him. Once you have turned it over to the Lord, let the Lord work on the problem and you keep quiet. Let's look at it this way: what if the grass didn't get done for weeks and the leaves totally covered the flower beds. What is more important, the grass and leaves or your marital relationship? Proverbs 11:29a (AMP) reminds us "He who troubles his own house shall inherit the wind . . ."

Most of us take our mates' comments on a deep personal level. We don't take time when our mate says, "Your hair looks like heck," to evaluate the comment honestly. The tears start flowing, or the words start flying without thought. First appraise the situation: "Is my hair a mess?" If it is, take the proper steps to correct it, don't automatically go on the defensive. If it isn't, realize that your man may have just had a hard day at the office and is taking the hostility he felt for his boss out on you; or perhaps he isn't feeling well. There are many reasons for critical outbursts which have nothing to do with you personally. Don't take everything on such a deep level, think through what has been said. If it is justified, correct the situation. If not, chalk it up to another source and let it rest.

(4) How do I deal with anger and arguments?

Kahlil Gibran expressed this problem beautifully when he wrote: "If your heart is a volcano how shall you expect flowers to bloom in your hands?"[1]

Anger in its scriptural context is an emotional reaction to a given issue. Anger and resentment are *not* parallel terms. Mark 3:5 states that Christ was angry. But instead of hoarding His feelings, He directed His energy to *rightly* correcting the disturbing situation. Because His anger was correctly dealt with and directed, resentment never took root in His heart; therefore, no sin was committed. This is a beautiful example of anger controlled, properly directed, and a problem solved.

Of course, most of us don't react this way. When we are rejected or put down, a restless, hostile feeling results. In the bed of hostility, anger grows. Anger gives us a feeling of power, which we usually turn on our mate.

I Peter 3:11 (AMP) says: "Let him turn away from wickedness and shun it; let him do right. Let him search for *peace—harmony,* undisturbedness from fears, agitating passions and moral conflicts and seek it eagerly. Do not merely desire peaceful relations but pursue, go after them!" God says it is not enough to merely want to have peaceful relations with your mate, but *you must pursue them* and with an act of your will go after it. (Prov. 17:14)

Anger or displeasure expressed in love can open new lines of communication. When a wrong has been done between you and your mate, no matter who is in the wrong, take the aggressive step. In love, approach your mate and seek reconciliation. Too many of us, when we are wronged, sit around waiting for our mates to apologize. As we wait we brood, and resentment begins to grow in our souls. If the apology is not received, bitterness also takes hold.

Paul told us that we should not let the sun go down on our anger, Ephesians 4:26. Most couples who end up facing a marital counselor are toting with them a gunny sack full of unresolved problems and disappointments which have turned to bitterness and resentment over the years. Instead of confronting the problems in love, they have played the old game of "not rocking the boat." Their boat may not have rocked for a while, but in time it has become so weighed down with repressed hostilities and unresolved problems that it is now on the verge of sinking.

Do you realize that most of us act as if our mates were clairvoyant? They do something that angers us, and what do we do? We sit sulking in the corner, waiting for them to recognize how much they have upset us. Often they are not the least bit aware of what is eating at us. If you don't deal with your problems biblically, daily, in loving confrontations, and solve them, you can stew for days and still your mate won't discern the reason for your attitude. He may not recall what he said, or perhaps he doesn't understand why his comments or suggestions have so upset you. This is just another reason for your daily heart cleansing. The Bible shares with us that whoever feels the strain of the situation, whether it is the one who was right or the one who was wronged, should go to the other, express his or her feelings, and seek reconciliation.

I am not saying that every little thing that annoys you about your mate, every trifling sin throughout the day, should be mutually confessed. Paul tells us that in I Peter 4:8 (Berkley): ". . . for love covers up many sins." As we grow in Christ, as we allow Him to lead and control our lives, we can learn the act of forgiving and covering our mate's little annoyances with love. But if you find that some act, a harsh word, a misunderstanding, has occurred between you and your mate, and that this has been eating at your guts all day, then before it becomes a sore, it is time to discuss it. Remember that these things are to be settled on the day when they occur, if at all possible.

The "Table of Harmony" is a place where a few minutes each day *every* member of the family meets and shares the experiences of the day, their joys and their sorrows. At the table, each person should have the opportunity to share any pressures or grievances that he feels have been inflicted upon him that day. The table is a place to discuss and *correct problems, not people.*

"Now, Anne, this really sounds juvenile," you might say. Well, can you imagine how many of the unpleasantries of your life could have been avoided if you had had the opportunity to express your displeasure before their pressure took root in anger and resentment? The Scripture must always be your guide as you discuss and settle problems at the "Table of Harmony." Again, I remind you, other members of your family aren't mind readers; they can only make changes that upset you if they are aware of them.

Few of us can immediately call to mind each verse or concept God has in His Word. Therefore as you gather around the "Table of Harmony," a good concordance and topical Bible will be of great help. Another invaluable help and instrument of growth would be a copy of *The Christian Counselor's Bible,* by Dr. Jay E. Adams. This Bible includes marginal notes on counseling principles, shaded passages of help, and an Index of biblical references helpful in dealing with specific problems.

If at any time the discussions at the "Table of Harmony" become angry or hostile, there again you should have a prearranged signal which tells the other members of the family that they've gone beyond dealing with the problem and are attacking the person. A signal such as asking for a moment of silent prayer, or a comment like, "You are touching my wires" will alert the others that each needs to rethink his responses.

Include the children at the "Table of Harmony." Don't do as many parents do and try to protect your children from your day-to-day pressures. Many problems with children can be averted if they understand emotional and financial strains the family is going through. The children will become less demanding and gain true insight into the responsibilities of the family unit.

The next time an argument begins to brew, keep this checklist in mind: (1) Make no judgmental statements; (2) Keep the conversation in the present tense (I Cor. 13:5 Phillips): "It (love) does not keep account of evil or gloat over the wickedness of other people"; (3) Refrain from all statements which involve blame; (4) Remember it's the problem that you are trying to correct, not the other person; (5) Occasionally what we say, and what is heard, aren't one and the same. In the beginning, you might repeat what you heard said, by repeating a person's statement back to him, prefaced by, "What I hear you saying is . . ." A lot of misunderstandings can be avoided; (6) Remember to share your feelings in touchy discussions—for instance, "I feel pressured," or, "I feel uncomfortable when you . . ." This helps to express the situation, and share how the problem is affecting you personally.

If you have made a mistake, first be sure that you have the situation corrected with the Lord. Then ask the Lord to help you select the proper time, when your mate isn't tired, or hurried, and share your failure with him. On the other hand, if you have done something that will hurt your mate deeply, and there is probably no way that he or she will ever know about your indiscretion, make your confession to the Lord (I John 1:9) and know that you are forgiven. There is no point in bringing hurt and distrust into the relationship.

When you do discuss your failure with your mate, know that he or she isn't likely to be surprised. Whether or not you realize it, he/she already knows that you aren't perfect! Often when we share our mistakes and failures with our mates, a closer bond of friendship and trust results. In being honest, you have allowed your mate a closer relationship with the "real" you. As humans we not only relate and become closer to each other through the good, successful things we accomplish, but in recognizing the vulnerable humanity in each other as we struggle and fail. Wonderful avenues of togetherness can be opened when we risk being ourselves.

When discussing displeasures and anger over a given situation, be sure that you *clearly* and *directly* ask for forgiveness. Don't assume that your mate or your children understand what you are seeking. Clearly say, "Will you forgive me?" and seek a clear response from them. If you are seeking to reconcile the situation and forgiveness is not clear, the reconciliation will also be on a rocky foundation. If your mate refuses to forgive, then commit the situation to the Lord, and claim His promise in Romans 12:18–19. You then will have done all that the Lord requires from you, and even though you may not recognize it at the time, you may have planted a softer spirit in the heart of your mate which will grow to the point that he or she can face forgiving and forgetting also. Love will ultimately forgive and forget. When you have done all this, you have fulfilled God's desire in Hebrews 12:14 (Berkley): "Seek eagerly for peace with everyone . . ."

Naturally you can't pull all these things off on your own power, your own strength. You need to pray: "God, it's just You and me. I am trusting Your power to enable me to respond to my mate in love, when You and I know I'd really like to slap him in the face. I am relying on Your promises and trusting, as I am faithful to apply Your concepts that You will work out the anger and hostility which tears at our home." As you do this you will begin to see wonderful transformations begin to occur in your relationship.

(5) How to deal with depression?

First, I would advise you to consult your physician to be sure that your depression isn't rooted in some physical malfunction. Depression, by and large, is emotional, but there are rare cases where there is a physical cause, and you need to check this out first.

Depression is basically rooted in a deep bed of self-pity. Self-pity is a constant introspection into one's self, one's problems, and what one has been deprived of or thinks he is being deprived of. Self-pity is a destructive force, and depression is its follower.

Since you have tried every other method of rising above the clouds of depression that darken every day, may I suggest that you take another look at the emotional causes. If you are having a mental war with resentment, worry, jealousy, guilt, bitterness, hostility, then you have just discovered the problem which has ignited your mental situation.

Jealousy, worry, resentment, etc., do not of themselves cause depression, but your reaction and handling of them does. Depression is caused by a cycle of events.

I realize that sinful reactions and habits are difficult to break, but if they aren't dealt with, you will be continually on the downward side of the roller coaster, a constant companion of depression.

As you move from wrong reaction to wrong reaction, from sin to sin, each failure to rightly respond only adds to the depth of your depressive cycle. Depression gives us a sense of failure, which is compounded as we frantically attempt to rise above our situation, and fail again. Depression and failure are common companions.

Now that we realize where depression originates, what can we do about it? *First of all, confess your wrong reactions to the situation to God.* Most of us fall into depression because we are relying on our "feelings" toward a given situation instead of putting God's directives into action.

The next time you are faced with an unpleasant job, don't stop to rationalize the situation, don't decide that it can wait until next week because you just don't "feel" like it. Do it! Don't wait for the "mood" to hit before you apply God's concepts to your marriage. You see, if you don't fulfill your God-given responsibilities, guilt builds up, the failure creeps in, and disgust and despair grow, then down the spiral you go.

Depression is basically a breakdown in self-control and discipline. Now you can't whip up these qualities in your life. The creation of this type of life within you is the work of the Holy Spirit as Galatians 5:22–23 states.

To correct this downhill slide, you do whatever it is that you know must be done. You face the problems which come your way. You respond in a biblical manner and you will have taken your first step to recovery.

If you hate housework, ask God to give you a deeper love for your family, and as you consider them instead of yourself, God will be able to change your attitude about your work. Just as the "feeling" of love is a by-product of action, so right desires, right actions are the by-product of obedience to God. When you are reacting to your situation in this manner, God will bless you, strengthen you, and in time you will find that many of the situations you dreaded the most are now pleasurable experiences.

In a previous book, I recalled one woman who had been plagued with severe depression and who beautifully expressed how she now does her housework. "When I place dishes in the dishwasher, I thank the Lord and remember the time when I didn't have one," she said. "When I wash the clothes, I think of the child who will be wearing them. When I make our bed, I thank God for the love He restored and the good times we have in that bed." God can change your attitudes as He did hers.

Once you have conquered the blues, continue to apply God's concepts to your life daily. Keep short accounts with God; in other words, don't let overt or mental-attitude sins build up during the day. If you are disorganized, make up a schedule for yourself, with your priorities in order, and each day go down the list and check off each duty as it is accomplished. Remember to *always* depend on God, His directives, His desires, *never* on your own "feelings." When disappointments, problems, or heartbreak come into your life, go to the Scripture and respond as God would have you, not as you "feel" like responding.

There are a few things which you might find helpful to avoid. If you know certain persons depress you, avoid them. Don't spend your time hashing over your daily problems with your next-door neighbor, or the guys at the bar. The end result of this type of action is that much sympathy is shared. Self-pity and self-centeredness is produced instead of Christ-centeredness. Keep your eyes on Him. He has promised to ever be with you, to ever strengthen you.

(6) How do you respond to a mate filled with mental-attitude sins? What do you do when your mate comes home from work totally filled with mental-attitude sins, ranting, raving, cussing about work conditions, the boss, the clients, etc.? He may be going on about what rotten things happened during the day; perhaps he is planning "sweet revenge." Maybe he is really cutting a fellow worker down to size. How are you to respond to him/her in this situation? Proverbs 26:4 (AMP) says: "Answer not a fool according to his folly, lest you also be like him." At a time like this, you have to concentrate on allowing the Holy Spirit to control you. Your responsibility is not to allow yourself to become involved in mental-attitude sins yourself and at the same time respond to your mate rightly. Usually, the best response is a very limited, *unemotional* one. For instance, "Honey, I can really understand how you would feel hurt," or, "Yes, I see the point you are making." Sympathetically listen, not approving or disapproving, just listen and allow your mate to vent his frustrations. As your mate is allowed to spill out all the pain and disappointments of the day, God will be able to deal with him to show him his error. In this way your marital relationship will not be damaged.

(7) How can I get my mate to admire and praise me? When you respond to God's Word as He would have you do, you will obtain honor from men. That is what Proverbs 4:8 brings out. Proverbs 3:3–4 makes the same point. Proverbs 27:2 (AMP) says: "Let another man praise you, and not your own mouth; a stranger, and not your own lips." So you will be praised, promoted, honored when you are relating to life, your mate, etc. as unto the Lord rather than for the praise of men. When the praise does come, and it will, you will be able to handle it, knowing that anything good about you has come through God's working in your life, not by *self-creation*. That reminds me of a joke I heard

about a boastful, arrogant man who was talking to a bunch of people at an old-fashioned church picnic. He had listened as first one person, then another, gave the credit for their success in life to the Lord. Finally, regarding them as weaklings, he proudly said: "Well, I am here to tell you that I am a self-made man." Silence fell on the crowd for a moment. Then a little old gray-haired lady looked him straight in the eyes and said: "Well, sonny, I'm glad you admitted it. You know the more I listened to you, the more I realized that you had to be the product of unskilled labor."

(8) How am I to deal with temptations which come into my life?

Whether your area of weakness is in the line of mental-attitude sins (jealousy, bitterness, self-righteousness), or overt actions like gossip, or being attracted to someone else's wife/husband, God's Word has an answer. Your first need, of course, is a personal relationship with Jesus Christ. You have to get plugged into the power source, or you won't have the strength to resist the pull of your old sin nature very long. Secondly, we as Christians have the privilege of talking to the Lord in prayer, and claiming His promises of victory over temptation. James 1:5 (NASV): "But if any of you lacks wisdom, let him ask of God Who gives to all men generously and without reproach, and it will be given to him." "So give yourselves humbly to God. Resist the Devil and he will flee from you. And when you draw close to God, God will draw close to you. Wash your hands, you sinners, and let your hearts be filled with God alone to make them pure and true to Him." (James 4:7–8 LVB)

Next time you feel the pull of your old sin nature, instead of reaching for the phone, hit your knees. You will find the results transforming, rewarding, and permanent. Remember James 1:12 (LVB): "Happy is the man who doesn't give in and do wrong when he is tempted, for afterwards he will get as his reward the crown of life that God has promised those who love Him."

(9) How do I handle fear?

To really make lasting changes you have to overcome your attitude of fear. If you think, "I'll apply this concept today, but

I'm scared to death about what may happen," you are defeated before you start. Your attitude is not one of trust, but one of fear. You relate that attitude to your mate in everything you say and do, and the relationship is resting on that proverbial time bomb. You can't transmit faith, trust, a solidarity in your life, if you are standing on a trembling base of fear. You can't on one hand relate to your mate that you have finally found the answers to your crumbling marriage, and on the other hand say that you are afraid to try them. You have to go one way or the other.

First of all, you must have placed your trust in Jesus Christ, as we discussed in Chapter 3. Now that you are God's child, you are His responsibility. How, then, does He expect you to live? Acts 17:28 (AMP) says: "For in Him we live and move and have our being." We are to live daily in Him, concentrating on Him, His promises, for fear and the controlling power of the Holy Spirit will not abide at the same time. If we are filled with Him, there will be no room for fear. II Thessalonians 3:3 (AMP) tells us: "Yet the Lord is faithful and He will strengthen (you) and set you on a firm foundation and guard you from the evil (one). You can trust Him to be utterly sufficient for your every need, your every fear." (I Thess. 5:24 AMP)

So what do you do now? You must do exactly what God has asked you to do in your life, and in your marital relationship. Do you realize that if you let fear stop you from being the right kind of mate, from serving God, from doing whatever possible to save your marriage, then fear has become your master, and that fear has now become sin because you have not trusted?

"But I'm still so afraid," you say. Yes, I know you are, but there is a power, a force stronger than your fear. Remember Romans 8:31 (AMP): "What then shall we say to (all) this? If God be for us, who (can be) against us?—Who can be our foe, if God is on our side?" Now you must supplant that fear with the strongest force on earth: *love*.

You love your mate, right? You love your children, you love God? Then take this love and put it in the place of your fear. If you are operating in love, on love, then you are on a positive mental-attitude wave length. When love is at the center of your actions, then you are Christ-centered and positive things are accomplished.

You begin by taking one step on faith. Remember Hebrews 11:6 (AMP): "But without faith it is impossible to please and be satisfactory to Him . . ." "But, Anne, I'm so weak, I have so little faith." Well, guess what? Christ spoke of that in Matthew 17:20 (LVB). It doesn't begin with the mighty faith of a man like Abraham. Christ said: "For if you had faith even as small as a tiny mustard seed, you could say to this mountain, 'Move!' and it would go far away. Nothing would be impossible." Now you know that even you have that much faith.

Certainly, the fear, the "feeling," doesn't disappear all at once, and mentally, for a good while, you will have to remind yourself of God's love, of God's support, of God's promises. If you find yourself worrying, or being afraid, just confess it as sin, because that is exactly what it is; it is not trusting. Claim I John 1:9 and step out.

(10) How do I deal with boredom in my life? Basically, this is a feminine problem, but it speaks to many of you men also. Proverbs 14:14 (LVB) says: "The backslider gets bored with himself; the Godly man's life is exciting." Most of the time when men or women complain of boredom, it is because they are trying to find fulfillment in things of the world that God never designed to bring fulfillment. Perhaps you are trying to have your mate meet a need in your life that only Jesus Christ can fill. Maybe you have sought ultimate fulfillment through education, sex, a career, pleasure, a job promotion, a new house; yet when these things were obtained, you found yourself still seeking, still carrying the gaping void with you.

If you are bored, re-evaluate how you spend your time. Ask yourself, "Have I been taking in God's Word daily?" If you haven't, then this is an area that needs correction. Check out your priorities. Have I been occupied with Christ first, my family second, and all other things in their correct order? Have I been centering my thoughts and concerns on my mate, or on myself? You may have gotten on the dead-end street, called "self," which leads to boredom. Perhaps after you have completely checked out your life, some of you do have some extra time. Don't feel that to be a "good" Christian you necessarily have to rush out and donate that time to hospital volunteer work, or to a "Christian" endeavor. God may have a unique message that He wants to share through you. Perhaps your hobby is painting, writing, gardening, etc. Even though you may feel you aren't directly sharing Christ in these outlets, know that if you are developing a God-given talent, He will open the most unusual doors, bring you in contact with people who need His message even though your activity isn't directly centered in evangelism. Just go to your Heavenly Father and ask Him to give you the opportunity to share the wonders and glory of knowing Him through your hobby or avocation, in your own personal manner, and then stand back, because He will.

(11) How do I handle sleepless nights and insomnia? "Anne, I can hardly make it through the day, and when I do I am jumpy and fussy with my family," a young woman complained. Certainly if you aren't getting the proper amount of rest, your reaction to any situation of strain will be less patient, thus putting tension on your marital relationship. If insomnia is a constant problem for you, first see your physician and be sure the source isn't physical. Now, I didn't say go and ask for sleeping pills, because if there is no physical reason for your lack of sleep, and you start hitting the pills, you will just be masking the real reason, and developing a dependence on the pills at the same time. Second, when you go to bed at night, prepare yourself and your bed for a comfortable sleep. Try different height pillows, different positions, possibly even different material blends of sheets. Third, exercise to the point of perspiration right before you go to bed; tension and exercise are rarely partners, they normally offset each other. Fourth, place a pen flashlight, a pen and notepad beside your bed; then if you happen to think of something during the night that you need to do the next day, you can just turn over and write it down. If you have a creative thought, write it down; with your night notes, you won't have to lie awake thinking over and over, hoping that particular idea, design, etc., will not be lost from your memory in the morning. Fifth, as you lie down to sleep, go to your Heavenly Father in prayer, talk to Him, ask Him to remind you if there is any unconfessed sin from the day, and if there is, confess it and clear the slate for that day. Then take your problems, worries, and strains

and commit them to Him. Ask His blessing on your sleep, claiming Proverbs 3:24 (AMP): "When you lie down, you shall not be afraid; yes, you shall lie down and your sleep shall be sweet." Psalms 4:8 (AMP) says: "In peace I will both lie down and sleep, for You, Lord, alone make me dwell in safety and confident trust." Again in Psalms 127:2b (AMP): ". . . for He gives (blessings) to His beloved in sleep." Know that it is God's will that you have a full and restful sleep. Commit your conscious and subconscious mind to His keeping and ask Him to take care of it, then thank Him, knowing you can rely on His Word.

(12) How to handle general irritations and problems? Perhaps there are things, situations which you didn't find under any of the other headings we discussed. When you are confronted with everyday annoyances you can always claim I Thessalonians 5:18 (AMP): "Thank (God) in everything—no matter what the circumstances may be, be thankful and give thanks; for this is the will of God for you (who are) in Christ Jesus." I know that you are reading this book right now because you want to know God's will for your life; then also know that whatever happens in your life, your attitude is to be one of thanks: "Lord, I just thank You that I have the opportunity to trust You through this problem."

As a problem or irritation arises, ask yourself, Is there anything I can do to correct this? If there is, do it. If there isn't, realize that God wants to use that to teach you something special in your own life. Proverbs 20:24 (LVB) says: "Since the Lord is directing our steps, why try to understand everything that happens along the way?" You may not be able to understand why a certain thing keeps happening to you, doesn't make a bit of sense to you, but be assured that God hasn't said you will always understand. He has said that when He is in control of your life, when He is working in your life, you can trust Him for whatever happens.

Stop for a moment and think about your problems and irritations. Are they actually happening, or are they situations which you are anticipating? For example, "what will I do if my husband leaves? if my wife has an affair? etc." Recognize that you are violating Matthew 6:34 (AMP), which says: "So do not worry or be anxious about tomorrow. It will have worries and anxieties of its own. Sufficient for each day is its own trouble." God has created you with the ability to deal with today, not tomorrow.

(13) What exactly is faith and how do I put it into practice? Faith comes through a total commitment of our lives and our beings to the person of Jesus Christ, through trusting and accepting His payment to make us acceptable to God. Faith isn't a mental activity; it is a total commitment, a way of life. Faith is taking God at His Word, and stepping out trusting Him to be faithful and fulfill His promises in our lives.

Faith is *not* a "feeling." We are never admonished to see and *experience* a *feeling*. We are told to learn what is ours in Jesus Christ and apply that day-by-day to our lives, as in Colossians 2:3. Your feelings and emotions can be affected by many internal and external causes and circumstances and are vacillating things on which to rely or make decisions. *Only* God's Word, His concepts, are solid, firm, and never changing. Living a life directed by feeling or emotion can be like a continual ride on a roller coaster. *Feelings* and *emotionally* controlled actions are the opposite of faith. Faith is trust in action, no matter how I feel. It is based on God's Word, Hebrews 11:1 and Hebrews 11:6.

God has given us a book full of promises which are ours when we claim them on faith. We can have traumatic ups and downs, but inside we can be at rest, relying on Him. This is the lesson He wants us to learn: to claim His promises and move into a moment-by-moment reliance on Him. Did you realize that the Scripture contains seven thousand promises? These are promises from God to you; they were given to you for your peace and blessing in *this life*. Many of you have trusted Christ for your salvation, and stopped there. You haven't grown because you haven't trusted.

Most of us handle trials and problems in similar ways. The problem hits, we run to the Lord, claim a promise, and in the next breath an idea occurs to us. We say, "Wait a minute, Lord, let me try this first." When "this" doesn't work, back to the Lord we go, and almost before the words are out of our mouths, another idea hits and off we go again. No wonder we don't progress, grow in faith—we are too busy trying this idea, then turning it over to the Lord, taking it back. What a mess. Mature faith is reached only when we realize we can't, only He can. We give the problem to God, trust Him to work it out, then sit back and watch Him perform a miracle in our lives. One of the most difficult, yet vital, things you will have to learn in your marriage, your Christian experience, is to *wait*. Waiting is simply keeping your hands, your mouth, yourself out of the way and relaxing while God takes over.

"But doesn't God help those who help themselves," you ask? Let me tell you, that is one quote you will never find in the Bible. God helps those who have faith and trust in Him to work the problem out. God helps the helpless. God helps those who learn and apply His concepts, His directives to their lives. Faith grows through constant reliance on Him, watching as He transforms you, your mate, and your marriage.

We have already discussed the importance of Bible study, but I am sure you realize that it is impossible to claim promises that you don't know, or put concepts that you have never read into action. This is why constant Bible study is so important. The more you know of Him, the more you will understand His love, the more you will begin trusting Him and waiting on Him. II Corinthians 5:7 (KJV) says: "For we walk by faith, not by sight." And Hebrews 11:6 (KJV) tells us: "But without faith it is impossible to please Him."

Faith is trust; trust is relying on Him, one moment at a time, one day at a time. It is seeing His wonderful healing power in your life, in your marriage, in action. Faith is the next step in your growth. If you recall, II Corinthians 12:9 (AMP) said: ". . . for My strength and power are made perfect–fulfilled and completed and show themselves most effective–in (*your*) *weakness* . . ."

(14) What do I do about my husband who is in the armed services and away from home much of the time? or about my traveling husband? I mean, how do I stay under His Shield of Protection when he is gone so much? What you need to do is sit down with him and come to agreements on what the policies of the home are to be. He is the president, remember? You are the vice-president, the one who carries out the policies when the presi-

dent is away from the office. It might be best, if the children are old enough, to call them in on this discussion so that they will clearly understand what he expects from them while he is gone. This will be a good example for the children to see, as you respond to your husband's leadership. If they misbehave while he is gone and you have to correct them, they will also understand that you are merely carrying out the policies that Dad set down.

(15) What about in-laws? A powerful question. When I first outlined this book, I intended to devote a complete chapter to this subject, but after surveying hundreds of evaluation sheets from many seminars, it appeared to me that though in-laws occasionally cause marital problems, they do not represent a major trouble area. God's concepts in this category are so simple and relatively brief that I decided to place the solutions in this chapter.

Do you realize that God was not surprised by the in-law problem? Even before there were any, He spoke to the question in Genesis 2:24 (AMP): "Therefore a man shall leave his father and his mother and shall become united and cleave to his wife, and they shall become one flesh." God recognized how vitally important it is for a couple to *leave* their parents, physically, emotionally, totally, and *cleave* unto each other, in other words unite into a new family unit, complete, separate, and apart from the parents of either.

The parent-child relationship is a *temporary* one; the marital relationship is meant by God to be a *permanent* one. God ordained this ultimate, one-flesh union. In this first reference to in-laws in Genesis, God makes it crystal-clear that the prior relationship of parent and child *must* be severed. Dr. Jay E. Adams says: ". . . the original relationship that existed when he was living in the home will not continue. When he marries, a man can no longer sustain the same relationship to his parents that he once did. It *must* change. He must now become the head of a new decision-making unit that we call the family. He can no longer continue many of the former ties to his parents.

"Modern society has failed to discover this important distinction. In our society, the parent-child relationship has become the more significant one, to the detriment of children and marriage partners alike."[2]

Dr. Adams continues by saying: "When a young man allows himself to be pulled apart by his mother and wife instead of obeying the Word of God, everyone suffers. If he leaves and cleaves in spite of what she says, it is always best for his mother, as well as for his wife and for himself. How crucial it is for mothers to know when it is time to tell the children to leave the nest. They must first teach them how to fly, then nudge them out when the time has come. It is important, then, for parents to understand that the most basic relationship is between the husband and the wife, not between the parent and his child.

"Perhaps a word to young people would be appropriate. If you want to do the best for yourself and for your parents, you will not demand so much attention and interest from your parents. You will not be anxious to squeeze every second that you can out of them. They have only so much time. They need to spend some of it with each other. It would be great for some of you now and then to say, 'Mom and Dad, I want you to go out and do things on your own. I'll be glad to babysit voluntarily.' You should do everything that you can to help your parents to find some time for each other. They need to do some things alone. Not only will your parents benefit, but in the long run this will greatly benefit you."[3]

God's Word is clear in relationship to in-laws. They are to be loved, honored, and respected. When they offer advice, or you ask it, you should consider their counsel, their experience, wisdom, and thank them for their care and concern in sharing their insights with you in this matter. Then you would do well to consider the years of experience they offer in their advice, along with your own knowledge and desires; then after family discussion, the husband is ultimately responsible for the decisions made in the marriage.

If your in-laws live in the same town, and you are having problems with either Mom dropping in too often, taking over, or interfering with the discipline of the children, stop it before it becomes a habit. If it's already out of control, if it is the wife's mother or father, it might be easier on them if their daughter has a *direct* talk with them. Be sure you share with them in love, tell them how much you appreciate their care, concern and interest in your family, but let them know that their casual drop-ins aren't always convenient and occasionally disrupt family plans or times of family intimacy. Kindly suggest that they call before they come for a visit. If the husband's mother or father is the problem, he should *firmly* and lovingly let them know that there must be limits on their visits. *Grandparents, please don't wait to be told that you are overstepping your bounds. Wait till you are invited to visit your children.*

Genesis states, and I highly agree, that two families were never created to live under the same roof. The problems and lack of privacy are monumental and create a corroding atmosphere, particularly in a young marriage.

Never make your mate feel that he/she is competing with your parents for your love or attention or devotion. This problem can arise when a young man is quite close to his mother and discovers that his new bride isn't quite the cook or housekeeper that Mom was. Trying to change or encourage your wife by making comparisons with your mother's cooking, care, or whatever, won't improve the new bride, and will cause hostile feelings between her and your mother. Some men continue this process until their wives feel that their mother-in-law is the "other woman" in their husband's life. Harmony between the generations cannot be established in this atmosphere, so be aware of this, and if you as a husband have been disrupting your marriage in this manner, ask your wife's forgiveness and never use this approach again. Compliments and praise will be more encouraging to her, and will stabilize her relationship with your mother, more than any other approach.

Women, we too are often guilty of comparing our young husbands to our adoring fathers with whom we once lived. I think in both instances the problem is intensified if the idolized parent is dead. My Jim, unfortunately, had to compete with a father whom I remembered as being bigger than life. In my immaturity, having lost my daddy before I could see or relate to him through mature eyes, I saw him as a faultless giant who could solve any problem, protect and provide every wish and desire. My attitude was not only wrong, it was unhealthy, and it was detrimental to our marriage. Jim couldn't compete—he was smart enough to realize there was no point in trying—but till I matured, he was continually sharing me with the ghost of my dad. I made no attempt to hide my feelings; I often let him know that I felt if Daddy were here, things would be different, or Daddy would never let that happen to me, or Daddy would have handled that differently. No husband or wife can compete with the ghost of the past. No matter how wonderful your parents are, what you recall, and what they were actually like, are two very different things. Most of all, you, as I, are out of line biblically. Your devotion is to be completely toward your mate, *completely*.

What about the elderly mother or father who isn't able to safely live alone any more? That is a problem. It is my personal belief that it first depends on the personality of the parent involved. Certain personalities would prefer rest communities where they can visit and relate to those of their own age, talk about the past, and commune with people who generally think and act as they do. Others may be too shy or weak or ill. These, I feel, should be afforded the comfort of residing with their children, if they prefer. If you reach this point with one of your parents, remember that their move into the home should in *no way* change the line of authority, nor should you allow their presence to cause abnormal disruption in the family activities and habits.

If you are having trouble loving, or even relating to, your in-laws, first re-evaluate your actions and mental attitude toward them. Then turn the situation over to the Lord, claiming His promise in Proverbs 16:7. If you're harboring resentment, hostility, bitterness, confess those sins, recalling Psalms 66:18 (AMP): "If I regard iniquity, in my heart the Lord will not hear me." Ask the Lord to love your in-laws through you. Begin to relate to them, speak to them, care for them, recalling that Christ said in Matthew 25:40b (AMP): ". . . I tell you, in as far as you did it to one of the least of these My brethren, you did it to Me." As you begin relating to your in-laws as Christ would, in time I believe you will find they'll become a blessing and joy, forming true family unity.

We have just discussed a number of areas of your life which in the past you may have failed to deal with correctly. The deeper you get into God's Word, the quicker you'll begin to recognize these trouble areas. When you do, simply confess them and then ask the Lord to make your spirit sensitive to other areas which may be causing problems in your marriage. Certainly, if you have had problems with fear, anger, resentment, bitterness, jealousy, these things probably won't disappear overnight, but as you are constantly allowing the Holy Spirit to lead you, visible changes will begin to occur.

GOALS: Daily become more aware of mental-attitude areas of your life which are not pleasing to God and which are tearing at your marital relationship. Also become more and more aware of the importance of being in God's Word, of claiming His promises, realizing that all the strength, power, and peace you need are simply waiting for you to ask for them. Most of all, be sure that you are keeping short accounts with God, and in the process beginning to relate to your mate as Christ relates to you.

ASSIGNMENTS:

(1) Memorize Galatians 6:7, II Corinthians 12:9 and 9:8.

(2) Read Hebrews 10:38, 11:1–40, and Psalms 66:18.

(3) Ask God daily to make you aware of improper responses, and then with an act of your will begin to respond as God would have you do.

(4) Make a conscious effort for the next week to say "Thank you" with a thankful spirit for everything that happens. As you begin to develop this spirit, it will spread to the rest of your family.

(5) Seriously ponder Proverbs 6:16–22 and you will see that of the six things that the Lord says He hates the most, all are what could be considered mental-attitude sins, with one or two exceptions!

(6) When you are in doubt about how to react in a situation, just think, "What would Christ do?" and you'll be on the right track.

(7) Continue to study the Word daily. You can't know the mind of Christ, or how to overcome trials and problems, until you know His Word. (Prov. 7:1–3)

(8) If you begin to feel down, remember Psalms 37:23–24 (AMP): "The steps of a (good) man are directed and established of the Lord, when He delights in his way. Though he falls, he shall not be utterly cast down, for the Lord grasps his hand in support and upholds him."

(9) Pick up a copy of Bill Bright's booklet "Have You Made the Wonderful Discovery of the Spirit-filled Life?" and read it.

CHAPTER 12

GOD, SCRIPTURE, AND DIVORCE

I constantly talk with couples who call on me, not to help them solve the marital problems they are facing, but to supply them with an excuse for a divorce. Most of these couples are Christians, but instead of searching for God's solutions for their marital strains, they are looking for something in Scripture to justify the dissolution of their marital vows. Maybe you fall into this category. In fact, perhaps this is the chapter you have been looking forward to, hoping that you can find in Scripture a way out of your problems. This approach isn't unusual. Most of us pray that our rationalizations can be blessed. As mere humans, we feel caught up in overwhelming situations, and our first instinct is to look for a way to escape.

Where divorce is concerned, most couples who are looking for a "loophole" in God's law usually realize their reasons are wrong. But they are still hoping that in their case some Scripture, some minister, or counselor will offer them a justifiable cause. Apparently, many persons in the counseling field are doing just that, because the divorce rate is increasing at an alarming rate. Too many couples seeking solutions, unfortunately, are being offered "loopholes," excuses and rationalizations instead of scriptural help.

As you read the next few pages on God's position on divorce, keep in mind that God didn't thoughtlessly set up rules. He knows exactly what will make you happy. He is *always* concerned about your happiness and is willing to do far more than you ask or even desire of Him. (Eph. 3:20) It says in John 10:10 (AMP): ". . . I came that they may have and enjoy life, and have it in abundance—to the full, till it overflows." That is the type of life and marriage that He fervently desires for *you!* Psalms 37:3–5 (AMP) reminds us of the method for obtaining this happiness when it says: "Trust (lean on, rely on and be confident) in the Lord, and do good; so shall you dwell in the land and feed surely on His faithfulness, and truly you shall be fed. Delight yourself also in the Lord, and He will give you the desires and secret petitions of your heart. Commit your way to the Lord—roll and repose (each care of) your load on Him; trust also in Him, and He will bring it to pass!" Just keep in mind, it says delight yourself in the Lord, not delight yourself in your desires. Keep these fantastic verses in mind while you read exactly what the Scriptures have to say about the blessed state of matrimony and the tragedy of divorce.

DIVORCE TODAY

I'm sure I don't need to tell you that divorce in the United States is increasing at an alarming rate. The divorce and annulment rate in America has increased 85 per cent since 1960. Since 1970, the divorce rate alone has increased 50 per cent! In most parts of the country, one out of every three marriages is failing, and in some portions of the United States there are now more divorces than marriages. Obviously, much of this change has been wrought by society's change of attitude toward divorce. Some of this change has been for the good. There was a time when a divorced person was almost alienated from proper society. On the other hand, divorce now, instead of being a state of social disgrace, is actually being encouraged by many, even Christians. (II Tim. 4:3–4)

In Christian circles, the views on the biblical teaching on divorce vary. Martin Luther, the reformer, took the position that divorce would cost a believer his salvation. Some teach that there is no ground for divorce; others say that there is only one ground. Still others see two clear grounds in the Scripture for divorce. Who to believe is often the overwhelming question to true Christians, seeking God's will for their lives. What you or I believe, think, or even hope are the grounds for divorce, doesn't matter. *What is important is what God says in His Word on this subject.* The only way to settle this issue is by an objective and inductive study of the Scriptures themselves.

GOD'S ORIGINAL PLAN

It was God's original plan for marriage to be a permanent state; divorce was not in the Genesis original. Obviously, in the beginning God meant marriage to be monogamous. There is no justification in God's eternal plan for polygamy, communal living, etc. All these are direct attacks on God's design for marriage.

God created marriage to be a *permanent* state. Marriage is intended to be honoring to God and personally fulfilling. I Thessalonians 2:12 (LVB) says: "That your daily lives should not embarrass God, but bring joy to Him who invited you into His kingdom to share His glory."

Marriage was created in such a way as to bring completion to both the husband and the wife. In the beginning of Genesis 2:18 (AMP) it says: "Now the Lord God said, 'It is not good (sufficient, satisfactory) that the man should be alone; I will make him a helper meet (suitable, adapted, completing) for him.'"

This was the original basis and intention for marriage. Idealistic? Not really. Learning God's concepts for a happy marriage is the key to this type of relationship.

In time, because of the fallen nature of man, God's beautiful original became tainted. Divorce entered the picture. As we search the Scriptures we realize that divorce is the result of sinfulness on the part of one or both of the marriage partners; more often than not, both are in some way to blame. Remember the Big "I." Does God really see divorce in this light? Yes. *He clearly states that divorce was a concession to sin.* Matthew 19:8 (AMP): "He said to them, 'Because of the hardness (stubbornness and perversity) of your hearts Moses permitted you to dismiss and repudiate and divorce your wives; but from the beginning it has *not* been so (ordained).'"

God's position on divorce is vividly stated in Malachi 2:16 (AMP): "For the Lord the God of Israel says: *I hate divorce* and marital separation, and him who covers his garment (his wife) with violence. Therefore keep a watch upon your spirit (that it may be controlled by My Spirit) that you deal not treacherously and faithlessly (with your marriage mate)." The Bible does not look kindly on the one who initiates divorce, as seen in Malachi 2:13–16.

Certainly the Scriptures, the mind of Christ, would have us avoid divorce if at all possible. The Scripture never *commands* divorce under any circumstance.

DIVORCE DEFINED

Divorce is defined by Webster in this manner: "divorce is a legal dissolution of a marriage; to get rid of one's spouse." For Christians, divorce is the dissolving of the marriage relationship for biblical reasons *only*. Divorce in both the Old Testament and the New is used as a legal term for the act of "removing the obligations of a marriage contract." For both Christians and non-Christians, God instructs us that legal channels *must* be followed if a divorce ever takes place. The institution of marriage has been given to the whole human race and therefore it functions under the God-given institution of government. (Gen. 9:1–7; Matt. 22:21) In other words, you cannot merely decide one day you have had it, turn to your mate and say: "I divorce you, I divorce you, I divorce you!" Though it would be cheaper!

As Christians you must realize that man's laws do not always parallel God's law. (Isa. 55:8–9) Because you have grounds for a divorce based on man's law, this does *not* mean these reasons are valid options for you as a believer.

DIVORCE AS SEEN IN THE OLD TESTAMENT

The Scriptures first speak about marriage and its intended permanence in Genesis 2:24. The divine purpose for marriage was that it be monogamous, permanent, complementary, and intimate. Divorce first reared its ugly head in Israel. At this time God permitted divorce as a concession to sin. As we see in Matthew 19:8, it was due to spiritual deterioration and negative volition toward God. God tolerated divorce, but it was intrinsically wrong.

Divorce as practiced in Israel was legally allowed for the reason of "uncleanness." (Deut. 24:1–4, Lev. 22:13, Num. 30:9, Num. 22:19, 29) "Uncleanness" was the only legitimate gounds for divorce in the Old Testament. The Hebrew word is *erwah.* It means something disgraceful, offensive (some people suggest such things as fornication, indecent exposure). This same verb, erwah, is used in Leviticus 20:18–19 in relation to sexual offenses. It is also found in Leviticus 18:6 and Deuteronomy

23:14. It could *not* mean adultery, for in that day the act itself was punishable by death. (Deut. 22:13, Lev. 20:10)

The Old Testament strongly emphasizes that divorce procedures were to be followed. First of all, a bill of divorcement had to be secured. This served as a deterrent to a quickie divorce. (Deut. 24:1) The procedure also protected the woman and served as proof of her lawful release from her marital obligations. Divorce dissolved the original union.

In the Old Testament there were three things which constituted a marriage; it was not based on a sexual union alone. To secure a marriage legally there were a dowry, a contract, and sexual relationship involved. There were also three things that could dissolve a marriage: (1) natural death, (2) execution for adultery (Deut. 22:22), and (3) divorce.

Just as we have liberal divorce laws today, divorce in the Old Testament became a problem through the abuse of the indecency clause of Deuteronomy 24:1. Husbands at that time were actually divorcing their wives for such things as burning the dinner. Thank heavens this isn't a legitimate ground today or, at one time or another, I imagine, we'd all have been thrown out.

DIVORCE AS VIEWED BY THE NEW TESTAMENT

In the New Testament we have the opportunity to see what Jesus Christ had to say about marriage and divorce. It is a wonderful opportunity, if we reflect on what the Scriptures have to say about the written word (II Tim. 3:16 AMP): "*Every Scripture* is God-breathed—given by His inspiration—and profitable for *instruction,* for *reproof* and *conviction of sin,* for *correction of error* and *discipline in obedience* and *for training* in *righteousness* (that is, holy living, in conformity to God's will in thought, purpose and action)."

Divorce in the New Testament is *restricted basically to marital unfaithfulness.* This is referred to as fornication. Fornication is a broad term and cannot be limited to premarital sex, as we see in Matthew 5:32. Fornication, or adultery, does not in itself dissolve a marriage relationship. The New Testament tells us that it takes two things to dissolve a marriage: unfaithfulness and a bill of divorcement.

We always find that the divine ideal is strongly stressed. In Matthew 19:3–12, we find a misquote of the quibbling Pharisees. Here, Christ clearly states that divorce in the Old Testament was tolerated only because of the sin in the hearts of the people. Divorce in these passages is clearly restricted to marital unfaithfulness (fornication). Remarriage is restricted in these verses, particularly in verse 9. Matthew 5:31–32 also speaks to this point. A believer only has the right to remarry if he has a scripturally legitimate divorce.

Divorce is next discussed in Mark 10:2–12. There are no legitimate grounds for divorce discussed here in Mark. Again, remarriage is restricted, and adultery is said to be committed by a party who wrongly dismisses his mate and enters into another marriage. In Mark we first find the Scriptures speaking of a wife initiating a divorce. (Mark 10:12) Luke also speaks to the subject of divorce. (Luke 16:18 and 18) Here again, divorce and remarriage are restricted.

We are truly blessed with insights from the Scriptures when we have the opportunity of reading Paul's writings in I Corinthians 7:10–16. (Before you decide these are merely Paul's ideas and can therefore be dismissed), remember that not only is *all Scripture inspired,* but Paul says that he is speaking about things that Christ didn't discuss, and he continues to speak, saying (I Cor. 7:10 AMP), *"I give charge, not I but the Lord."*

You as a believer are not to initiate a divorce because your mate is an unbeliever. If your unbelieving mate is willing to remain married to you, then, according to I Corinthians 7:12–14, you are to stick with it. Before you start screaming, please make a serious note of the positive benefits of this marital situation as we see in I Corinthians 7:14 (AMP): "For the unbelieving husband is set apart (separated, withdrawn from heathen contamination and affiliated with the Christian people) by union with his consecrated (set apart) wife; and the unbelieving wife is set apart and separated through union with her consecrated husband. Otherwise your children would be unclean (unblessed heathen, outside the Christian covenant), but as it is they are prepared for God—pure and clean."

The NASV Ryrie Study Bible has a very clear interpretation of this verse: "The presence of a believer in the home sets the home apart and gives it a Christian influence it would not otherwise have. A believing partner, therefore, should stay with the unbeliever. However, this does *not* mean that children born into such a home are *automatically* Christians. They are holy in the sense of being set apart by the presence of one believing parent." As we progress we will note other positive benefits of keeping God's law and one's marital vows. For instance, James 1:12 (AMP): "Blessed, happy, to be envied is the man who is patient under trial and stands up under temptation, for when he has stood the test and been approved, he will receive (the victor's) crown of life which God has promised to those who love Him." Isn't that wonderful? Not only are there a multitude of earthly benefits for those who keep the faith with God, but tremendous eternal rewards awaiting us also.

The *second* biblical ground for divorce appears in I Corinthians 7:15 (AMP): "But if the unbelieving partner (actually) leaves, let him do so; in such (cases the remaining) brother or sister is not morally bound. But God has called us to peace." Other translations of this verse use the words "not under bondage" or "not enslaved." In the original language of the Scripture, these words all denote freedom, the fact that the believing partner is thereafter not bound to keep the marital contract. The verse says nothing about remarriage directly, except where it notes that the believing partner is free from the marriage contract, is no longer in moral bondage, which gives him/her the biblical right to remarry. Therefore, here is the *second* and *only* other scriptural reason for divorce: desertion by an unbelieving mate.

This doesn't mean divorce is in order if your mate has a temper fit and leaves home for a couple of days. Remember, God is always aware of your motives, and if you use His law wrongly, if you push that unbelieving mate out the door so you can claim desertion, then God will be aware of it, and you won't have biblical grounds for divorce in His eyes.

Before we proceed, take a moment and see how the last sentence of this verse reads. Even though it gives the believer a biblical right to a divorce, still it closes in saying (AMP): "But God has called us to peace." Peace as it is used in this verse refers to reconciliation. Whenever possible, the Lord would have it that we should do our utmost to rectify our problems and reunite our marriages, *whether to a believer or to an unbeliever.*

To those of you who are married, seek to make your marriage as happy as possible. Remember that God didn't supply us with concepts, directions, and commands simply to fill a book. *He* was the original architect of marriage and the family. *He* knows what will bring our ultimate fulfillment and happiness.

Sometimes our thinking as Christians is rather twisted. We are willing to trust our ultimate destiny to God through belief in His Son Jesus Christ, but from that point on, we try to run our lives by man's standards, applying man's solutions, and then wonder why we fail. God gave us concepts directed to our marriages so that they might be the happiest, most rewarding relationships on earth. Think about our poor human logic here for a minute. Since God loved you enough to send His only Son to die for you personally, then why can't you accept the fact that He also knows what is best for you here in time? Believe me, as many others have discovered, He does; His concepts work. *Remember: divorce is man's solution; problem-solving, happiness and reconciliation are God's answers!*

SCRIPTURE AND THE CHURCH

Unfortunately, in the past the church has often been terribly harsh in its treatment of the divorced. Often it has positioned itself higher than Christ in its unforgiving attitude and rejection of the divorced. Neither the believer nor the church has the right to go beyond the Scriptures in its judgment of those who are divorced. As the living body of Christ, we must be as willing as He is to forgive, and never to make the error of putting a stigma on everyone who is divorced. Often, neither the church nor the believer knows whether or not they are dealing with the "innocent" party. It is our responsibility to treat divorced people on a grace basis, just as God treats us. Frequently, our scale of sins does not coincide with God's scale. In our self-righteousness we forget what Christ had to say about pride, hypocritical judging, and gossip.

Those who are divorced or remarried should not be excluded

from church membership. The Scriptures do not legislate against their membership. (I Cor. 6:9–11, Eph. 2:1–6, 5:1)

THE "WHAT IFS" OF DIVORCE

A book could be written on the "what ifs" of divorce. I sincerely hope that the preceding pages have made the grounds of divorce and God's position on divorce clear, but in this section I will try to deal with the major "what ifs."

What if in the marriage of two believers, one is unfaithful? Biblically, the offended party has legitimate grounds for divorce, but divorce should only be sought as a last resort. Divorce is never automatic. It is only permitted. Remember Matthew 18:21, 22 (AMP): "Then Peter came up to Him and said, 'Lord, how many times may my brother sin against me and I forgive Him and let it go? As many as up to seven times?' Jesus answered him, 'I tell you, not up to seven times, but seventy times seven!'" God would have it that if at all possible, you work always in the direction of reconciliation.

What should a believer do when a *believing* mate has been unfaithful? The Scriptures provide for the exact procedure in Matthew 18:15–17.

First, if your mate wrongs you, you are to go to him in private and in Christian love, share with him his default of you.

If he refuses to listen, or correct the wrong, then again in love, you are to take with you one or two others "so that every word may be confirmed," and again confront him with his wrong, and ask him if he will not turn from it.

If he still refuses to listen and repent, you are to go to your pastor and let him deal with the situation.

If your mate is still hostile and refuses to alter his behavior, then you as a Christian have done your duty as God set forth in the Scriptures.

I recently came in contact with a woman whose husband had been involved in a long-standing affair, and after she had done everything in her power to change the situation, she followed God's directions in Matthew. Today, the marriage has been mended and the affair ended.

The procedure may sound a bit foreign, or possibly ridiculous, but God provided it for a purpose, and if there is a way to reach your mate, God will work in and through it as you are obedient to follow His commands.

What if in a marriage of two believers the marriage is so strained that there is physical or mental pressure which the "innocent" party can no longer bear?

First of all, re-evaluate your situation. Learn God's concepts and *earnestly* apply them to your marriage. Recall how one person can change a situation by allowing the Lord through the power of the Holy Spirit to change him. Perhaps a new you would create a new mate. It is *not* your job to change your mate. Leave that to God. Concentrate on allowing God to remake you in the image and likeness of Jesus Christ. Remember, God is a judge of the thoughts and intent of your heart. The grounds of undue mental pressure are often used by those wanting to rationalize their situation and to cop out on their responsibilities and problems. There are no biblical grounds for divorce in this situation. But if one of the believers feels that he must leave, then they are to remain unmarried.

I Peter 5:7 (LVB) says: "Let Him have all your worries and cares, for He is always thinking about you and watching everything that concerns you." Trust God to make the necessary changes in the situation, and remember, He works on a different time schedule, but He is always faithful. He will never fail you, never! In this circumstance, if the believer does leave, the Scripture does *not* provide for remarriage. (I Cor. 7:10–11)

II Corinthians 6:14 (AMP) says: "Do not be unequally yoked up with unbelievers—do not make mismated alliances with them, or come under a different yoke with them (inconsistent with your faith). For what partnership have right living and right standing with God with inequity and lawlessness? Or how can light fellowship with darkness?"

If you happen to be reading this book, and you haven't yet married, *please* take God's position opposing marriage to an unbeliever seriously. In fact, you are treading on thin ice if you even make a practice of dating unbelievers. I have seen some beautiful Christians make a complete wreck of their lives by this practice. If you constantly date those who do not know Jesus, you are risking emotional involvement and much unhappiness. You may think that you are involved in the love of the century, but one day when the rosy glow has dimmed, you'll discover that one who is truly committed to Christ and married to an unbeliever is constantly being pulled in different directions. If you are seeking to know God's right man or right woman for you, if your current love isn't committed to Christ, you can certainly mark him or her off the list.

What about the verse in II Corinthians 6:14 (AMP): "Do not be unequally yoked up with unbelievers . . ." Does this apply to those married to unbelievers, or those who are trying to reconcile their marriages to unbelievers? *No.* Certainly this verse is dealing with marriage, but it is also dealing with friendships, alliances, etc. The verse is written for those who are choosing marital partners for the first time. It certainly *doesn't* give a believer the right to leave an unbelieving mate. When you study God's Word, you can't pick out one verse and hinge your decisions on that one verse until you have studied all that God has to say on the subject. We can clearly see from other verses, like I Corinthians 7:14, that God expects you to stay with your unbelieving partner. He wants you to apply His concepts to your relationship, and by being the right kind of Christian mate, to perhaps help bring your husband or wife to a personal knowledge of Jesus Christ. Where there is any hope of the relationship being reconciled, this certainly would be God's will; remember His word on divorce in Malachi 2:16.

What if in a mixed marriage (believer and unbeliever) the unbelieving husband wants his wife to take care of the home, stay married, raise the children, but he wants to run around with other women, and generally do as he pleases? The believer certainly has grounds for divorce. (Matt. 19:9) But remember, divorce is rejection of God's ideal, and with God's help nothing is beyond change, even a situation like this. Many thousands of women have faced it, applied God's concepts, and in time found that they could again put complete trust in their once wandering husband. Often these marriages have become the most fulfilling, rewarding relationships on earth. *Always look to yourself first,* using God's concepts. Analyze what *you* may be doing either to contribute to or create the present situation. Very few situations are totally one person's fault. Remember Matthew 18 and forgive "seventy times seven." Certainly, you as a Christian should do everything possible to avoid divorce. If your husband wishes to leave, you should allow him to leave, but let him make the first move toward divorce court.

It would probably help if you did a thorough study of the principles of suffering as taught in the Scriptures. If you don't know where to begin on this subject, if you'll write me, I will be glad to help you get a correct start in this study. Please remember, during this difficult time, that you do *not* have the right to refuse sexual relations. I Corinthians 7:5 (AMP): "Do not refuse and deprive and defraud each other (of your due marital rights) except perhaps by *mutual* consent for a time, that you may devote yourselves unhindered to prayer. But afterwards resume marital relations, lest Satan tempt you (to sin) through your lack of restraint of sexual desire." Denying sexual relations is usually an act of revenge, which is un-Christian, and normally results in cutting off your nose to spite your face. It certainly is against God's will, and it can bring disastrous results.

Should this situation ever reach the point that the unbelieving husband does desert, then you again certainly have grounds for divorce.

What if one becomes a Christian after marriage and an unbelieving mate is hostile to the believer for this commitment (won't let his or her mate attend church, or pressures against it)? I Corinthians 7:12 speaks to this problem. There are no grounds for a Christian to leave a non-Christian on this basis. The believer should make the very best of the situation; try to be the best example of Christian love and understanding. Often, this problem arises because the unbelieving mate suddenly feels left out of your life, feels no common ground of communication. It may be that you, as a new believer, have become so excited about the person of Jesus Christ and learning the Scriptures, that in your desire to have your mate know Jesus too, you have become preachy, pushy, and are actually driving your mate away.

In a "mixed marriage," often the church (or Jesus) becomes a focal point of jealousy. Sometimes constant preaching or Bible reading in the presence of the unbeliever can cause great guilt problems. Comments such as, "I'm not worried about the problem, I know Jesus can handle it," or overt prayer, any sign of faith, can cause these situations to develop. Without words, you may be saying, "You are wrong in your thoughts, actions, etc." or, "I want you to change." You can clearly see how these feelings would cause hostility on the part of the unbeliever. It is difficult for your mate to understand what has happened in your life. And by your actions and words you may be making it even more difficult. If your mate is totally hostile to your attending church, try to eliminate this fear of alienation from you by taking your Bible study through tapes or study groups, which do not occur at a time or place that offends your unbelieving mate. The Christian involved certainly should not be the one to initiate a divorce based on these circumstances. If the believer does divorce an unbelieving mate, it becomes an act of rebellion against God, and the believer must either remain unmarried or be reconciled to his or her mate.

If you are concerned about the children involved in such a situation, I am sure that the believing mate can make right provisions for teaching the children, or having them taught at a time and place which will not upset the unbelieving mate. Remember that one of the greatest testimonies for Christianity your children will ever contact is the life that you lead before them. Explain God's line of authority to them; also explain the situation in the home in a loving way. Have a private time of prayer together for the unbelieving parent. God will honor your obedience, and your children will have a living example of God's Word.

What if two unbelievers are married and one becomes a Christian and the unbeliever leaves? I Corinthians 7:12–16 speaks to this point: If you, as a Christian mate, have done *everything* in your power to apply God's concepts to your marriage, if you have lived with your unbelieving mate as God would have you do, and the unbeliever still willfully deserts you, then you are no longer "under bondage." You are free to divorce and remarry. I would suggest to you in all cases where divorce seems the only solution, that whenever possible, you allow the unbelieving partner to make the first legal moves. Verse 15 states the second reason for divorce. I would caution you, however, not to use this verse as a "loophole" when you have actually driven your unbelieving mate away. Of course, if adultery is involved in the situation, the believer has grounds for divorce.

What if one has biblical grounds for divorce (fornication or desertion) but the state law categorizes the reason under another heading, such as "irretrievably broken," or "incompatibility"? The dissolution of your marriage is based on the act of fornication (sexual unfaithfulness) or desertion, plus a bill of divorcement. Whether you have the right in the eyes of God, *not the state,* is the issue. First use Matthew 18:15–17 and try to resolve the problem through the church. If it is totally impossible, the believer has the right to use whatever law on the state books is most in accord with his own situation.

What if a person wants to remarry and the divorce was based on the biblical reason of fornication or desertion? The Scriptures neither command nor forbid marriage; either is a proper and available choice for the "innocent" party involved. The Scriptures still encourage forgiving and restoration of the first marriage as a more ideal situation.

What if one is divorced, has remarried, and has just discovered that unscriptural reasons were involved. Should one go back to the first partner? There is no biblical basis for this. (I Cor. 7:17–24) It would be a situation where two wrongs don't make a right. The first marriage has been completely dissolved (in the eyes of God), since a divorce, a new marriage and a new sexual relationship have been established. The second marriage cannot be dissolved by divorce on improper grounds in an attempt to correct a past mistake. Just thank God that when you became His child that all your past sins were forgiven. Encourage your spirit by rereading Romans 8:28.

What if your former mate has become a Christian since your divorce and wishes to become reconciled, and (the marriage has not been totally dissolved) because remarriage has not taken place? In that case, you should seek reconciliation and remarriage. This gives you a wonderful opportunity to be a silent witness for Jesus Christ by being a loving and righteous (not goody-goody) mate. Perhaps you can be instrumental in bringing your mate to a deeper relationship with Jesus Christ. Remember, however, that even though the marriage has not been completely dissolved, there should be *no* sexual relations until you are officially married.

What if the "innocent" party in a divorce remarries. Can the "guilty" party then remarry? If you are a Christian and happen to be the guilty party, sit tight. Study the doctrine of divorce and remarriage. Learn God's concepts for a good marriage, so that if and when you do remarry you don't duplicate the mistakes of the past. Remember, you might be led to perpetuate the divine ideal and remain in a single state. If the "innocent" party in the marriage has remarried, the marriage has been irretrievably broken, and the guilty party may remarry. If the innocent party remains unmarried, the guilty party does *not* have a biblical right to remarry.

BUT MY NEIGHBOR SAID . . .

Many tragic mistakes have been made by well-meaning neighbors, relatives, and friends. All these people love you very much, and it hurts them when you are suffering. Unfortunately, they are usually long on sympathy, which drives you into destructive self-pity, and short on biblically constructive solutions. I'll bet that for those of you who have tried this, if you will be honest with yourself, you'll find you've spent about 90 per cent of your time discussing what awful things have been done to you and about 10 per cent of the time discussing what someone your friend knows did in the same situation. Right? Or worse, you might do as a friend of mine and I did before I knew Jesus. We plotted and planned the most awful forms of revenge. One night, we planned to gather up all her husband's odd socks and send them to his girlfriend and ask her to mate them up. Another friend of mine dumped her husband's dirty laundry on his honey's doorstep! Of course, these are just funny things. I won't even go into the cruel things we contrived for fear I might give you some ideas that you haven't thought up for yourselves. Before you rely on anyone's opinions on marriage, divorce, marital relations, problems, solutions, be sure that you check the Scriptures for *yourself*. God is going to hold *you* responsible for the actions and decisions you make. In the back of this book is a list of Scriptures which deal with basic family problems, responsibilities and concepts. These have been listed to help you read and check God's Word for yourself.

WHAT ABOUT A CHRISTIAN COUNSELOR?

I wish I could say, if you feel the need of third-party help, just go to your phone book and look up a Christian counselor. But I can't. Sadly, sometimes the only thing you may find Christian about some is the name. In the past forty years, more and more people have gone into this field, but obviously fewer and fewer marriages are being saved. Sitting here in Atlanta, there is no way I could recommend a counselor in Cowpen, South Carolina, or Marble Falls, Texas. There are a number of problems involved, the main one being that everyone who calls him- or herself a "Christian" counselor may or may not base his or her procedures on the Scriptures. Christian counselors can be the greatest help in the world; they can lead you through the Scriptures, point out your problems, and from the Word, show you how to correct them, or they can be as destructive as any quack on earth. Because this is such a problem, I have contacted two large interdenominational groups which train very competent counselors. Someone trained by one of these groups should be convenient to almost every area of the country. If you have a simple question or problem, please feel free to write me, but if you feel the need of a third party in your home town, a list of agencies which can put you in contact with Christian counselors is listed in the appendix of this book.

As you think about the subject of divorce, please recall that God didn't simply take a strong stand on the subject and leave you helpless in a miserable marriage. He has provided us with all the help, all the answers to *any* problem that we will ever face. He has eternally promised to be sufficient, to be faithful. (Heb. 13:5) He has even promised to make us at peace with our enemies, and if some of you feel right now that your mate is your greatest enemy, read God's promise in Proverbs 16:7 (AMP): "When a man's ways please the Lord, He makes even his enemies to be at peace with him."

In our search of the Word we find that God's ideal is that two believers should be united in marriage, that this is the ideal state. Unfortunately, many people don't fall into this ideal situation, and their marriages are wounded and broken. Some who are reading this don't have serious problems; they are just tired and want out. For everyone, no matter what the situation, you can clearly see that the Scriptures allow for divorce on two grounds only: fornication (sexual unfaithfulness) and the desertion of a believer by an unbeliever. As you consider your own situation, remember that God knows your heart, that He wants more than anything in the world for you to be happy, and because He does, He has provided all the directions and concepts to help you find peace and happiness right where you are. He doesn't ask that you save your marriage alone; He is waiting for you to ask for His help, His leading. He is only a prayer away.

GOALS: Your goal is to better understand God's divine plan, and to become aware of your commitment as a Christian to do everything possible to save your marriage, or, if you are separated, to reconcile your relationship.

ASSIGNMENTS:

(1) Reread I Corinthians 7:10–15, I Peter 3:1, Ephesians 4:30–32, Matthew 19:7–9.

(2) Memorize Matthew 19:6 and Malachi 2:16.

(3) Check to be sure that you are trusting Christ for *every* area of your life, and that your priorities are in Godly order.

(4) Continue to work on your relationship as "unto the Lord." (Col. 3:23–24)

(5) Remember Hebrews 4:15 and 16, which tell us that Christ Is vitally aware of all our thoughts, feelings, pain and heartbreak, and that He will provide the help and strength that you need. Read Philippians 4:19 and John 15:7.

(6) Read and reread God's concepts and study them so that they become second nature to you as you act and interact with your mate.

(7) Continually take your problems and anxieties to the Lord in prayer, recalling His promise in John 14:14 and 18 (AMP): "Yes, I will grant—will do for you—whatever you shall ask in My name (presenting all I am). I will not leave you orphans—comfortless, desolate, bereaved, forlorn, helpless—I will come (back) to you." Also read I Thessalonians 5:17.

(8) Continue to be the mate that God designed you to be, and turn whatever corrupting force is eating away at your marriage over to Him. He is your supreme lawyer. (Eph. 6:10, Heb. 10:30)

(9) When considering divorce, please spend much time studying God's Word, seek God's solutions, and know God is aware of the thoughts and intentions of your heart. In most cases the choice is: Do you want your way? or God's? (James 1:2–5)

(10) Don't become dismayed, impatient, feeling God is failing to deal with and supply your needs. God's timing is *perfect*. Learn the blessing of waiting upon the Lord. Refer to Isaiah 30:18, 40:31, and Psalms 25:3, 40:1, 62:5.

AFTERWORD

THE SURVIVOR'S REWARD

I am sure many of you have already begun to apply God's concepts to your relationships and can testify to the joy and truth they contain. Some already have miraculous stories to tell about the transforming power of Jesus Christ and the dramatic impact that God's directives have made in your own personal marital situation. You have trusted, obeyed, applied and marveled as Christ stepped in, took over, and turned tragedy to triumph. I know that some of you who picked up this book as your last hope, have found the truth of Psalms 34:17, 18 (AMP): "When the righteous cry for help, the Lord hears, and delivers them out of their distress and troubles. The Lord is close to those who are of a broken heart, and saves such as are crushed with sorrow for sin and are humbly and thoroughly penitent."

You've discovered that Christ is constantly aware, not only of our overt actions, but also of the pain and sorrow in our souls. He Himself was a man of sorrows and is ever aware of the heartbreak and pain that His children are suffering. But more than that, He has supplied the concepts, directives, and answers to every problem that you face, and all He asks is that you are willing.

Hearts that were broken, homes that were cracking under strain, are now experiencing the fulfillment of growing together. Many of you are beginning to discover the excitement of raising children in a home where mom and dad care enough, that through Christ's power you've saved your marriage and your family. Perhaps for the first time in your marital life you are experiencing a home that is warm, and you are learning the joy of building happy memories for yourselves and your children. You have come to understand the truth the Psalmist shared in Psalms 16:11 (AMP): "You will show me the path of life; in Your presence is fullness of joy, at Your right hand there are pleasures forevermore." You are learning the unexplainable joy of becoming a survivor.

Of course, I don't want to mislead you. Survivors do miss

something! You'll never have the opportunity of facing failure. As a survivor, you won't know the pain and heartbreak of a broken home, the fighting over who will take what, or who can visit the children and when. As a female survivor, you won't understand the fear and difficulty of possibly having to re-enter the working field after years of being a homemaker and wife. As a man, you will never know how it feels to hear your children call another man "Daddy." There are many things survivors miss: dinners alone, the horrible lonely Sundays, or the plastic parties where you continually search for the "right" one again. You may never understand what it's like to continually have your guts torn in a mental search for the reason for your marital failure. Yes, survivors, there are things you will never know, never experience, but take it from those of us who have been on both sides of the fence, you ought to thank God every day that you have bypassed these depressing experiences.

I could fill a book with the comments that people have made when they honestly applied God's concepts and directions to their marital relationships. You clearly saw what they did for Jim and me, Melony and Todd, Lorna and Blake, and others. These same answers are waiting for you. All God asks is that you are willing. If your marriage has been blessed by applying God's concepts, I'd love to hear how the Lord has blessed your relationship.

As we discussed in Chapter 11, you don't need to worry that love is dead because the "feeling" has waned. In story after story, comment after comment, you have seen God's eternal truths working in and through lives to change and mold them into beautiful, exciting new relationships. It doesn't matter whether your relationship has been torn by adultery, alcohol, drugs, role-reversal, sexual frustration, or a communication breakdown; *there is hope, there are answers.* You have just come face to face with people who met these problems and survived.

As you begin this wondrous journey of trust and reliance on Jesus Christ, and consistently apply His concepts, you'll experience joy unlimited. When you become a survivor, you'll discover that in surviving your marriage has become stronger. Little problems, day-to-day upsets which used to bring fear to your heart, are no longer frightening. You have faced the brink and survived. You'll learn that you have acquired an appreciation for the "little" things you may not have noticed before, or taken time for in the past. These will be precious moments to be cherished, moments to be thankful for. Your senses will be heightened; you'll be aware of every special moment, every quiet time, the beauty of an evening walk, the comfort of just lying in bed shielded and held in the arms of a love that was tested and survived.

There is one pitfall that remains. You have read, you know God's concepts, you understand His ways, you have seen His directives work in the most traumatic marital situations, but you may still be standing on the brink waiting. Many people wait too long, sit and intellectually think through all the possibilities and ramifications before they put them into practice. All of us find that it is much easier to discuss concepts, discuss God's directives, than to step out and put them into practice. You can spend your time discussing this method versus that until the day you walk into divorce court. Discussion and debate are not substitutes for faith. (Heb. 11:6) *Love is something that has to be lived, not discussed or debated.*

You are standing on the brink of the most wonderful experience of your life. You can step out with God's Word and discover that God will guide you through the dark to the most glorious morning of joy. Psalms 29:5b (AMP) says: ". . . Weeping may endure for a night, but joy comes in the morning." Are you ready for that exciting experience?

As you commit yourself to Jesus Christ and apply His concepts to your marriage, you can almost sit back in wonderful amazement as through you He works out the right plan, the right solutions for your unique situation. The rewards you will receive are boundless. The most precious is knowing that you were obedient to God, His Word, and that He will abundantly bless you for that. You have upheld the marital vow you made before God.

I'd like to close with the clearest, most beautiful description of love that has ever been written. I Corinthians 13:4–8a (AMP): "Love endures long and is patient and kind; love never is envious nor boils over with jealousy; is not boastful or vainglorious, does not display itself haughtily. It is not conceited—arrogant and inflated with pride; it is not rude (unmannerly) and does not act unbecomingly. Love does not insist on its own rights or its own way, for it is not self-seeking; it is not touchy or fretful or resentful; it takes no account of the evil done to it—pays no attention to a suffered wrong. It does not rejoice at injustice and unrighteousness, but rejoices when right and truth prevail. Love bears up under anything and everything that comes, is ever ready to believe the best of every person, its hopes are fadeless under all circumstances and it endures everything. Love never fails—never fades out or becomes obsolete or comes to an end."

You can know this type of love, this renewal in your own life and marriage through a total dependency on Jesus Christ, and daily application of the concepts He shared with each of us in the Scriptures. When you become a survivor you will know the full meaning of Song of Solomon 2:16 (AMP): "My beloved is mine and I am his!"

For information on Bible Study Courses; Women's Tape Classes; Tape Series for Teens; God's Principles for Raising Children Tapes; or to correspond personally with the author, please write:

Anne Kristin Carroll
℅ Love's Outreach
P.O. Box 888312
Dunwoody, Ga. 30338

For information concerning Christian counselors in your area please contact:

Christian Counseling & Educational Foundation
1790 East Willow Grove Ave.
Laverock, Pa. 19118

Christian Counseling Center
354 West St.
Valparaiso, Ind. 46383

Christian Counseling Center
1 Lakeside Plaza, Suite 509
Lake Charles, La. 70601

The Narramore Christian Foundation
Box 5000
Rosemead, Cal. 91770

Chapter 3

1. "Jesus Christ and the Intellectual," booklet by William R. Bright, produced by Campus Crusade for Christ International, Arrowhead Springs, San Bernardino, Cal., 1968.

Chapter 5

1. "Heart to Heart," by Lois Wyse, from *Love Poems for the Very Married* (Cleveland: World Publishing Co., 1967).
2. Tolstoy, from *The Kingdom of God Is Within You,* p. 33.

Chapter 7

1. Theodor Reik, quoted in *The Art of Understanding Your Mate,* by Cecil G. Osborne (Grand Rapids: Zondervan, 1970).
2. Henry Ward Beecher, quoted in *The Encyclopedia of Religious Quotations,* Ed. Frank S. Mead (New York: Pillar Books, 1976), p. 411.
3. *Christian Living in the Home,* by Dr. Jay E. Adams (Grand Rapids: Baker Book House, 1972), pp. 89–90.

Chapter 8

1. *The Recovery of the Family,* by Elton Trueblood (New York: Harper, 1953), p. 54.
2. *The Act of Marriage* by Tim and Beverly LaHaye (Grand Rapids: Zondervan, 1976), p. 44.
3. Ibid., p. 266.
4. Ibid., p. 291.

Chapter 9

1. "Letting Out All the Reins," by Mary Cholmondeley, from *Leaves of Gold,* Rev. ed. (Williamsport, Pa.: Coslett Publishing Co., 1960), p. 53.

Chapter 10

1. "Kismet," by G. K. Chesterton, from *Leaves of Gold,* Rev. ed. (Williamsport, Pa.: Coslett Publishing Co., 1960), p. 10.

Chapter 11

1. *Sand and Foam,* by Kahlil Gibran (New York: Knopf, 1967), p. 36.
2. *Christian Living in the Home,* by Dr. Jay E. Adams (Grand Rapids: Baker Book House, 1972), p. 51–52.
3. Ibid., p. 52.

RECOMMENDED READING

(Including books which have been
influential in the author's life and works)

The Saving Life of Jesus Christ, by Ian Thomas. Zondervan. Grand Rapids, Mich.

We Became Wives of Happy Husbands, by Anne Kristin Carroll and Darien Cooper. Victor Books. Wheaton, Ill.

You Can Be the Wife of a Happy Husband, by Darien Cooper. Victor Books. Wheaton, Ill.

Do Yourself a Favor . . . Love Your Wife, by H. Page Williams. Logos Books. Plainfield, N.J.

The Total Man, by Dan Benson. Tyndale House. Wheaton, Ill.

Man of Steel and Velvet, by Aubrey P. Andelin. Pacific Press. Santa Barbara, Cal.

The Liberation of Planet Earth, by Hal Lindsey. Zondervan. Grand Rapids, Mich.

The Terminal Generation, by Hal Lindsey. Revell Company. Old Tappan, N.J.

The Late Great Planet Earth, by Hal Lindsey. Zondervan. Grand Rapids, Mich.

The Act of Marriage, by Tim and Beverly LaHaye. Zondervan. Grand Rapids, Mich.

What Happens When Women Pray? by Evelyn Christenson. Victor Books. Wheaton, Ill.

Time for All Things, by Dr. Charlie W. Shedd. Abingdon Press. Nashville, Tenn. 37203

How To Be a Christian Without Being Religious, by Fritz Ridnour. Regal Books. Glendale, Cal.

Satan Is Alive and Well on Planet Earth, by Hal Lindsey. Zondervan. Grand Rapids, Mich.

Dare to Discipline, by James Dobson. Tyndale House. Wheaton, Ill.

The Christian Counselor's Manual, by Dr. Jay E. Adams. Baker Book House. Grand Rapids, Mich.

Say It with Love, by Howard G. Hendricks. Victor Books. Wheaton, Ill.

Spirit Controlled Temperament, by Tim LaHaye. Tyndale House. Wheaton, Ill.

Promises to Peter, by Dr. Charlie W. Shedd. Word Publications. Waco, Tex.

What to Do About Worry, by Dr. Jay E. Adams. Presbyterian and Reformed Publishing House. Nutley, N.J.

Godliness Through Discipline, by Dr. Jay E. Adams. Presbyterian and Reformed Publishing House. Nutley, N.J.

Set of Pamphlets ("Fear," "Worry," "Marriage," "Depression," "Hooked," and "Anger") by Dr. Jay E. Adams. Presbyterian and Reformed Publishing House. Nutley, N.J.

Prayer, by O. Hallesby. Augsburg Publishing House. Minneapolis, Minn.

Joni, by Joni Eareckson, with Joe Musser. World Wide Publications. Minneapolis, Minn.

Character Skeletons, by Bill Gothard. (Available by writing to IBYC, Box One, Oak Brook, Ill. 60521.)

Devotions for the Children's Hour, by Kenneth Taylor. Zondervan. Grand Rapids, Mich.

The Christian Counselor's Bible, by Dr. Jay E. Adams. Presbyterian and Reformed Publishing House. Nutley, N.J.

What You Should Know About Alcoholism, by Don Tracy. Dodd, Mead. New York, N.Y.

Drugs and Alcohol, by Kenneth L. Jones, Louis W. Shainberg, and Curtis O. Byer. Harper & Row. New York, N.Y.

Christ and Your Problems, by Dr. Jay E. Adams. Presbyterian and Reformed Publishing House. Nutley, N.J.

The Amplified Bible. Zondervan. Grand Rapids, Mich.

Nave's Topical Bible, by Orville J. Nave. Moody Press. Chicago, Ill.

Christian Living in the Home, by Dr. Jay E. Adams. Baker Book House. Grand Rapids, Mich.

Tramp for the Lord, by Corrie ten Boom with Jamie Buckingham. Revell. Old Tappan, N.J.

Between Christ and Satan, by Kurt Koch. Kregel Publications. Grand Rapids, Mich.

Limiting God, by John E. Hunter. Zondervan. Grand Rapids, Mich.

It's Intended for Pleasure, by Dr. Ed Wheat and Gale Wheat. Revell. Old Tappan, N.J.

How to Overcome Evil, by Dr. Jay E. Adams. Presbyterian and Reformed Publishing House. Minneapolis, Minn.

A MARITAL CONCORDANCE

LOVE OF MAN AND WOMAN

Matt. 5:43–48
John 15:12
I John 4:7–11
Prov. 17:9
I Cor. 16:14
Eph. 5:2
Matt. 6:21
Rom. 14:15
Ps. 133:1
Song 8:6–7
Rom. 13:8–10
Heb. 10:24
Prov. 15:17
Luke 6:31–37
I Cor. 13:1–13
Prov. 10:12
I Cor. 14:1
Eph. 5:25, 33
Prov. 27:5

MARRIAGE AND GOD'S LINE OF AUTHORITY

Prov. 5:18–19
Matt. 19:5–6
Col. 3:18–20
Ps. 128:3–6
Deut. 7:12–13
Prov. 11:29
Rom. 13:2
I Cor. 13:1–13
Heb. 13:4
Prov. 3:3
Mal. 2:14–17
I Cor. 10:31
Eph. 5:20–33
I Pet. 3:1–16
Prov. 12:7
Ps. 127:1

The marriage ceremony includes a vow before God. Therefore, the following Scriptures relate to God's position on vows.

Num. 30:2–16
Eccles. 5:4
Zech. 8:17
Deut. 23:21, 23
Lev. 19:12
Mal. 3:5
Prov. 2:16–17
Ps. 50:14
Hos. 10:4
Zech. 5:4

WOMEN AND WIVES' RESPONSIBILITIES

Prov. 5:18–19
Prov. 18:22
Prov. 25:24
I Tim. 2:11–15
Ps. 128:3
I Cor. 7:2–5
Eph. 5:22–24, 33
Gen. 2:18, 23–24
Prov. 14:1
Prov. 21:9
Prov. 31:10–31
Titus 2:3–5
Prov. 12:4
I Cor. 11:3, 8–12
Col. 3:18–21
Gen. 3:16
Rom. 7:2
Col. 3:22
Prov. 11:16
Prov. 21:19
I Cor. 7:4, 14, 16, 34
I Pet. 3:1–6
Prov. 19:13–14
I Cor. 14:34–35
I Tim. 3:11
I Tim. 4:1
Prov. 9:13

MEN AND HUSBANDS' RESPONSIBILITIES

I Tim. 5:8
Gen. 2:23–24
Mal. 2:14–16
Eph. 5:22–33
Num. 30:10–15
Titus 2:6–8
Prov. 5:15–19
I Cor. 7:3, 5
Col. 3:18–19
I Pet. 3:7–12
Eccles. 9:9
I Cor. 11:3, 8–14
Ps. 128:3–6

CHILDREN AND THEIR RESPONSIBILITIES

Prov. 19:13
Prov. 3:1–4, 15
Gen. 28:7
Prov. 13:1
Prov. 10:1
Prov. 23:13–26
Prov. 1:8–9
Prov. 5:1–2
Col. 3:20
Jer. 32:39
Matt. 15:4, 5
Gen. 47:12, 30
Gen. 45:9–11
Ps. 119:9
Prov. 4:1–4, 10–11, 20–22
Lam. 3:27
II Tim. 2:22

II Tim. 3:15
Gen. 46:29
Lev. 19:3, 32
Matt. 18:4
Ps. 148:12–13
Eph. 6:1
Titus 2:6

SEX IN MARRIAGE

Gen. 1:27, 31
I Cor. 7:3–5
Prov. 5:15, 18–19
Prov. 31:22
Gen. 2:24
Heb. 13:4
I Tim. 4:4–5
Prov. 11:25
Song 7:1–4, 6:1–10
Gen. 3:7
Gen. 18:12
James 1:5
I Tim. 1–4

SEXUAL IMMORALITY

Gal. 6:7–8
Gen. 20:3
Prov. 5
Matt. 5:28, 32
Gal. 5:19, 21
I Thess. 4:3–7
Rom. 1:22–32
Eph. 3:17
Job 31:1
Prov. 6:24–33
Prov. 23:27–28
Matt. 15:19
II Cor. 12:21
Lev. 18:20
Eph. 5:5–6
I Cor. 6:8–20
II Pet. 2:18–19
Prov. 2:16–19
Matt. 19:9
Heb. 13:4

DIVORCE

Gen. 2:23–24
Eph. 5:22–23
Num. 30:9
Lev. 18:6
Deut. 21:10–15, 17
Matt. 19:3–12
Rom. 7:1–3
Mic. 2:9
Matt. 19:4–6, 7–9
Deut. 24:1–4
Num. 22:19, 29
Deut. 22:13, 18–19
Deut. 24:1
Mark 10:1–12
I Cor. 7:10–16
Mal. 2:13–16
Lev. 22:13
Lev. 20:10, 18–19
Matt. 5:31–32
Luke 16:18
Jer. 3:1

MENTAL ATTITUDE

Prov. 16:1–3
Prov. 6:16–19
Prov. 23:7
Matt. 7:1–5
Matt. 5:22–26

SALVATION

Rom. 3:20–26
Col. 2:9–10
John
Rev. 3:20–21
Luke 19:10
I John
Rom. 5:12–21
Luke 15:2–7, 10
Eph. 2:8–9

PRAYER

Matt. 7:7–8
I Thess. 5:17–19
I Tim. 2:5
Ps. 116:2
Luke 11:10
Ps. 66:18
Matt. 6:5–13
Matt. 18:19–20
Rom. 12:12

PROMISES OF STRENGTH AND SUPPORT

Deut. 31:6
I Cor. 10:12–13
Heb. 4:15–16
Phil. 4:6–13
Isa. 43:2
Ps. 107:5–7
II Cor. 12:9
Matt. 19:26
Heb. 13:5
Luke 18:27
Rom. 5:3–10
James 1:2–15
Rom. 8:18, 37–39
Col. 3:22
Eph. 3:20